Civil Rights and
the Idea of Freedom

CIVIL RIGHTS
AND THE IDEA
OF FREEDOM

Richard H. King

The University of Georgia Press

Athens and London

Published in 1996 by the University of Georgia Press
Athens, Georgia 30602
© 1992, 1996 by Richard H. King
This University of Georgia Press edition is published by arrangement
with Oxford University Press, Inc., 198 Madison Ave.,
New York, NY 10016
The paper in this book meets the guidelines for permanence and
durability of the Committee on Production Guidelines for Book
Longevity of the Council on Library Resources.

Printed in the United States of America
00   99   98   97   96   P   5   4   3   2   1

Library of Congress Cataloging in Publication Data
King, Richard H.
Civil rights and the idea of freedom / Richard H. King.
p.   cm.
Originally published: New York : Oxford University Press, 1992.
Includes bibliographical references and index
ISBN 0-8203-1824-8 (pbk. : alk. paper)
1. Afro-Americans—Civil rights.   2. Afro-Americans—Civil rights—
Moral and ethical aspects.   3. Civil rights movements—United
States—History—20th century.   4. Civil rights movements—United
States—Moral and ethical aspects.   I. Title.
[E185.61.K55   1996]
323.1′196073—dc20   95-41594

British Library Cataloging in Publication Data available

To Charlotte
hela tiden

Contents

Preface
to the New Edition

Although the last decade or so has seen an outpouring of writing about the civil rights movement, the reasons behind this rush to publish are by no means clear. The cynical might see the steady stream of monographs, biographies, and narrative histories as a product of the "publish or perish" imperative in American universities, in this case primarily among American historians. Yet journalist Taylor Branch, the author of the prize-winning *Parting of the Waters* (1988), has shown that his documentary is scarcely subject to such academic pressures. Nor was Henry Hampton's award-winning documentary *Eyes on the Prize*, whose first installment was a six-part series that was then followed by an eight-part continuation, aimed primarily at an academic audience, although it has clearly been a boon to those who teach about the civil rights movement. As of yet, films made about the civil rights movement (or some aspect of it) are few and far between, with Alan Parker's *Mississippi Burning* being the most prominent example. Indeed, it might be better all the way around if Hollywood steered clear of the topic, if Parker's film is anything to go on.

What explains this fascination and to what uses might it be put? One answer is that concern with the civil rights movement needs no utilitarian justification. That is, the question all but answers itself. Or if that response is too minimal, an answer might be that many Americans are concerned with their pasts, as African Americans, as Southerners, and as Americans. Moreover, professional historians, like most academics, are generally a liberal group, and the movement could be seen as the last—and for that matter, the first—interracial movement of any consequence in recent history, all this being reason enough to learn about it. Yet this fails to explain why the civil rights movement appeals to those outside the United States—why the actions, the music, and the images generated by the movement still resonate on a global scale. Particularly during the world-historical events of 1989, from Eastern Europe to China, evocations of the movement were not difficult to detect. All this suggests that the civil rights movement still has the capacity to interest and to inspire people in many different places and circumstances.

And yet there are undeniable countertendencies at work as well. Within the African-American community in the United States and outside the United States as well, a certain backlash has made itself felt. Beginning in the 1970s and culminating with Spike Lee's film *Malcolm X*, there has been a tendency to demote Martin Luther King, Jr. from his position as the representative figure—and hero— of the civil rights movement and to elevate Malcolm X as the figure who best embodies the aspirations and dilemmas of African Americans. Some observers have been concerned that the divisions between what the two men represent might become an insurmountable barrier, while others have emphasized the way that both King and Malcolm X speak to contemporary African-American (and possibly general American) concerns. From this point of view, their respective visions are not contradictory but complementary. Indeed, it is a muted suggestion and theme of *Civil Rights and the Idea of Freedom* that the civil rights movement King has come to represent and the black power and consciousness movement that Malcolm X inspired share a deep concern with the restoration of black self-respect and pride. Certainly the younger, more radical members of the Student Nonviolent Coordinating Committee (SNCC) proclaimed that theme with particular vehemence. But it is also easy to overemphasize what the movement and Malcolm X had in common and to strike for a too easy reconciliation.

In general, fascination with the figure of Malcolm X represents an estrangement from the specifically Southern and Christian cast of most movement rhetoric. Why the ethos of the urban ghettos and Nation of Islam ideology has come to seem more accessible even to people outside of the United States is puzzling, but my experience has been that both black Britons and predominantly white British university students often find it easier to relate to Malcolm X than Martin Luther King, Jr. It is easy to patronize King as a dreamer and regard the ideals of the civil rights movement as utopian while viewing Malcolm X as a hard-nosed realist with a viable blueprint for the future. Needless to say, such judgments will not survive serious scrutiny without fundamental qualification.

Yet there was, and perhaps still is, something more substantive driving this questioning of the relevance of the civil rights movement. First would be the claim, coming once from black nationalists and now from Afro-centrists, that the civil rights movement was too integrationist and too concerned with voicing its claims in the constitutional and/or universalist terms of the so-called white liberal mainstream. In other words, the civil rights movement was neither black nor radical enough. Believing in a somewhat different form of radicalism would also express doubts about the movement by noting that, in concentrating on legal and political changes, the movement had failed to address, not to mention solve, the economic and social plight of African Americans. In the face of the Republican political hegemony since 1968 and the drift rightward of the Democratic Party, continued harping on the inspirational qualities or value of the movement seem counterproductive, mere exercises in nostalgia.

In other words, such tendencies exemplify something more serious than just the preference for Malcolm X over King—the consignment of the civil rights movement to the category of irrelevance and of "merely" history. Though once inspiring, so this view laments, the movement no longer has much to say to the contemporary world, if for no other reason than that its essential goals—the dismantling of Jim Crow and the systematic disfranchisement of black voters in much of the Deep South—have long since been achieved and its basic philosophy of praxis—nonviolent direct action—has long since proved to have limited effectiveness both inside and outside the United States.

Indeed there are tendencies in the academic historiography of the civil rights movement that inadvertently reenforce this drift toward irrelevance. One arises from an overemphasis upon the specifically Southern and black roots of the movement and from the alleged uniqueness of black politics. This is not to deny that the movement's emotional and experiential roots were in the Southern black community, but to see that fact as determining rather than delineating the nature and destiny of the civil rights movement is to deny the open-ended quality of historical development. Put generally, this tendency to particularize the movement by historicizing it, to consider the context within which it emerged as all-determining, makes it difficult to imagine how a similar movement might emerge elsewhere or why the characteristics of the movement might be worth study or analysis other than as quaint curiosities.

A second tendency, one also manifested in the recent historiography of the movement and mentioned in the text of *Civil Rights and the Idea of Freedom*, challenges the idea that the civil rights movement represented a definite break with the past and that it was something qualitatively different than what had preceded it. Claims along these lines state that the origins of the civil rights movement can be detected in the 1930s and early 1940s. Thus, by extension, the period running from Montgomery to Memphis was continuous with, and not that much different from, what had come before.

The problem with this point of view is that it threatens to deny the uniqueness of the movement altogether. In terms of Anglo-American historical thought, it represents a kind of Whiggism in the writing of the movement's history—a tendency to see the civil rights movement prefigured in every protest by black Southerners against any example of racial injustice going back to the 1930s. In other words, it represents a failure to distinguish between protests against violations of civil rights, the failure to enforce the separate but equal principle, or the efforts of black and white workers to organize unions, on the one hand, and the civil rights movement as an increasingly self-conscious movement with its own internal dynamics and momentum on the other hand. Overall, this tendency illustrates the historian's obsession with finding—or imposing—continuities in the past and his or her fear of anything that calls historical continuities into question. Indeed, there is a covert sort of commitment to inevitability of development in this position.

What is worrisome about these tendencies to situate the civil rights movement too strictly in the context of its origins and in the alleged continuity of historical development is that it risks rendering the movement unavailable for other people and places and future historical moments. By making the movement too specifically Southern and African-American in ethos and by making it too much the product of what came before it, the movement is in danger of becoming irrelevant. Thus, paradoxically, because the civil rights movement was something unique as an historical movement, it remains available for study, contemplation, use, criticism, and even admiration.

Now that these concerns have been addressed, it remains for me to spell out what I think is still worth considering in the movement. This involves focusing on what I believe to be its political dimensions. *Civil Rights and the Idea of Freedom's* primary purpose was to explore the various political meanings and uses of the idea of freedom in the experience of the movement. In doing so, I was inevitably forced to examine the concept of politics in general and the various traditions—biblical, liberal, communitarian/republican, and democratic—intertwined in the movement. Here I would like, briefly, to reiterate and expand on a few aspects of what the history of the movement offers that might illuminate the deliberations of political theorists of various persuasions in the contemporary world.

First, to reemphasize something that I mention in passing in the book, the civil rights movement illuminated the meaning of politics (and the political in general) in so far as it made clear that the state and the political realm were not necessarily synonymous and that, to advert to Hannah Arendt's political thought, the political realm emerges wherever there is talk and action together in public in reference to public affairs. From this point of view, the contemporary communitarian movement could learn considerably from movement history and thinking. In particular, it might learn that attempting to mobilize people without offending anyone, trying to appeal in too bland a fashion across all ideological boundaries, will succeed only in rendering the movement toothless. A strong movement will provoke strong enemies; until it does so, the communitarian movement threatens to develop all the political excitement that organizations like Common Cause once did, that is, not very much at all. In addition, the communitarian movement should admit that it is a political movement, aside from whether it is aligned with one, two, or more political parties. Americans need to be reeducated to the fact that politics is not defined solely by what goes on in Washington and/or among the traditional political organizations.

Though the civil rights movement defined its goals sharply, it was able for a time to balance the particular and the universal, group needs and larger public concerns, and the regional and the national. Indeed, not only were the achievement and preservation of that balance prerequisites for the movement's survival, they were also central to the operative definition of what the movement essentially was. Much of the current debate among political theorists over the relative merits of liberalism and communitarianism takes place against the background of the following worry: how to create a political movement rooted in specific communities and concrete needs and desires, yet possessing a vision that is philosophically committed to a

Preface to the New Edition

kind of universal regard rather than the partial-sightedness, even parochiality, of any particular group? Indeed, in retrospect, the main task and great achievement of Martin Luther King, Jr. was keeping these opposing tendencies within the movement and within the black community from flying apart. In this respect he, rather than Malcolm X, made things most difficult for white Americans since he gave them few hostages to fortune—no excuses to reject black demands out of hand.

Put another way, the civil rights movement as a whole presented a fascinating combination of a predominantly communitarian ethos with liberal goals. To be more precise, the movement made skillful use of liberal goals to achieve ends informed by more than merely liberal values. It is hard to know which of the poles—liberalism or communitarianism—should be given priority. In a recent review of John Rawls's *Political Liberalism* (1993), one of the leading communitarian critics of liberalism, Michael Sandel, reflected on the costs of separating political and moral reasoning in public debate and in the process made the following reference to the movement by stating, "With a few notable exceptions, such as the civil rights movement, American political discourse in recent decades has come to reflect the liberal resolve that government be neutral on moral and religious questions . . . without reference to any particular conception of the good" (107 *Harvard Law Review* 1793 [1994]).

It is worth studying Sandel's observation a bit, since there are several things noteworthy about it. First, it is relatively and distressingly rare to find reference to concrete historical events or movements in the writings of contemporary political theorists. In fact, one of my main aims in *Civil Rights and the Idea of Freedom* was to alert political theorists and historians of political thought to the rich possibilities that the civil rights movement offered to their deliberations. The example of the civil rights movement has not escaped Sandel, but it is not clear if the movement has had much influence on communitarian thought in general.

Moreover, the communitarian case advanced by Sandel has the strength of acknowledging that the particularist loyalties of ethnicity, race, community, and religion can have more than a negative or nugatory role to play in the life of a liberal polity, constructed around equality before the law and tolerance of ideological diversity. In the case of the civil rights movement, religious language, moral imperatives, and visions of community ("the beloved community") enriched rather than stifled the public discourse of the 1960s. Whatever the case, a communitarianism that has learned from the history of the civil rights movement could point to the way communal loyalties can and will be brought into play within a liberal polity. But communitarian thought might also be forced to consider constructing some sort of rank ordering of admissible communal commitments, some of which would be seen as valuable and others inimical to the effort to form a public consensus around the common good that communitarians so desire in a polity as diverse as the United States. Indeed, this might sharpen the communitarian vision and dissipate some of its aura of being "all things to all people."

Yet the historical example of the civil rights movement presents similar opportunities and challenges to a theoretical political liberalism. For instance, the way the civil rights movement was able to bring its religious and moral vision based on what Rawls has called a "comprehensive conception of the good" into congruence with the secular provisions of liberal constitutionalism might confirm Rawls's contention that various individuals and groups can come to an "overlapping consensus" on certain political values and institutions from quite different moral and ideological vantage points: Protestant/Catholic/Jew/Muslim; black/white; and radical/liberal/conservative. Indeed, political liberals, neutral on overarching religious, moral, or philosophical doctrines, might plausibly maintain that the best political framework for a truly multicultural society is provided by theoretical liberalism.

The history of the movement should also remind Rawlsian liberalism that its liberal vision remains otherworldly to the extent that it fails to acknowledge that racial loyalties, religious commitments, and ethnic allegiances cannot be simply checked at the door when matters concerning the public realm are at issue. A political liberalism that does not consider commitments to binding communities of belief and belonging to be a potential strength rather than an automatic weakness will have little purchase on most of our loyalties. Yet the political liberal of the Rawlsian type can, in contrast to the communitarian, more easily construct a lexical ordering of particularist loyalties, some of which are admissible and others of which are inimical to a liberal order.

The final political point to be drawn from consideration of the movement is the flip side of my earlier point regarding the balance between individual rights and communal loyalties that the civil rights movement maintained for most of its existence. I refer to the likelihood of failure to which most twentieth-century history attests. Liberal national or multicultural orders are exceedingly frail and thus their preservation is a considerable achievement. Indeed, modern Western history has seen three great multicultural empires: the Austro-Hungarian Empire, the Soviet Union, and the United States. Two of them have perished. Whether the remaining one will survive as a diverse cultural order worth living in is one of the most important political questions facing the United States. My suggestion is that reconsideration of the life and death of the civil rights movement as an experiment in political thinking and behavior might illuminate some of the ways mistakes can be avoided and opportunities can be grasped in the future.

RICHARD H. KING
Nottingham, June 1995

Preface

Remembering the origins of a book is about as difficult as recapturing those early experiences that shape our lives. Indeed, Freud suggested that the crucial memories of our early years, even and especially those that seem clearest and most authentic, are often composites of fantasy and experience that never happened the way they reveal themselves to us in memory. They are what he called screen memories (*Deckerinnerungen*). Furthermore, the degree of their distortion is proportional to the conflicted nature of the memory in question.

At any rate I have two memories which help explain why this book eventually came to be written. The first concerns a meeting I attended in Jackson, Tennessee, in the summer of 1965. I was teaching summer school at Lane College but had also spent some time under the wise and shrewd guidance of the college treasurer and local civil rights activist, Albert Porter. He took me to several black churches in nearby Haywood and Fayette counties where we helped set up a couple of "freedom schools." I was from East Tennessee and the flat, swampy part of the state might as well have been another country. It seemed (and was) like the Mississippi Delta, a place name filled with mysterious and frightening resonances even for a white Southerner.

It was in this strange yet also somehow familiar background that I attended a meeting with Mr. Porter. As I remember it, the meeting was held in a recreation center in the black section of Jackson and its purpose was to organize the local group that would apply for funds from President Johnson's War on Poverty. There was nothing world-historical at work here exactly; still, the reason why that meeting lodged in my memory, and was in fact quite vivid and moving at the time, was that I observed how a group of people, in this case black Southerners, for the first time confronted the "fact" that they were a group who had a choice. They could organize themselves, elect officers, then debate what their community needed and apply for funds. What I witnessed was a crucial part of the process of people—including myself—becoming "political," a process which had begun several years before in Montgomery and Greensboro and then spread throughout the South.

The other experience, an intellectual one, happened about the same time, perhaps that summer. Sometime around then I read Hannah Arendt's *On Revolution*, a work which culminates with a long discussion of the way people in certain settings organize themselves relatively spontaneously into councils or *soviets* or *Räte*, there to debate and decide on new forms of political action and organization. For Arendt, the council system was the embodiment of free action in concert and the core of the revolutionary tradition she wanted to rescue from Marxist-Leninist models of or liberal-social democratic explanations for modern revolution.

I spent the 1965–66 academic year teaching at Stillman College in Tuscaloosa, Alabama. There I came into contact with SNCC workers who were organizing the Lowndes County Freedom Organization. Periodically, they would come to nearby Tuscaloosa for "R&R" and to escape the life-threatening tension involved in organizing in Black Belt Alabama. What struck me at the time, and since, was the way Arendt's highly abstract meditation on revolution and politics as species of political freedom spoke so directly to what I heard from the SNCC workers and what I saw happening among the people whose political awakening the civil rights movement had been all about. Later I met a friend who had had roughly the same set of experiences—involvement in the movement in its last stages in the mid-1960s. She too had read *On Revolution* during that time and she too had been forcefully struck by its power to illuminate what she had experienced and seen happen.

The point of relating these two incidents is to suggest what compelled me some two decades later to begin work on an analysis of the civil rights movement that would be most centrally influenced by the work of Hannah Arendt. In doing so it has been far from my intention to import complex European theories into American political experience just for the sake of it. It is fair to wonder about the appropriateness of such an application. My response can only be that I have found nothing written by an American, white or black, academic or activist, which brings alive in such cogent and powerful form as does Arendt's work what I take to be the essence of the civil rights movement—the search for freedom.

But to talk of "essence" risks transforming a movement into a static model, thus denying differences or changes within the movement during its short and at times unhappy life. More dangerously, it also risks re-creating the movement as an object of nostalgia. Thus I use Arendt and others not only to analyze the various ideas of freedom in the civil rights movement but also to trace the burgeoning splits within the movement as well as its decline and dissolution, a process that had an internal dynamic as well as external causes.

If there is a coherent view of history at work here, it might loosely be called republican; in Nietzschean terms, monumental. I am deeply suspicious of this form of historical consciousness which at worst combines nostalgia with the uncritical apotheosizing of individuals and groups, one of the ingredients in the poisonous brew known as fascism. A more salutary function of this form of historical awareness is to call us back not literally to first principles and institutions so much as to a contemplation of what was central to the movement and what might be retained or revitalized from it. Moreover, events over the last three years in China, the Soviet Union, and Eastern Europe suggest that the kind of politics, the sort of freedom, and the nature of political authority which Arendt so powerfully defined in her work show that neither a reading of Arendt nor of the civil rights movement through Arendtian spectacles is merely an academic exercise or an exercise in sentimentality. If it remains such after reading this book, either the reader or I—or both of us—has failed.

As usual writing a book incurs many debts for which mere thanks is inadequate. Though this book must travel, I suppose, under the aegis of intellectual history, I have done some archival research in its preparation. The civil rights movement is perhaps the first historical movement to be so extensively documented through oral history and captured on film. Besides the several excellent published compilations of interviews with participants in the movement, there remains much unpublished material to be used. Particularly valuable is a collection of transcribed interviews with a vast array of participants and observers of the movement that is found in the Civil Rights Documentation Project at Howard University in Washington, D.C. The head of the Oral History Department of the Moorland-Spingarn Research Center, Dr. Elinor D. Sinnette, was particularly helpful in facilitating my research there. Louise Cook granted access to the King Library and Archives at the Martin Luther King, Jr., Center in

Atlanta, Georgia; and Diane Ware, research assistant, offered friendly aid when I consulted some of their manuscript collections having to do with Mississippi Freedom Summer in 1964 as well as newspapers such as *Southern Courier* and *Southern Patriot* and several important pieces of academic research dealing with Martin Luther King. Finally, Howard Gotlieb of the Mugar Memorial Library of Boston University made available various documents dealing with Martin Luther King. I thank him as well.

In addition, I made an effort to view as much film footage of the movement as possible in order to recapture the mood of the movement and the times that escapes embodiment in print. In the summer of 1985, I spent several days at the National Archives in Washington looking at newsreels and special network programs on the civil rights movement from the 1950s and 1960s. My special thanks go to Patrick Sheehan and Sarah Rouse of the Library of Congress Film Division who helped me track down several television specials on the movement from the 1960s as well as Elie Landau's four-hour documentary film *King: From Montgomery to Memphis*. Finally, of course, every student of the civil rights movement, as well as every American citizen, is deeply indebted to the superlative documentary *Eyes on the Prize*, produced by Henry Hampton.

Without a certain amount of financial support for travel and research, a book such as this becomes even more difficult since the archives are in the United States and I live in Britain. The Research Fund of the University of Nottingham helped make a two-month research trip to America possible in the summer of 1985, and the British Academy provided travel money to come to the States in the spring of 1987 for a few weeks. While still living in America, a summer stipend from the National Endowment for the Humanities allowed me to begin work in earnest on this project. Most important, I participated in an NEH Summer Seminar in 1982 led by Professor Richard Flathman of Johns Hopkins University on the topic "Political Freedom." It is impossible to overestimate the importance of this seminar in providing the background in political theory that informs my book. Suffice it to say that Dick Flathman was a fascinating and exemplary teacher-leader-theoretician and my colleagues in the seminar were as congenial and intellectually stimulating a group as I have ever had the privilege to be a member of.

Over the last several years I have presented papers on the topic of civil rights to various groups in Britain and America. In England,

groups at the British Association of American Studies (B.A.A.S.), the
University of East Anglia, the University of Sussex, and Oxford
University have listened and criticized. I presented part of the
material on Martin Luther King at the symposium "We Shall Overcome: Martin Luther King, Jr.—The Leader and the Legacy," in
Washington, D.C., in October 1986. Vincent Harding and Mary
Berry offered useful comments on my paper at that time. In America,
invitations to present aspects of my study at Brandeis University and
the University of Virginia have been much appreciated. In particular
Thadious Davis, Ralph Luker, and J. Mills Thornton commented on
aspects of my study at the Southern Intellectual History Group
meeting at Chapel Hill in March 1990. Finally, my year at the
University of Mississippi (1989–90) and association with the History
department and particularly the Center for the Study of Southern
Culture was invaluable in bringing my work to completion in a
congenial setting. The center has a large collection of videos, dealing
not only with Southern literature and culture but also with Southern
politics, in particular the video transcriptions of two major confer-
ences sponsored by the center dealing with "The Media and Civil
Rights" and "The Law and Civil Rights." The staff at the center,
especially Associate Director Ann Abadie, were helpful beyond any
reasonable expectation and made my time there a genuine pleasure.
That Mississippi is not "now" what it was "then" can be attributed to
many factors, forces, and people. One of them certainly is the Center
for the Study of Southern Culture under Bill Ferris's direction.

I have been extremely lucky in teaching in such a congenial setting
as the American Studies department at Nottingham. In particular,
colleagues such as Pete Messent, Dave Murray, and Douglas Tallack
have provided intellectual encouragement (and challenges) to what
they see as a quaintly liberal approach to political and social change,
despite my protestations that Europeans don't know how many
mansions there are in the house of American liberalism. Critical
theorists take a dim view of my approach here but my colleagues in
the School of Critical Theory at Nottingham have created an atmo-
sphere of theoretical excitement and vitality that exemplifies the
intellectual value of Marxism and post-structuralism, both of which
are coming under demagogic attacks of late from people who should
know better.

Homage should also be paid to the extraordinary work of scholars
who have written on the civil rights movement in the 1980s and

particularly to journalists such as Pat Watters whose reactions to and thoughts on the movement have influenced me quite a bit. Ray Arsenault and Paul Gaston have both been good friends and valuable sources of information about the South and the movement over the years. Three friends—Larry Friedman, Steve Whitfield, and Jim Turner—read the entire manuscript and offered needed encouragement and/or stern warnings about difficulties. Jim Turner was particularly helpful at one juncture when I had begun to wonder if I was making sense to anyone at all. Larry and Steve have become regulars at this and I thank them once again for their intellectual companionship as well as personal friendship. Over the years, Sheldon Meyer of Oxford University Press has provided encouragement and Rebecca Schneider's close attention to sense and syntax along with her insightful questions about vagaries in the text have even made the process of responding to copyediting enjoyable.

The most profoundly felt gratitude is perhaps the hardest to express in a straightforward way in such a public setting. But my book is dedicated to my wife, Charlotte Fallenius, whose presence has made all the difference.

Nottingham   R. H. K.
September 1991

Civil Rights and
the Idea of Freedom

Introduction

Where the civil rights movement in the United States once seemed to herald an historical "break" of major proportions, the 1980s saw the appearance of several works in black intellectual and cultural history identifying what V. P. Franklin has called a tradition of "core values"—freedom, resistance, self-determination, and education—which formed during slavery and upon which the movement of the 1950s and 1960s drew for intellectual sustenance. Moreover, historically oriented sociological studies have reconstructed the dense institutional matrix of Southern black colleges and churches, NAACP chapters, and "movement centers" staffed by independent white and black activists from which the civil rights movement emerged and by which it was sustained. Even before the bus boycott in Montgomery in 1955–56, there had been a mass campaign against bus segregation in Baton Rouge in 1953. And as Taylor Branch points out in his 1988 book *Parting the Waters*, the Greensboro sit-ins of February 1960, which touched off the direct action phase of the movement in earnest, had been preceded by "similar demonstrations in at least 16 other cities" in the "previous three years."[1]

Another example of this tendency to push the origins of the movement back in time, inevitably lessening the significance of the events of the 1950s and 1960s, can be seen in a recent article in the *Journal of American History* which has suggested the early 1940s rather than the mid-1950s as the true inception of the civil rights struggle.[2] According to this argument, during the World War years the black population in the South and North entered for certain into the processes of urbanization and industrialization. In plants all over the country black workers were organized by CIO unions around issues of working conditions, wages, and hours, while membership in traditional civil rights organizations such as the NAACP and the Urban League increased, as did black participation in politics at all levels. Such a focus implies that the later direct action campaigns, most prominently Greensboro and Nashville, Albany and

3

Birmingham, the 1964 Freedom Summer campaign in Mississippi and the grand finale of the Selma to Montgomery march in early 1965, duplicated the efforts made two decades earlier or, more startlingly, that they failed to address social and economic issues which union campaigns of the 1940s had made central.

This recent emphasis on the movement's ideological and institutional continuity with the past tends, wrongly I think, to minimize what was different, even unique, about the civil rights movement of the 1954–68 period. Paradoxically, what began as an effort to explain the emergence of a "new" historical phenomenon ends by undermining its novelty. No doubt the civil rights movement did not emerge *de novo*. Antecedents to intellectual and cultural aspects of the movement there certainly were and most of Chapter 1 will be spent examining them. But with all that said, the freshness, even inexplicability, of the movement should not be underplayed for the sake of an historical pedigree; nor should we succumb to the temptation to erase the distinction between priority and effective causality, what logicians name the fallacy of *post hoc, ergo propter hoc*.

With this we arrive at the issue which is one of the main concerns of this book. The position I will be challenging has been expressed most succinctly by J. Mills Thornton when he writes:

> From the perspective of the ideal of individual liberty, the Civil Rights Movement ended because, with the Civil Rights Act of 1964, the Voting Rights Act of 1965 and finally the Fair Housing Act of 1968, the movement had achieved its goal.[3]

I will be arguing, however, that what was unique about the civil rights movement was not *just* the attainment of individual liberty through the dismantling of the Jim Crow system, though this was, as Thornton has suggested, the most readily identifiable goal of the movement. Rather, first tracing out the *various* meanings of individual and collective freedom as they turned up in the rhetoric and thinking of movement participants and leaders, I will then focus upon what I take to be the other important goal of the movement—the effort to create or make evident a new sense of individual and collective identity, even self-respect, among Southern black people through political mobilization. This is not to claim that the civil rights movement invented self-respect and pride or that it was uniquely successful in securing such a self-conception. Rather that for the first time—or for the first time in a long time—such ideas took on a collective, political meaning.

By extension, I want also to suggest that the differences in the goals of the Southern civil rights movement and the (largely) Northern- and Western-based black pride and black consciousness movements which appeared in the late 1960s and early 1970s have been over-emphasized. Differences there most certainly were—in strategy and tactics, informing vision and ideological emphasis and, of course, goals. But what united the two phases of the black insurgency, what Martin Luther King and Malcolm X did share, was the goal of constructing a new sense of self and of black culture. And what was first a political goal became, in the 1970s and 1980s, the impetus for the academic and intellectual rediscovery and reinterpretation of the Afro-American cultural and historical experience.

At the base of this project is my effort to understand the experience of political involvement undergone by movement participants. How did participants talk about their experience of sitting-in at a lunch counter or trying to register to vote in Selma or attending mass meetings in churches in rural West Tennessee or in the Delta? What terms did they use most often? If such experiences are neglected, it becomes easy to view the civil rights movement as a kind of mopping-up operation, one which changed nothing fundamental, however important it may have been in fulfilling the nation's ideals and securing the rights of its black citizens. Ironically this latter view of the movement tends to be shared by those who stress the purely legal and mainstream political goals of the movement, such as Thornton, and the black power/consciousness movement that followed upon the successes—and failures—of the civil rights movement. Under the relentless, even scornful scrutiny of figures such as Malcolm X and Eldridge Cleaver, marches, mass meetings, freedom songs, non-violence, Fannie Lou Hamer, and Martin Luther King seemed at best quaint and at worst part of the problem not the solution. From this "radical" perspective, the religious, participatory democratic and liberal dimensions of the movement seemed hopelessly reformist or bourgeois or "white"—and usually all three together.

Indeed the historiography of the movement has generally ne-glected much, if any, discussion of the "new" notion of politics the movement seemed to embody. Most histories of the movement, as well as works analyzing the legal and constitutional issues that emerged with and from the movement, assume that it can best be understood from within the institutional and conceptual confines of post-war liberal pluralism with its emphasis upon the pursuit of interests and defense of political and legal rights as the *raison d'etre* of politics. The great merit of works such as Pat Watters and Reese Cleghorn's *Climbing Jacob's Ladder* (1967), Watters's *Down to Now* (1971), Stokely Carmichael and Charles Hamilton's *Black Power* (1967), and David Garrow's *Protest at Selma* (1978) is that for them the pursuit of rights and assertion of interests do not exhaust the definition of what politics involves or might be.[4] Much of what follows in this study is devoted to exploring the experience of the "political" in the civil rights movement and the way that experience failed to fit comfortably, if at all, within the confines of coventional liberal politics.

The larger point here is that the politics of pluralism assumes that politics centers appropriately on power, narrowly conceived in terms of control and domination, working one's will against the resistance of others or assuring a way toward co-existence with others. On this definition mainstream liberals, hard-boiled realists, and radicals are in essential agreement. As Willie Ricks, the Student Nonviolent Coordinating Committee (SNCC) field worker who coined the phrase "black power," explained in 1966 during the first flush of the black power movement: "We had moved to the level of verbalizing our drive for power—not merely for the vote, not for some vague kind of freedom, not for legal rights, but the basic force in any society— power."[5] The problem with this view of politics is that it either implies that "after the revolution" politics will still be about power, in which case the revolution will have been in vain, *or* that some mysterious transformation in human nature will cause the reign of domination to fade away. In either case, when political opposition does appear after a revolution, the justification exists to suppress it as traitorous rather than treat it as normal.[6] And the emphasis upon securing rights as the main aim of political or legal action may lead, as has been pointed out, to the position where rights and politics will be seen as mutually exclusive, causing a kind of depoliticalization to set in.[7]

What then was the conception of politics at work in movement activities? The "new" politics of the 1960s has been characterized by Wini Breines as "prefigurative" rather than "strategic," by Jane Mansbridge as "unitary" as opposed to "adversary."[8] But the paradox is that though this new politics seems unique and utopian when set beside the pluralist theory/practice of mainstream American politics, it bears a certain family resemblance to pre-modern civic humanist or republican impulses recast in decidedly modern democratic and even communitarian anarchist terms. In this respect the political culture set in motion by the civil rights movement fell outside the hegemony of the "liberal" tradition so strongly argued by Louis Hartz.[9]

In the process of political involvement, to which I will return in Chapter 2, many participants in the movement arrived at a new sense of themselves as neither beleagured, isolated individuals nor as oppressed masses but as newly empowered citizens who were part of a collective, public process of deliberation and action. They no longer felt so dependent upon the benevolence of white Northern friends nor so fearful of the hostility of their white Southern enemies. And they embraced the specifically political meaning of taking responsibility for their own lives, a meaning which had little or nothing to do with the economic or moral individualism so endemic in the dominant culture. Indeed this assumption of responsibility might be seen as the modern democratic form of political virtue.

This is not to claim that participants in the movement were unconcerned with gaining their rights or defending their interests. Nor is it to claim that participants in the movement were better or more moral people than their adversaries or temporizing allies. In some cases this was so; but not always. Indeed my purpose here is not to emphasize the "moral" nature of politics in the civil rights movement as opposed to the corrupt and compromised politics of mainstream America or of Southern segregationists. Rather I want to stress the "political" nature of the politics of the civil rights movement. For the strategies and goals of the movement, of various campaigns, and especially of grass-roots efforts at community organizing were often arrived at through extended political discussion, argumentation, and persuasion and carried out with considerable participation by people other than those belonging to the movement elite. When this process worked at its best, not only were individual participants' senses of selfhood enlarged as the goals of the group coincided with the most democratic traditions in the political culture of the United States, but, more importantly, the movement forced the polity to act on its own best impulses and original principles, that is, for the common good or in the public interest.

Finally the most politically innovative thing about the movement was the way that, faced with the intolerably restricted and occluded nature of the public realm in the South, the movement reilluminated and then expanded that realm. Put another way, the movement revivified the potentially subversive idea that the "State" was not always or necessarily identical with the political realm and that *raison d'etat* was not synonymous with the *res publica*. In this it served notice that conventional understandings of politics and the political had become seriously atrophied and were in need of radical rejuvenation.

Observant readers will have noticed that I have gradually moved from issues of historiography to matters basic to political theory and political culture. While further analyzing the limits of what historians have said about the political culture of the movement, I want to discuss how the movement both generated and deployed political ideas, most importantly the idea of freedom, and how, in turn, the uses of freedom within the movement fit with—or expanded upon—the conventional understandings of freedom in contemporary political culture and thought. From this perspective, I will suggest some ways in which a movement such as the civil rights movement can serve as a valuable resource for contemporary political theorists who have devoted surprisingly little attention to it. For as Don Herzog has suggested, political theorists "need to exploit the considerable resources of history and social theory" much more than they have up to now. [10]

Such suggestions imply a judgment upon much recent American political thought, one which mirrors my criticism of the historiography of the civil rights movement for its indifference to political ideas. First, recent academic political thought, particularly the influential and rich liberal political theory, as exemplified in the work of John Rawls especially, is unconcerned with historical context or concrete historical specification. Symptomatic of this problem, perceptive critics of liberal political philosophy such as Michael Sandel and Ian Shapiro themselves fail to ventilate their works with very much historical "reality," preferring to engage in a purely "internalist" argument. [11] For instance, most critics of liberalism, particularly from the Left, fail to account for the persistent appeal of liberal modes of thinking, particularly the contemporary prevalence of "rights" talk everywhere. Musty claims that liberalism's appeal is a misunderstanding because of its original dependence on individualistic conceptions of the self or that it is just an ideological cover for capitalist conceptions of the market fail to confront the fact that contemporary liberalism's willingness to take rights seriously has been practically the only ideological/conceptual bulwark against totalitarian concepts of the State and Party, whether on the Left or Right, in the nearly half century since World War II.

Moreover, critics of liberalism fail to acknowledge that though rights in liberal theory are assumed to bear exclusively on the individual, rights-talk and claims have been taken up by groups of all sorts in protest against social exclusion and political/legal oppression. One need only point to the women's movement, now in many respects a world-wide movement, to dissident popular movements such as Solidarity in Poland and those in the Soviet Union and Eastern Europe generally, and of course to the on-going struggle in South Africa to see the necessity, if not the sufficiency, of liberalism in the contemporary world.

A related shortcoming of recent political thinking in general, not just of liberal political thought, has been the tendency to focus on static conceptual states—rights, justice, equality, and freedom—while neglecting the experiences that make up actual political involvement. Observing that "Political theorists seldom capture spontaneous responses to the experience of political life," Nancy Rosenblum contends that it is a "perfectly reasonable expectation that political theory mirror [participants'] experience of political life, including affective ones."[12] I concur heartily with Rosenblum's observation and thus focus my ensuing discussion of the experience of politics in the civil rights movement around such constitutive experiences as the risk of life involved in much of the political action undertaken by participants in the movement, the emergence of feelings of self-respect and self-determination, the growth of a sense of solidarity, the capacity for making political judgments, and finally the experience of what Hannah Arendt has called "public happiness" within the civil rights movement.[13]

More generally, to "do" political theory without understanding the experience of political action is akin to trying to appreciate an opera by studying the libretto without listening to the music. Extensive documentation of that experience in the South exists in the form of published and unpublished interviews and oral history collections.[14] Such a source presents a tremendous opportunity for us to understand more about what was existentially involved in the rhetoric and ideas of freedom—freedom not just as a concept or status, but as an experience with a history.

A Note on the Nature of the Text

As things stand now, the literature of the civil rights movement includes plenty of first-rate general histories of the movement; exhaustive studies of major civil rights organizations such as SNCC, the Congress of Racial Equality (CORE), and the Southern Christian Leadership Conference (SCLC); fascinating analyses of campaigns in towns and cities of the South, ranging from Chapel Hill, North Carolina to Tuskegee, Alabama; and biographies of and autobiographical reminiscences by leaders of the movement. What is missing so far is anything approaching an intellectual history of the movement, specifically a political-theoretical analysis of its rhetoric and thinking.

Attempting to fill this gap, what follows will not depend on a narrative line to move it along, though the book is arranged in roughly chronological order. My organizing image is rather the triptych viewed from a vantage point directly in front of it. Chapter 1 will provide that vantage point by unpacking and analyzing four basic meanings of freedom in Western political thought, illustrating them with examples from United States and specifically Afro-American history and thought. Chapters 2 and 3 belong together as one "panel" of the triptych. They address the general experience of politics in the civil rights movement, moving on to more abstract reflections upon the relationship between self-interest and self-respect in political thought and action. Chapters 4 and 5 make up the middle panel and are devoted to the way Martin Luther King's life and thought embody the four previous meanings of freedom previously identified; Chapter 4 being the more descriptive and its successor more analytical. The final panel, comprised of Chapters 6 and 7, traces the shift in thought and rhetoric undergone by workers in SNCC which involved a narrowing of the meaning of freedom and the radicalization of its meaning. Here the influence of Frantz Fanon will be especially of interest, since Fanon's position represents the ultimate destination of the drive for self-respect in the movement. In the conclusion, I move away from the close focus on the civil rights movement and look briefly at the fate of freedom and political action in the contemporary world.

Finally, I should say that my focus upon political ideas does not imply that I assign ultimate causal force to them. It does attest to my firm belief that neither individual nor collective political action can be properly understood without taking into account the way ideas (i.e., values, beliefs, ideologies) shape, guide, and occasionally determine what people want and how they go about getting it. It also assumes that the "goods" that people attempt to gain through politics are not exclusively material ones and that the ideas they deploy in the process of attaining these goods are neither mere "smokescreens" behind which lurk so-called "real" interests nor products of "false consciousness."

CHAPTER 1

The Repertory of Freedom

Free at last! Free at last! Thank God Almighty, we are free at last!

Martin Luther King, March on Washington, August 1963

Freedom in its various guises has been a central theme in Western thought. At any particular place and time, the dominant meaning of freedom and its sphere of primary relevance (sacred or secular, personal or collective; economic, social, cultural, or political) will vary. The set of ways of defining and applying freedom in the political thought and culture of the West is what I will call the "repertory" of freedom.[1]

Not surprisingly, freedom, as much or more than most political concepts, is "essentially contested."[2] Thinkers over the centuries have argued about the relationship of free will to political and social freedom, questioned whether freedom is a unitary concept at all, and, if not, sought to enumerate various types of freedom. Even at a popular level, usage of the term has ranged widely. When individuals and groups refer to themselves as "free," they usually mean more than that they are not legally enslaved or that they have legal protections and entitlements as citizens. A person can be a slave, yet possess what some would call a kind of autonomy or "mental" freedom, while a legally free person can be a slave to drugs or alcohol.

Of course the term freedom can be subject to Orwellian distortions or pressed into the service of suspect causes. At one time the "free world" included several nations ruled by highly repressive regimes, while the mechanisms of the "free" market may severely restrict my comings and goings. The infamous Rousseauean claim that we may "force people to be free" has bothered more than just conservatives. Closer to the theme of freedom in the civil rights movement, a perfectly acceptable liberal principle—"freedom of choice"—became a way for white Southerners to avoid sending their children to integrated schools in the 1960s.

In this chapter I will delineate what I see as the four basic meanings of freedom in Western and American political thinking and see how they relate to Afro-American thinking about and experience of freedom. In doing this I hope to establish the repertory of freedom, the traditions of freedom-talk which the civil rights movement was both conscious of and, at times, unconscious heir to, and explore the ways the movement revitalized and enriched those traditions.

The rhetoric of freedom permeated the movement from the beginning. Martin Luther King's first book, written out of his experience as leader of the Montgomery bus boycott, was named *Stride Toward Freedom* and he ended his now famous "I Have a Dream" speech in late summer 1963 with the words of "the old Negro spiritual—free at last! free at last! thank God Almighty, we are free at last!" "Freedom songs," a new type of music different from spirituals, gospel, blues, or protest songs, were first made part of movement activities in Albany, Georgia in 1961–62. The Mississippi Summer Project of 1964, spearheaded by SNCC but carried out under the aegis of the Council of Federated Organizations (COFO), was known as "Freedom Summer." Out of that effort came the Mississippi Freedom Democratic Party (MFDP) which made an unsuccessful bid to be seated at the Democratic convention in Atlantic City in August of that same year. Informal schools set up by volunteers to teach basic literacy and impart the rudiments of black history and political education were known as "freedom schools," while the "freedom house" was the name of movement headquarters in various Mississippi towns. Indeed the rallying cry of the civil rights movement until the mid-1960s was "Freedom Now!"

It is tempting to dismiss such freedom-talk as a species of sloganeering and little more. Indeed one participant in the movement remembered that "none of us knew exactly what it meant, but we were saying freedom."[3] Still, easy skepticism on the topic begs the question of why the rhetoric of freedom resonated so powerfully with the aspirations of Southern blacks and occasionally Southern whites. And to minimize the importance of the rhetoric of freedom fails to take seriously how participants in the movement themselves articulated what concerned them and assumes that "we" somehow know better. More generally we should reject the notion that interests not

words are what really move people to political action and question the
related assumption that to be concerned with political rhetoric and
ideas is to be unreasonably high-minded. Political acts of cruelty are
as often motivated by ideas as by interests. But before unpacking the
various meanings or dimensions of freedom, we need to ask what the
"logic" of freedom-talk was.

There was surprisingly little explicit talk about equality as such in
the civil rights movement. Indeed, it may be that equality concerned
whites more than blacks since the argument about racial equality was
(and essentially is) an argument among white people. Black people
assume equality to be the case, by and large; and perhaps the relative
paucity of references to the term among movement participants or
leaders may have derived from the sense that it was demeaning for
black people to argue the case at all. In addition, freedom itself could
be understood to subsume equality in so far as a sense of self-respect
and pride, characteristics of a new, free self, implied an assertion of
equality. Finally, when terms such as "equal rights" or "equal
protection of the laws" were deployed, they did not refer to the
capacities of black people but to their relationship to the law,
whatever their capacities. That is, neither individual nor group
capacity is relevant to the question of equal rights.

But the link between rights-talk and freedom-talk is both closer
and more complicated. Dominated as the legal and political culture of
the United States has been by rights-talk, it comes as a surprise to
note the relative infrequency of reference to rights within movement
rhetoric. One reason may be that rights are legal/constitutional
entities, more the concern of lawyers and judges than of grass-roots
movements. Furthermore, an individual may be said to "possess" a
right. But it is not a disposition or state of mind; a "right" has no
psychological dimension and denotes an external relationship to state
power or social pressure. For that reason to be a rights-bearer lacks
the emotional resonance of the claim to be a "free" man or woman.
Finally, demanding, exercising, or protecting rights is sometimes
close in meaning to what political theorists call "negative" freedom.
Thus some sorts of rights-talk can also be seen as freedom-talk,
particularly when rights are thought of as privileges (a black person
should have the right to apply to the University of Alabama) or
immunities (black people should not be hindered from sitting anywhere on a public conveyance). Rights, in other words, are particular
specifications on and codifications of freedom in general.[4]

Explicit concerns with justice were frequent in movement rhetoric—one thinks of King's frequent evocation of the biblical image of "justice roll(ing) down like waters." But the justice sought was to be brought about by white people, particularly white authorities. It was a demand from black people that white people take responsible action. Also, as with rights, justice refers primarily to an external relationship between whites and blacks and concerns the distribution of various social, economic, and political-legal goods rather than a state of mind. A black person wanted to be free, but not to feel or be just. Indeed, only when a person is free can he or she be called to account for acting unjustly or praised for doing justice. Like equality before the law, the possibility of being just is something that presupposes freedom.

Finally, of course, power was increasingly important within the civil rights movement. Indeed, one mark of the sea-change in the movement after the mid-1960s was the decline of freedom-talk and the emergence of the rhetoric of power. Still, as is the case with rights, certain meanings of power coincide with certain meanings of freedom. If, as Michel Foucault claims, the term power is normally taken to be synonymous with repression and restriction, then power and freedom seem to stand in sharp opposition.[5] If, however, power is understood as the capacity to act or speak or think in ways of one's own choosing, if we understand it as "self-determination" or being "one's own master" as Frederick Douglass said, or if it implies empowerment, then power and freedom may overlap in meaning. Like freedom—and unlike justice—power implies a potential or actual capacity for action; unlike rights, power may refer to a psychological state as well as to an objective condition, i.e., one feels powerful. Thus we can see the way freedom-talk could easily turn into power-talk and recognize the ambiguous but close relationship between the two concepts.

The Repertory of Freedom

In addition to the general importance of political freedom in Western thought, there exists a specifically American obsession with freedom deriving from the actual presence of chattel slavery in the North American colonies and then, after independence, in the United States.[6] In American thought and experience, "freedom" and "slavery" have referred to an actual status as well as being concepts and tropes for certain conditions or states of mind. And, however important their African cultural heritages may be, Afro-Americans have shared in this high rhetorical, intellectual, and practical commitment to freedom by virtue of the experience and memory of enslavement as well as by their internalization of the dominant political culture.

Moreover, at the center of the biblical culture that whites and blacks, slaves and free people came to share were two powerful and compelling stories of the move from slavery to freedom—the Exodus story of the deliverance of the children of Israel from slavery in Egypt to the Promised Land and the spiritual deliverance from the bondage of sin to freedom in Christ as promised in the New Testament. From the beginning, collective and individual, literal and spiritual deliverance were "packed into" the idea and narrative of freedom at the popular as well as at the high cultural level. Thus when we combine the historical presence of slavery/freedom with the biblical narratives of deliverance from slavery, the intellectual and cultural precondition for the centrality of the idea of freedom within the civil rights movement becomes clear.

The modern debate about freedom, particularly political freedom, has generally been argued in terms of dichotomies, though the two terms of the dichotomy have shifted significantly over time. In the American context, John Winthrop's famous "On Liberty" (1645) is often cited as the *locus classicus* of two fundamental meanings of freedom or liberty.

> There is a twofold liberty, natural (I mean as our nature is now corrupt) and civil and federal. The first is common to man with beasts and other creatures. By this, man, as he stands in relation to man simply, hath liberty to do what he lists; it is a liberty to do evil as well as good. . . . This is that great enemy of truth and peace.

Winthrop then contrasts this pernicious natural liberty with "civil and federal" liberty which

> is a liberty to do that only which is good, just and honest. . . . This liberty is maintained and exercised in a way of subjection to authority.[7]

Winthrop's dichotomies are pre-modern insofar as they still assume the inseparability of secular and spiritual liberty, but they do anticipate the later dichotomy of "positive" and "negative" freedom, though the valorization of the two types of freedom will shift considerably.

If we turn specifically to the political-legal sphere, another dichotomy begins to emerge, at least in America, by the 1770s. This way of differentiating types of liberty grouped "civil liberties," the protection of personal rights, including property, on one side and "political liberties," the right and duty to participate in and have one's consent solicited as to the forms and policies of government on the other.[8]

Such a purely secular, binary opposition received its most eloquent and generally influential expression from the French liberal, Benjamin Constant, whose "The Liberty of the Ancients Compared with That of the Moderns" (1819) was written in reaction to the frightening connection between liberty, virtue, and terror that had emerged during the French Revolution. In Constant's historicizing typology, there were two fundamental types of liberty. The modern notion of freedom was one in which the citizen was subject to laws rather than "arbitrary will." In contrast (implicitly) to Winthrop's thinking that the individual was free by and through obedience to the spiritual and secular law, Constant's essentially "liberal" notion was that, as long as citizens were not treated arbitrarily or capriciously and themselves obeyed the law, a major prerequisite of freedom had been met. But modern liberty also included freedom of property, expression, movement, association to "discuss" and "profess," and freedom to "exercise some political influence on the administration of government." By way of contrast, citizens in the ancient world "collectively but directly" had engaged in deliberation, voting on laws, and serving on juries. More importantly, there had been little or no protection of privacy nor did any presumption in favor of protecting private liberties exist. In the ancient world "laws regulated customs." Generally, then, Constant identified "sharing of the social power" as the essence of classical freedom and "guarantees accorded by institutions to these [private] pleasures" as capturing the essence of modern freedom.[9]

Several things are worth observing about Constant's formulation of the two basic ideas—and experiences—of liberty. First, what Winthrop had called natural liberty had been domesticated, as it were, and its assessment reversed. Modern liberty became the freedom to pursue particular and private interests within a framework of laws which demanded only external obedience to the secular law rather than creedal adherence to a spiritual law. Secular and religious spheres were separated; indeed religious freedom, along with freedom of property, became the two paradigmatic examples of modern, "negative" freedom. Constant, along with contemporaries such as John Stuart Mill, was instrumental in formulating what came to be known as the liberal or "negative" concept of freedom, a type of freedom which stressed the right of individuals to choose their own beliefs and values; to act upon desires and interests as long as they did not fundamentally infringe upon those of other people; and the right not to engage in politics, all within a framework of laws and institutions arrived at through what Constant referred to as a "representative system" of government[10] based on the "consent of the governed" (to use the American phrasing) rather than their direct participation. Thus Constant's "modern" conception of political freedom drew the crucial axes of difference between the private and the public, between individual rights and communal obligations and privileges rather than between the natural and the spiritual. And in contrast with Winthrop, the former not the latter of each opposition was preferred.

No American, as far as I know, expressed these two contrasting views of freedom so clearly. But in modified form they were at issue, for instance, in the different understandings of what constituted citizenship in the years between the founding of the Republic and its Reconstruction in the late 1860s. For instance, by 1866 radical and moderate Republicans were separated by their contrasting views on the nature of citizenship. Did the fact that freedmen were now also citizens entail the political right to vote and hold office or did the possession of civil rights, i.e., equal treatment in protection of person, family, property, and contracts exhaust the attributes of citizenship? Where radicals held voting and holding office to be "essential attributes of citizenship," the moderates (not to mention more conservative Republicans and Democrats) held that "voting was a privilege" and not inherent in being a citizen.[11] From this perspective, the argument about federalism and the relative power of the national and state governments has, throughout American history, been a disguised or displaced debate about the nature of citizenship and ultimately the nature and entitlements of freedom.

To be sure the radical Republican view of citizenship and freedom hardly gave the same pride of place to political participation as had the ancients' view. Political power in America was invested in representative bodies at the national and state level rather than in institutions of direct democracy, while the Bill of Rights provided protection against (federal) infringement of individual liberties and guarantees of certain individual rights. Still the maximalist notion of freedom within what nineteenth-century Americans called "republican" government implied both civil rights and liberties (the liberty of the moderns) and political rights, a remnant of the importance of participation in the exercise of political power found in the classical conception of freedom. That political rights were never explicitly guaranteed in the Constitution—the Fifteenth Amendment only forbade certain types of discrimination in enfranchising citizens—is one of its great weaknesses, a legacy of the notion that voting was a privilege too important to be left to just any citizen without qualification. But the "spirit of the laws," the political culture at its most expansive, was consonant with what might be called the "political" liberalism of Constant, Mill, and Alexis de Tocqueville, each of whom thought that political freedom, not being a matter of indifference, should not be left to languish. We must, claimed Constant, anticipating Tocqueville and Mill as well as John Dewey much later, "learn to combine [the two types of liberty] together"; for "political liberty . . . enlarges [the citizens'] spirit, enables their thoughts and establishes among them a kind of intellectual equality which enhances the glory and power of a people."[12]

There was yet another way that the formal freedom to pursue one's private concerns and the freedom to participate in the political life of the community needed supplementing in the post-Revolutionary era. This was through the provision, material as well as educational and cultural, of resources to citizens. Political freedom, it was argued, would remain empty if there were no time or resources or economic wherewithal to gain meaningful access to the public realm. In general the recognition that what might be called the opportunity of freedom had to be supplemented with capability led some to see the provision of capability, spiritual and material, as a vital part of freedom itself.

In the American context, the development of a public school system, derived largely from the Jeffersonian/republican notion of the necessity of an educated citizenry, reflected the idea that formal freedom needed substantive content. By the end of the nineteenth century, the lack of material as well as educational capability, the particular problem of the poor and excluded, was recognized as bearing on freedom. For instance, W. E. B Du Bois identified the "negative and positive sides" of freedom in terms of access and capability when he wrote in 1915 that Negroes must have

> freedom on the one hand and power on the other . . . These shackles must go. But that is but the beginning. The Negro must have power: the power of men, the right to do, to know, to feel and to express that knowledge, action and political gift. He must not simply be free from . . . he must have the right to vote and rule over the citizens, white and black . . .[13]

Here of course "right" is, as already discussed, used not just in the sense of a protection from the state or from social oppression but also as an enabling "freedom to," as a form of empowerment.

Similarly, at about the same time, Randolph Bourne turned his acerbic pen to the political plight of the immigrants:

> If freedom means the right to do pretty much as one pleases, so long as one does not interfere with others, the immigrant has found freedom, and the ruling element has been singularly liberal in the treatment of the invading hordes. But if freedom means a democratic cooperation in determining the ideals and purposes and industrial and social institutions of a country, then the immigrant has not been free . . .[14]

Yet this expansion of the notion of freedom, the attempt to make both terms of the dichotomy equally valid and to give substantive content to formal freedom, has not gone unchallenged, particularly in Anglo-American political thinking. The strongest and best-known counterattack came from Isaiah Berlin in his enormously influential "Two Concepts of Liberty" (1958). Berlin claimed to be writing in the liberal tradition of Constant and Mill and, indeed, his essay revoiced Constant's critique of the republicanism of the French Revolution which, Berlin implied, had returned in the more ominous form of twentieth-century totalitarianism, under the guise of Marxist-Leninist ideology and politics.

But there were important differences in the positions of Constant and Berlin. Though Berlin ranged widely over the history of Western thought, his was a decidedly prescriptive (as opposed to historical) discussion of freedom. In truth Berlin did not believe there were two conflicting forms of freedom, since "positive" freedom simply wasn't freedom properly so called: "Everything is what it is—liberty is liberty not equality or fairness or justice or culture or human happiness or a quiet conscience."[15] Thus what might be called the "weak" point of Berlin's essay was a "rectification of names," an attempt at clarifying the vocabulary of political discourse and jettisoning misunderstanding about terminology.

There was, however, a "strong" version of Berlin's thesis. Not only was freedom univocal in meaning, but positive freedom was a dangerous concept which had wrought considerable damage and would continue to do so unless it was abandoned. Thus despite Berlin's commitment to value pluralism, his hostility to dogma, and his generally keen sense of historical differences, he clearly reified the concept of freedom and impoverished, as much as clarified, its meaning. This stands in marked contrast with Constant who explicitly historicized his preference for modern liberty: "Since we live in modern times, I want a liberty suited to modern times."[16]

Indeed, Berlin stood closer to Winthrop than to Constant to the degree that he accepted the terms of Winthrop's binary opposition though he inverted Winthrop's valorization of them. Natural liberty became Berlin's negative freedom—"absence of interference" or "absence of obstacles to possible choices and desires" in Berlin's terms[17]—while what Winthrop called civil or federal liberty was roughly the same as Berlin's idea of positive freedom. What linked Berlin and Winthrop was the belief that the essence of civil/positive freedom consisted in obedience to some higher authority or standard or value, i.e., it was really a species of obedience. Moreover, according to Berlin, such a position implied there was a "true" or "rational" self different from one's given empirical self. And if this were the case, then some sort of an elite, in modern times usually a political one (as illustrated by the doctrine of the vanguard role of the Party), was needed to determine what that higher standard was to which the real self should adhere and then "to force empirical selves into the right pattern" and to punish them for failing to achieve it.[18]

Had Berlin stopped there, his position would have been quite tenable. He was clearly reflecting (on) the bleak postwar mood caught by Orwell in his idea of "doublespeak" and by Camus and Koestler in their explorations of the casuistry of political murder. Still the way Berlin had sundered freedom from anything to do with politics, except to say that "the chief value for liberals of political—'positive'—rights of participating in government is as a means for protecting what they hold to be an ultimate value, namely individual—'negative'—liberty," was startling. Though Berlin insisted that to deny the label of freedom to political participation was not to downgrade it, and that, as he later wrote in a 1969 addendum to the 1958 essay, "participation in self-government is, like justice, a basic human requirement, an end in itself," there can be no doubt that the Berlin of the 1958 essay belongs to the strand of the liberal tradition that undervalues political participation and not to the tradition of political liberalism to which Constant, Tocqueville, and Mill belong.[19]

Most important for our purposes is an analysis of Berlin's concept of positive freedom, for it is not at all clear, as C. B. MacPherson has observed, that the various characteristics Berlin attributed to positive freedom comport very well with one another nor that we should deny them all the name of freedom. There seem to be at least four different idea-clusters grouped under Berlin's positive freedom umbrella: 1) provision or prerequisites for making a choice or acting, i.e., capabilities; 2) individual autonomy or variants on it such as "self-expression" or "self-realization," "the desire to be governed by myself" or "to be [my] own master"; 3) collective political self-rule and political participation; and 4) acting in accordance with a higher standard (Christian Truth, Marxist Laws of History, Kantian Duty, or Hegelian Reason) and realizing the true self thereby.[20] My sense here is that autonomy and political participation need to be separated out and retained as meanings of freedom.

Berlin is by no means the only thinker who separates freedom (of the negative variety) from autonomy. Indeed some define freedom in negative terms solely to exclude autonomy, since the latter concept is, as Nancy Rosenblum has noted, "more than just free selection, it is determining one's own desires and values." Gerald Dworkin differentiates autonomy from freedom ("the ability of a person to do what she wants . . .") by linking it with self–rule or -determination arising from scrutiny and reflection on one's wants. Harry Frankfurt's well-known position, to which Dworkin's is closely related, could be understood as defining freedom as the ability "to do what one wants to do" and free will (or autonomy in our terms) "to want what he wants to want." Generally, J. R. Schneewind suggests that autonomy now refers to the ability "to look at our lives and actions from, among others, the point of view of the self-legislator." And finally Richard Flathman sees autonomy as involving "continuing assessment of ends and purposes . . . independence of mind . . . willingness to try out novel ideas and to experiment." It is an "achievement."[21]

What is interesting about such accounts is that though autonomy and negative feedom are differentiated, no one agrees with Berlin that autonomy necessarily involves adherence to some higher law, categorical imperative, or metaphysic. It has become, in other words, as Schneewind particularly emphasizes, a psychological capacity roughly equivalent to moral self-awareness. Nor, it should be added, is there an inherent requirement that the language of self-determination or -mastery is necessary to elucidate the concept of autonomy.

Still, there are dangers which may arise from confusing negative freedom and autonomy. Early in *Walden*, Thoreau writes:

> It is hard to have a Southern overseer; it is worse to have a Northern one; but worst of all when you are the slave driver of yourself.[22]

Here Thoreau himself confuses—at least for rhetorical purposes—negative freedom (not being a slave) with autonomy (freedom from an employer or public opinion or one's self-image). Indeed the way Thoreau glides from one to the other is one of the reasons why Berlin and others object to the equation of autonomy and freedom. Yet Thoreau redeems himself by identifying precisely what can be pernicious about autonomy, even as an internal state—the lack of criteria for what counts as valid or real desires and the tendency to be harder on ourselves than we should be.

Still, once these dangerous elisions and possibilities of confusion are registered, I see no compelling reason to refuse to see autonomy as a valid form of freedom, one which is neither synonymous with negative freedom nor a covert form of obedience to higher law or reason or a way of handing over choices to a spiritual elite or of justifying obedience in the name of freedom. My respect for your freedom forbids my tearing up your ballot for George Wallace for president, while my concern for your autonomy, your ability to make reasoned choices, tempts me to refuse your ballot and subject you to further political education. Indeed, the politicization of autonomy, as we shall see, is extremely dangerous; and we should give negative freedom priority over autonomy in an explicitly political context where state action is concerned and insist that one's moral capacities or choices, insofar as they do not impinge obviously on others and are within the law, are not the proper business of the state.[23] But this should not prevent us from considering both autonomy and negative freedom as types of freedom.

The historical case is even stronger for including political participation and self-rule among the types of freedom. Indeed the civic humanist or republican tradition in the West, originating in the classical period, identified freedom with the participation of a virtuous citizenry in the deliberations and decisions of the polity. However much of that tradition has been lost to us, what does remain, as we have seen, is the idea that a free people is a self-governing people, one whose government is founded on the consent of the governed and demands their active participation.

The most powerful contemporary expression of freedom as political participation has come from emigré political theorist Hannah Arendt, whose work of the late 1950s and early 1960s constitutes the best response to Berlin's "Two Concepts of Liberty" essay of 1958. Not only was Arendt's influence on the student Left in America—or at least on some of its early leadership—significant, as was her later influence on dissident movements in Eastern Europe, her "theory" of freedom was as close as anyone came to anticipating—and illuminating—the specifically political nature of the activities of the civil rights movement.[24]

There are several ironies in the fact that Arendt posed the main challenge to Berlin's understanding of and enthusiasm for negative freedom. Both were Jewish and emigrés, though Berlin came to England from Riga, Latvia at an early age, while Arendt fled Germany after the Nazi takeover and arrived in New York in 1941 after several years in Paris and a period in internment camps. Yet while Berlin grew up to join the British academic-intellectual establishment, becoming one of its most admired members, Arendt was marginal to institutional academic power for most of her life; indeed, her experience in Germany had taught her considerable suspicion, even contempt, for the political capability of academics.

Arendt and Berlin also shared several common intellectual concerns. Despite what seem superficial similarities between the political thought of Rousseau and Arendt, Arendt was every bit as hostile to the French thinker's influence as was Berlin; and both agreed on a specifically political reading of Machiavellian ethics. Moreover, like Berlin, Arendt always stressed the dangers of deductive thinking and abstract truth claims in the political sphere. She characterized the "human condition" in terms of "plurality," the sheer variety of perspectives arising from the diversity of human beings, and emphasized the importance of argument and persuasion versus demonstration and deduction in the political realm. Finally, even more than

Berlin, she took the "burden of our time" to be the emergence of totalitarianism in Europe.

But what most sharply differentiated the two thinkers was that Arendt's assessment of the contemporary experience of "dark times" led her to locate one of the crucial preconditions for totalitarianism in the radical split between public and private spheres of thought and action leading to the destruction of a public realm or space of political action. By contrast, Berlin, and others like him, tended to identify the rise and essence of totalitarianism with the politicization of all spheres of existence and the invasion of the private realm by the all-powerful state. It was but a short step from his position to one which looked askance upon mass political participation altogether.

In her essay "What Is Freedom?" Arendt first really voiced her claim that "the *raison d'etre* of politics is freedom and its field of experience is action." To be sure, humans had to "be liberated . . . from the necessities of life"; and she later allowed in *On Revolution* that "freedom of movement" and "freedom from unjustified restraint" were the "results of liberation." But such (negative) freedoms are "by no means the actual content of freedom, which . . . is participation in public affairs, or admission to the public realm." What was required to be free was "the company of other men" and "a common public space" into which one "inserts himself by word and deed."[25]

Arendt was aware of how strange her identification of freedom with political participation sounded in a period dominated by an interest-group conception of politics on the one hand and the metapolitics of the Cold War on the other. She acknowledged that the experience of totalitarianism tempted one to accept the "liberal credo: 'the less politics, the more freedom'" and more generally to buy into the modern separation of "freedom and politics."[26] Nor did she accept the Christian or the Kantian equation of freedom with free will or autonomy. Hers was the position of the Greeks and Romans that freedom was first of all a public, political fact in the world.

Put another way: Arendt equated acting with freedom: "to be free and to act are the same." Indeed what she meant by acting was not just any form of movement or "behavior" but that which seemed to "begin something new." Political action was akin to acting in the theatrical sense, since it required an audience and a "space of appearance" in which "virtuosity" was to be displayed. But Arendt was not interested in aestheticizing politics as such. Besides virtu-

osity she saw "courage" as a prime requirement for political action,
since "in politics not life but the world is at stake," by which she
meant that the highest priority of political actors should be the
preservation of the possibility of human action and the institutions
that protect it. Thus she defined freedom in terms of the qualities of
the actor, the place of action, and the effects of action.[27]

Though so strangely conceived as to be unassimilable when it
appeared, Arendt's account of the relationship between politics and
freedom is of immense pertinence for an understanding of the civil
rights movement, particularly the public virtuosity and the courage
of its participants. Moreover what differentiated Arendt's position
from the mainstream of republican thought or Hegelian *Staatslehre*
was her refusal, particularly in *On Revolution*, to identify the public
realm or space of freedom with the institutions of the state. The *polis*
was "the organization of the people as it arises out of acting and
speaking together . . . no matter where they happened to be."[28] It
could be called into being and manifested wherever people gathered
publicly to speak and act on matters bearing on their common life.
Protection of individual rights and privacy were important to Arendt;
but, inverting Berlin, they were not the essence of but only prerequisites for genuine political freedom.

If we draw back and survey the various conceptions of freedom
discussed so far, we can generalize by identifying four principal
meanings of freedom within American/Western political thought that
link up with the language of freedom within and the goals of the civil
rights movement.

1) **Liberal freedom.** The conceptual core of this position is negative freedom. Individuals are free from arbitrary legal or institutional
restrictions, arbitrary being defined as not equally applicable or not
rationally justifiable or arrived at by commonly agreed upon procedures. All citizens are treated equally. In addition their private
concerns and interests are protected by rights and liberties which
create a sphere of non-interference against state depredations or
social pressure. Political rights are part of the bundle of rights, but
the state or public is indifferent to whether or why citizens participate
in politics, the assumption being that they will do so, directly and
through representatives, to protect and advance their interests.
Otherwise, the tendency is to see politics as a bother or at worst a

danger. Generally, individual commitments or values, adherence to creeds or religions, is a matter of indifference to the laws of the polity. Beyond the fact that one's main obligation as a citizen is to preserve the existing structure of laws, there is no notion of the public or common good. With all sorts of accretions and embellishments, this has historically been the dominant understanding of freedom within mainstream American political culture, particularly and in a strongly normative sense after World War II. In reference to the civil rights movement, liberal freedom is protected or guaranteed by the Reconstruction amendments, while the First Amendment provides a valuable charter for civil liberties and personal freedoms.

2) **Freedom as autonomy.** This position derives from, or is at least related to, a certain cluster of characteristics of positive freedom (as defined by Berlin) such as autonomy, self-determination, pride, and self-respect. Generally speaking it refers to proposed or achieved changes in sense of self or personality; to internal states rather than the achievement of tangible gains as such. It may be the product of political education and/or the outcome of political action. This process of becoming free from an old sense of self and from relationships of oppression or dependency can resemble a kind of religious conversion or therapeutic transformation. Indeed, it is probably only in the twentieth century, or at least since the French Revolution, that politics has been seen as a context of and for self-transformation of the sort captured under this form of freedom.[29] In the view of freedom as autonomy, politics is still a means not an end, but politics does take on more than an external relationship to the self and its desires. In other words politics becomes not just an arena where interests are pursued but also a process of self-transformation. In the rhetoric and thinking of the civil rights movement, this form of freedom found expression in the powerful idea(l) of "somebodyness" and "self-respect."

3) **Participatory freedom.** In the modern world of liberal constitutionalism, this form of freedom has made its presence felt only with considerable difficulty. The close link between citizenship, voting, holding office, and the general rhetoric of popular sovereignty reflects its continuing hold. Involvement in politics is not just a right or even a duty, but a positive thing, a practice which has its own rules and standards. Besides voting and holding office, participatory freedom can be expressed in citizen meetings for deliberation and planning, and in mass demonstrations and public action generally. The purpose of politics in this conception of freedom is to perpetuate

institutions which will maintain public participation in the exercise of
power and keep the public realm open to all citizens. But if such
institutions are lacking and participation is difficult, even impossible,
as was the case for black Southerners in many parts of the region up to
the 1960s, the people affected are denied the possibility of fulfilling
their full human potential as well as their citizenship rights.

And finally there is

4) Freedom as collective deliverance. As liberation from external
control, often from an occupying people or from captivity, this vision
of freedom is found not in philosophical theories or texts, but, as
already mentioned, in the "Exodus" story in the Old Testament.
Thus it appears less as an idea or concept than as a narrative of
deliverance, journey, and arrival.[30] In the Western political tradition, collective liberation has often been prefigured by the example of
the children of Israel and, in the American context, by the Puritan
exodus from England and the establishment of a "New Zion" in North
America. Moreover, this narrative of freedom and ultimately of
"national Christianity" seems to be more congenial to Protestant than
Catholic peoples, since it focuses on dissidence and secession.[31]
Finally, as we shall see in the civil rights movement, freedom as
collective deliverance is ambiguous as to whether it is a story of being
freed or of self-liberation, of chosenness or self-initiated rebellion, of
going home or expelling an occupier from one's home, or finally
whether it is of a religious or secular nature. This narrative of freedom
is silent as to the nature of the political institutions of the people in
question, or as to how much freedom or obligation, rights or duties
individuals have within the collectivity. The central concern is the
nation not the republic; individuals are designated generally as
subjects rather than citizens or rights-bearers.

Freedom and Black Political Culture

I have developed this repertory of freedom in order to show the way
black political movements, including the civil rights movement, have
drawn upon, modified, and developed these four forms of freedom.
This implies that the civil rights movement did not operate in a
vacuum, at least not a cultural or religious vacuum. There was a
continuity of religious institutions and practices, rituals, stories, and
theologies linking the slave experience with protest movements well
into this century, just as there were forms of music (both sacred and

secular as well as political protest) and literature (the prototype being the slave narrative) running throughout the Afro-American experience. But politically the threads connecting the first and second Reconstructions were less straightforward. Still, if we look at the meanings of freedom that emerged in the transition from slavery to freedom, we can give some historical density to the four models of freedom relevant to and articulated in the civil rights movement.

The ideological sources of black political culture are generally the same as those of the dominant white political culture, but different experiences—liberation from slavery—and emphases—the persisting importance of Afro-American modes of religious ritual, symbolism, and theology—had to be accommodated. Obviously for black Americans slavery and freedom possess an intensity of significance largely absent in the white political culture, since slavery had actually been experienced by the relatives of many participants in the movement. Not only could this not be said of any white Americans; for many, even most Americans of European descent outside the South, no real history of family slaveholding or meaningful connection with the institution had ever existed.

Moreover, the centrality to black theology of the Exodus story meant that slavery/freedom was understood on a figural-spiritual level by many black Christians. Thus slavery and freedom referred to more than "just" a secular experience or status, for they were also spiritual or sacred experiences of a people whose experience was part of God's purpose and plan. Freedom, according to this spiritual interpretation, was a destination in sacred history as well as a goal of action within secular history; it was a future condition implying a fundamental transformation in individual and group life.

Finally slavery and freedom possessed some of the same resonances in black as in white religious and political culture. The terms could refer to the condition of the individual soul. One was a slave to the world, but now free in Christ. More complexly, one became free (spiritually) by freely choosing to live in perfect obedience to God's word and will, the obvious source of Winthrop's second idea of freedom.[32]

In the political context, the great American story of the fight for independence from colonial domination and the ostensible commitment to a natural rights idea as found in Jefferson's Declaration of Independence profoundly influenced white and black Abolitionists from the beginning of their struggle, whatever the blindness, not to mention hypocrisy, of Jefferson and the Founding Fathers on the matter of slavery. Thus besides the religious provenance of Afro-American freedom-talk, a secular vocabulary of republicanism, revolution, and rights, derived from the American and (later) Haitian wars of independence, existed for useful appropriation. Indeed, "the language of Natural Rights," claims Daniel Rodgers, "has been the central subversive strain in American political life."[33]

Besides the Exodus model of group liberation and the rights and revolution rhetoric, there were the examples of the three (abortive or unsuccessful) slave revolts in the first third of the century. Moreover, once slavery had ended, Afro-Americans sought to put into practice the cluster of ideas and impulses associated with the "free-labor" ideology of mid-century Republicanism, a vision derived in part from the "possessive individualism" of the liberal tradition, the connection of property and autonomy inherent in the civic humanist tradition, and bearing a certain rhetorical resemblance on a mundane level to the quest for personal and spiritual autonomy deriving from German Idealism domesticated for American uses.[34] The vision of independent, self-sustaining black citizens, farming their own land and determining their own destinies, was for many the logical result of emancipation and the proper goal of Reconstruction. As one banner in a freedom parade in Charleston, South Carolina in February 1865 read: "We Know No Master But Ourselves." This adumbration of freedom as autonomy makes the point that Eric Foner has stressed in his *Reconstruction* that freedom was less a clearly defined concept than a "terrain of conflict" during Reconstruction.[35] Indeed this has been the case throughout American history, a point which the various uses of the term freedom during the civil rights movement confirms quite clearly.

Overall, during Reconstruction freedom implied, first, a change in the legal status of former slaves from that condition to legal freedom. Less obvious or acceptable to many whites was that this free status also included "civic equality," the security of person and property, protection against harrassment and serious intimidation meted out by hostile whites. This essentially "liberal" cluster of freedoms was then augmented, according to Foner, by "desire for independence from white control, for autonomy both as individuals and as members of a community itself . . ."; or as Vincent Harding has asserted, "[F]reedom for black people meant taking care of themselves."[36] In practice this meant everything from the choice of surnames to freedom to travel to search for lost relatives or better opportunities. It was also manifested in the desire to control the spheres of work and ownership, churches, schools, and ultimately the right to vote and hold office. In other words, the first task of freedom was the creation of the basic institutions of civil society, guaranteeing their legal and constitutional protection, and ultimately achieving the needed autonomy to sustain a free way of life.[37]

Reconstruction also saw two great surges of political mobilization among black men, which constituted a tremendously important expansion of the public realm for blacks and a just as frightening phenomenon for most Southern whites. The first rush came just after the war was over; the second with the onset of Radical or Congressional Reconstruction in 1867. In both cases freedom took on a more explicitly political dimension and "politics emerged as the political focus of black aspirations." Crucial in this second upsurge were the Union Leagues which served as centers of political education, offered economic aid and social services, and even helped organize schools. In the early elections of Radical Reconstruction, voter turnout among freedmen was 90 percent and the "loss of suffrage" was identified with the "loss of freedom."[38] Writes Harding, himself a veteran of the civil rights movement, in the accents of the second Reconstruction and with Arendtian cadences, black people were

> now meeting in public not only to discuss the political affairs of the state and the nation . . . but to challenge the political legitimacy of their former owners, overseers and oppressors . . . freedom meant above all the right to participate in the process of creating it . . . not only the right to vote, but the right to participate in all the political decision-making processes.[39]

In addition to these forms of freedom—deliverance from slavery, a new status, institutional autonomy, and participation in politics—the concern with pride and self-respect, the inner prerequisite for independence, ran throughout antebellum black thought and experience. For instance in his *Appeal* (1829), perhaps the first explicitly Afro-American jeremiad, David Walker took the Exodus story and rung an interesting change on it by claiming that white Christians treated their slaves worse than the heathen Egyptians had treated the Children of Israel. Indeed, he seriously doubted that whites would repent, though unless they did they were "ruined." But he also addressed his comments to "afflicted, degraded and slumbering brethren" and attacked their servility.[40] Though his evocation of the biblical story of slavery might have led Walker to a nationalist-migrationist position, he refused to concede America to the whites. Rather black people must be "united" and their "greatest happiness shall consist in working for the salvation of the whole body." Asserting that "America is more our country than it is the whites [sic]," he ended his diatribe by quoting the Declaration of Independence.[41]

Walker's militant vision of "black messianic armed resistance" derived in part from the perception that slavery perpetuated itself by numbing the minds and spirits of the slaves. Frederick Douglass was also to stress the connection between the willingness to fight for freedom, casting off the aura of dependency and creating pride: "If we are elevated, our elevation will have been accomplished through our own instrumentality." Or as one black soldier said during the war: "Now we sogers are men—men de first time in our lives." Less dramatic or extreme demonstrations of pride and self-respect were encouraged by the black churches. Bishop Arnett, for instance, called for everyone to "assist in delivering the African race from physical, mental and moral bondage," for "[i]f the whites would not respect them, they could at least respect themselves."[42]

Henry Highland Garnet was one of those who drew the theoretical and practical implications of the baleful logic of dependency. At the Colored National Convention in 1848, he contended:

> To be dependent is to be degraded. . . . we must become equally independent with other members of the community. That other members of the community shall be as dependent upon us, as we upon them.[43]

Garnet's position represented an abandonment of a Christian ethic of non-resistance: "To such Degradation it is Sinful in the extreme for you to make voluntary submission."[44] Such a view implied the complicity of slaves with their own enslavement and that at some level a choice of slavery and degradation rather than death had been made. Indeed, behind Garnet's advocacy of resistance lay a momentous question that has remained embedded in Afro-American thinking: Was the degradation of slavery "only" external, a condition free whites imputed to black slaves or was it a condition internalized by some, even if not all, slaves? Was degradation real or only apparent?

In 1854 Martin Delany offered a fascinating meditation on the themes of citizenship and self-determination. Taking Rome as the historical precedent, he noted that enemies and aliens were non-citizens, while the citizen was "one who might enjoy the highest honor in his own town . . . and country and commonwealth." The upshot, however, of this precedent was, Delany suggested, that Afro-Americans could never be full citizens and hence fully free since America was not their home. Voting would always remain a privilege rather than a right in such a situation.[45]

The argument was made explicitly collective when Delany asserted that to be free a people "must be their own rulers" or at least possess the "acknowledged right to govern." But because no people are free "who themselves do not constitute a ruling element of the country in which they live," a condition certainly true of Afro-Americans, the suffrage as such was useless since they were not part of the dominant or ruling element. Were the signs of difference eradicable, as, for instance, with economic status, equality might be attainable in theory. But since the principle of difference in the United States was color, there was no realistic possibility of its eradication. All this amounted to a closely argued brief for emigration of some sort. Behind it was the assumption that no political order founded on what we now call a pluralistic society was viable. "Universal brotherhood," contended Delany, was really "universal acknowledgement of Anglo-Saxon rule." If return to Africa was impossible, some sort of link between "black and colored persons" should be established.[46]

Delany's mixture of historical, sociological, and political-theoretical argument is fascinating because it is one of the few attempts by black or white abolitionists to break out of the religious and/or republican rhetoric, i.e., what Vincent Harding has called "The Great Tradition," in order to rethink the meaning of and conditions for political freedom in the widest sense. Indeed, Delany's position shares a good bit with the older classical civic humanist equation of citizen equality, political participation, and power. Furthermore Delany uncovered—or at least made explicit—one of the traditional assumptions underlying republican government: the existence of a homogeneous population rooted in a particular place. Because Afro-Americans were aliens, Delany had to bleakly conclude that they would never be incorporated into the polity. To assume otherwise was to be complicit in one's own degradation.

Though something like what I have called the "repertory of freedom" may be said to exist, the question remains as to the relationship between these aspects of freedom in the inherited black political culture and the civil rights movement of the 1950s and 1960s. Was there a causal relationship, a conscious linkage of traditions of political thinking, or were these essentially nineteenth-century currents anticipations without essential connection to the explicit thinking of participants in the civil rights movement?

One answer has been given by Ronald Walters his essay "The Boundaries of Abolition" (1973). There Walters noted that many activists and historians of the 1960s claimed that there was a linear connection between abolitionism and the protest movements of the 1960s. Walters, however, was struck more by the discontinuity between the two periods and movements. Gandhi had exerted more influence on the movement than Garrison: "It [abolitionism] was rediscovered largely by academics and not by men and women centrally involved in agitation." Yet writing at the beginning of the next decade, Vincent Harding constructed his "collective history of the freedom struggle" as a "long, continuous movement, flowing like a river . . . toward the ocean of humankind's most courageous hope for freedom and integrity." In *There Is a River*, Harding's epic narrative has only followed that river into the Reconstruction experience. But it takes no great leap of the imagination to guess that, as Harding brings the story forward, he will continue to assume continuity and progress in his narrative.[47]

Part of the problem in this debate has to do with the degree of consciousness being asserted. Walters is speaking of explicit ideas and the conscious influence of thinkers and movements. On this point, it is hard not to agree with him that the ideas and visions which guided the civil rights movement of the 1950s and 1960s, particularly up to the early 1960s, owed relatively little to an explicitly Afro-American vision of politics or to the radical spirit of abolitionist thought. If one were to identify the influence of various political traditions on the early movement, one would point to the importance of:

1) socialist, Marxist, and radical New Deal traditions which older black activists Bayard Rustin and Ella Baker used to shape both new civil rights organizations—King's SCLC and SNCC;

2) Gandhi and American pacifism within CORE, first in the 1940s and then for early movement leaders such as James Lawson;

3) the academic influence of Gandhi, Thoreau, and Marx on the

student Martin Luther King and other young college students in the
early days of the movement;

4) the influence of existentialist ideas of self-definition and action,
especially those of Albert Camus, upon students and, to a certain
extent, King;

5) the influence of neo-orthodox theologians such as Reinhold
Niebuhr as well as Social Gospel and liberal theology upon King and
some of his ministerial colleagues.

But symptomatic of the gap separating the civil rights movement
from its political heritage is the difficulty in finding any mention in
the 1950s (or the early 1960s) of the significant 1930s debate among
black liberals and radicals under the aegis of the NAACP—or anything matching it in the later decades. Once the Depression set in,
some black activists and academics, as well as political leaders, began
challenging the leadership of the NAACP to expand the scope of its
work beyond what Harold Cruse was much later to call "non-
economic liberalism" which had as its goal the securing of black legal
and political rights via the strategy of "protracted legal struggle" in
which the law, according to crucial figures such as Charles Houston,
was an instrument to "foster and order social change."[48] This NAACP
position was the contemporary version of the "Great Tradition" of
liberal freedom.

Opposed to this mainstream legal and constitutional emphasis of
the NAACP were those influenced by socialist and Marxist (or even
radical union) ideas who saw the crucial task as one of improving the
"desperate economic conditions of the black masses" by forging an
alliance with the white working class. For some this position was a
crucial step toward revolution and for others a step toward interracial
unionism. As one of the major spokesmen of this position, Ralph
Bunche, put it, it made little sense for the Negro to "become a special
ward of the Supreme Court."[49]

And finally there was the position of W. E. B. DuBois who left the
NAACP and the editorship of *Crisis* during the decade because of his
disagreements with the national policy of the NAACP. DuBois called
for the black community to turn inward toward economic cooperation
and the strengthening of institutions such as schools, churches,
hospitals, and cultural organizations. The idea was to encourage "self-
help" and "racial pride." Like the more orthodox radicals, DuBois
saw economic problems as central. But unlike Bunche and other

radicals, he saw little hope in a black-white alliance since "the split between black and white workers" is "greater than between white workers and capitalists." Moreover DuBois's focus was as much upon consumer action as it was upon changing or taking control of the means of production. Nor did DuBois see any future in encouraging Garveyite migrationist schemes.[50]

This was an important debate in terms of ideas as well as practical proposals. But it, and relatively broadly debated issues of political vision and strategy for black Americans, disappeared from view after the end of World War II. The vision of an interracial alliance of the poor and working classes soon came a cropper and perished first of racial tensions, then of the Cold War and a certain modicum of prosperity. Nor did nationalist/migrationist ideas of collective liberation or community solidarity on a large scale have much general appeal in the South, perhaps because they seemed so implausible in that setting. DuBois's concern with racial pride would reemerge quite strongly in the 1960s, but there was little to link it with the political ideas regnant in the early movement, except perhaps for general acquaintance with the issues dividing DuBois and Booker T. Washington in the early years of the century.

Though Negro History was still taught in many black schools and some black colleges on into the 1950s, Negro History Week was hardly observed. By the "middle of the decade," report August Meier and Elliott Rudwick, "sales of [John Hope] Franklin's survey [*From Slavery to Freedom*] reached the vanishing point." The important point here is not that the civil rights movement drew upon or was ignited by black political and cultural thought in any explicit way, but that these traditions were rediscovered and made more accessible, at an academic and at a popular level, precisely by the far-reaching intellectual and cultural excitement generated by the movement. There were "[b]eginnings of curriculum revision" from 1963–65; and this was, claim Meier and Rudwick, "one of the most significant by-products of the current Civil Rights Revolution."[51]

And yet continuities there were. The NAACP was the main remaining heir to the abolitionist tradition. Though its intellectual energies were devoted to legal and jurisprudential matters, it was the only civil rights organization that counted in the South down to the late 1950s. Indeed the NAACP's focus on securing liberal freedom was of continuing relevance in the post–WWII world precisely because such little progress in the legal status and only slightly greater gains in the political power of black Southerners had been made. The number of registered black voters increased significantly even before the 1960s, a trend helped along mightily by the Supreme Court decision ruling white primaries unconstitutional in *Smith v Allwright* in 1944. But segregation itself remained pretty much in place down into the main decade of civil rights protest.

The other great cultural continuity was supplied by black Christianity and the black church. Leadership, sites of organization and action, forms of protest, as well as the stories, imagery, and ideas drawn from that tradition enriched mightily the secular currents of political and legal thinking. Moses and Christ, visions of salvation combined with narratives of liberation and themes of the individual and the collective: all persisted, even flourished, down into the years of the movement.

Perhaps the discontinuity/continuity issue is overdrawn. Clearly there were certain institutional, cultural, and political traditions available to the civil rights movement as it emerged in the mid-1950s. But none of these traditions, separately or collectively, provided the impetus for the movement's growth in strength and success in the early 1960s. In fact, as Clayborne Carson has pointed out about the student-initiated events of the early 1960s:

> The sit-ins, rather than emerging from radical intellectual ferment, reflected the students' general acceptance of the direction of racial reform in the United States. . . . With the exception of a few demonstrations about cafeteria food and student regulations, no significant protest movement had taken place on black campuses since the 1920s.

While it would be a great exaggeration to say that this was generally true of political activism among Southern blacks, it is the case that since the end of the WWII there had been, says Carson, "a narrowing of the range of political alternatives available to blacks. . . ."[52] Thus the intellectual and cultural preconditions for the emergence of new forms of political action in the South seem in retrospect quite bleak.

Finally several unexpected intellectual and cultural shifts had to occur before the civil rights movement could become what it was to become. First, the positive political potential of the black church had to be realized and utilized, rather than, in the manner of many black academics and intellectuals, dismissed as the (familiar) opiate of the masses.[53] In particular the music and the great unifying narratives of black Christianity, above all the Exodus story, had to be turned to explicitly political purposes. Not the place of work but the place of worship became the organizing center of the black movement in the South; not unions but action organizations became the vehicles for political and social change. Second, the relatively obscure ideas of non-violent direct action and civil disobedience had to be brought to the South, made convincing to black leaders, and then applied on a mass scale. All of this was to begin happening with the Montgomery bus boycott. Third, leaders and followers had to realize that the goal of liberal freedom, the destruction of segregation and disfranchisement, could only be achieved through new and dramatic forms of political action. Thus not the ballot box alone—which was foreclosed as a possibility in parts of the South—nor the court system but streets and public places became the sites where political power was to be exerted. Lastly, the drive for individual and collective self-respect and pride had to be linked with political action and thus, whether as a prerequisite or as a goal, become politicized.

Of course not all of these conditions were met before things began happening. The Supreme Court decision of 1954 was of catalytic importance, as was the general decolonization of Asia and Africa. The personality and rhetoric of Martin Luther King dramatized the situation in a way that the leadership of the NAACP never had been able to do. Like most great movements of historical change the civil rights movement was a great surprise.

CHAPTER 2

The Experience of Politics

All my conscious life I have wanted
to be a citizen—that is, a person
who calmly speaks his mind.

Leningrad electrician (1968)

If any single event touched off the activist phase of the civil rights
movement, it was the Montgomery bus boycott of 1955–56. Triggered by the refusal of a black seamstress, Mrs. Rosa Parks, to take
her place at the back of a city bus when the driver demanded it, this
grass-roots movement led by the young Martin Luther King lasted
for just over a year, from late in 1955 to late the next year. For the first
time since the Depression, political initiative shifted from Washington back out into the country itself, in this case to the courts, schools,
lunch counters, courthouses, streets, and jails of the South. The civil
rights movement would grow by fits and starts, shift strategies and
tactics, until the political and legal order that deprived black Southerners of their civil and political rights had been substantially dis-
mantled by the passage of the Civil Rights Act of 1964, which forbade
segregation in public accommodations, and a Voting Rights Act in
1965, providing for federal protection in the form of voter registrars
for those who wanted to register to vote in several of the Southern
states (or parts of them) where obvious patterns of disfranchisement
existed.

Setting

At the peak of movement activity in, say, 1962–65, there were efforts
at grass-roots organizing to match or even surpass the efforts of the
CIO-inspired union organizing of the 1930s or the Populist insur-

39

gency of the 1890s. Central to this effort was the Voter Education Project (VEP). Begun in 1962, VEP was funded by private foundations with the encouragement of the Kennedy administration which hoped that the involvement of the civil rights organizations in voter registration would divert their energies from mass demonstrations, sit-ins, boycotts, and freedom rides. With VEP support, civil rights workers, especially from SNCC, fanned out across the South, even and especially to hard-core areas such as the Mississippi Delta and the black belt regions of central and southern Alabama and southwest Georgia.

During this period the emphasis of SNCC organizers fell upon the creation of indigenous community organizations and the encouraging of local black people to generate their own leaders. The original organizing philosophy of SNCC, to which we will return later, was participatory politics in its purest sense and directly shaped much (white) New Left thinking during the first half of the decade.[1] The direct action approach of the King-led SCLC, highlighting as it did community mobilization, demonstrations, and other approaches such as picketing and boycotts, attracted greater national attention than did SNCC. But SCLC too was concerned with mobilizing grassroots support, though in a more massive, less differentiated form. While the ostensible goals of both organizations were relatively conventional up to around 1965, the forms of action they embraced were refreshingly new, at least in the immediate historical context. It was not so much that Rosa Parks or the four North Carolina A&T students at Greensboro, whose actions on February 1, 1960 ignited the sit-in movement, acted without precedent as that these initiatory events were exploited and developed so skillfully. In William Chafe's words, the forms of action developed in the movement "circumvented those forms of fraudulent communication and self-deception of whites." As a "new language," they expressed a determination to seize the initiative in formulating goals and strategies away from local white and, often, local black elites.[2]

Perhaps the most innovative form of political expression was the mass meeting. Like most insurgent movements in the United States, the civil rights movement originated outside existing party structures.[3] But unlike both the Labor and Populist movement, it flourished away from the workplace and was not integrally related to the sphere of production. Mass meetings were usually convened in churches, whether they were large urban edifices such as King's

Dexter Avenue Baptist Church in Montgomery, or small, one-room, wooden buildings deep in the countryside. They were events/sites where participants could express fear as well as resolution, anger as well as understanding, and where strategies could be effectively formulated. The psychological function of the mass meeting was not just cathartic; it also enabled action. Emotions were not expressed in order to be defused; rather their expression became a way of channelling fear and anger into effective collective action.[4]

Besides the testifying, preaching, and planning, "freedom songs" were also a crucial semantic and syntactical element, as it were, in the new language of public action. They were an amalgam of traditional spirituals, secular music such as blues, rhythm and blues, and even calypso, and the protest music of the 1930s, itself often of black provenance. Though containing a political subtext, spirituals were explicitly religious and generally centered on the *topos* of deliverance from bondage. Freedom songs on the other hand were explicitly political—religious language was usually secularized, e.g., the spiritual "Amen" became "Freedom" and "No More Mourning" became "Oh Freedom"; biblical figures such as Paul and Silas began to sound as though they were jailed civil rights workers who couldn't raise bail money (in "Hold On"); and the names of familiar adversaries such as Alabama's governor George Wallace or Dallas County, Alabama's sheriff Jim Clark were often worked into the lyrics. For instance, the spiritual "Rocking Jerusalem" became "Oh Pritchett, Oh Kelly," referring to the police chief and mayor, respectively, of Albany, Georgia during the movement campaign there in 1961–62. Still, the tunes and the words of the original songs were familiar enough and the setting for their performance was still the black church, making the origin of many of the freedom songs impossible to overlook.[5]

Specifically, where the spirituals conveyed the slaves' yearning for collective liberation and their sense of chosenness, the freedom songs often added a more explicit message of collective resistance, of standing fast, as in "We Shall Not Be Moved" and "We Shall Overcome." Chosenness, liberation, and resistance were not so much articulated conceptually as conveyed through imagery and anecdote drawn from biblical narratives, especially those concerning the children of Israel, the historical experience of emancipation, and the contemporary freedom struggle. Finally, what united spiritual and freedom song was the message, as Bernice Reagon put it, that ". . . Where I am is not where I'm staying." The movement, according to Reagon, made all the traditional "material, songs and prayers" come alive. For the first time, they "made sense."[6]

If there was a subtle mix of continuity and discontinuity, similarity and difference between the semantic contents of spirituals and freedom songs, the latter also worked "syntactically" to link the historical struggle of emancipation from slavery with the contemporary struggle for other kinds of freedom. But not only did the songs link past and present, they also mediated between speech and action, without being synonymous with either. Unlike speech, the freedom songs were less concerned with conveying information or arguing a position than with expressing resolve and public solidarity. The songs were also ways of punctuating talk and action, relieving tension and fear, summing up a general stance, and preparing for action. Thus freedom songs were particularly striking ways of making a collective presence known to the outside world—and to the participants themselves.

More generally, mass meetings helped bridge the gap between religious allegiance and political action. The black church had always been a proto-political organization and the movement wisely used rather than rejected this tradition. Where Southern blacks had once appeared primarily as religious beings in public, their churches were now transformed into political spaces and appearing in public took on an openly political significance. Indeed, the difficulty in separating sacred and secular or deciding, in retrospect, whether the black church was a source or merely a "site" of political organization, is revealed by the words of one middle-aged black man in Fayette County, Tennessee: "If you can't help 'em be a good citizen, you don't help 'em be good Christians . . . and making people good citizens is righteousness and nothing else."[7]

Close behind the mass meetings in importance as an innovative political form were citizenship schools, an offshoot of Myles Horton's Highlander Folk School in Grundy County in East Tennessee. Founded by Horton in 1932 as a center for training union organizers, by the 1950s Highlander had shifted its focus to racial matters and was perhaps the only place in the South at that time to hold interracial meetings and workshops dealing with race relations, political education, and leadership training. A graduate of Union Seminary in New York and influenced, as Martin Luther King would later be, by the then radical theologian Reinhold Niebuhr, Horton's philosophy of organizing was: "learn from the people; start their education where they are." In the context of the early days of the civil rights struggle, Horton stressed that the "burden and the responsibility is on the whites, but the burden of change is on the blacks." Horton, said SCLC's James Bevel, who attended Highlander (as did Martin Luther King, SNCC's John Lewis, and most significantly Rosa Parks during the summer before her momentous refusal): "made us deal with the fact that we were cowards and that we were lying, and were not being serious about who we said we were."[8]

Key figures in the development of the citizenship schools were Septima Clark and Esau Jenkins of South Carolina and Bernice Robinson, all of whom came together at Highlander in the mid-1950s. Clark was particularly crucial in developing the idea of citizenship schools with the aim of equipping black people at the grass-roots level with literacy skills and knowledge of the workings of governments and of their rights as citizens. The procedure was to train people at Highlander, and black women responded with particular eagerness to this chance of involvement in the movement as teachers who could then return to their communities to teach others. Later SCLC was to take over the administration of the citizenship schools from Highlander. Between 1957 and 1970, 897 citizenship schools were established; in 1964, 195 were in operation. Hosea Williams, later an aide to Martin Luther King, had been a supervisor of a citizenship school in Savannah, Georgia, while Mississippi's Fannie Lou Hamer had attended such a school in her native Sunflower County.[9]

Indeed, not only did the church and the citizenship schools represent new spaces of political action; so did the courthouses and even at times the jails. In their willingness to spend time in jail, protesters undermined the traditional negative connotations of jail and turned it from a place of shame to one of political honor.[10] Thus even the wretched jails of small Southern towns became public spaces, an irony in its own right, since of all civic institutions, places of incarceration are the quintessential private place of dishonor where rights are drastically curtailed and citizens become subjects.

From Setting to Experience

In analyzing the experience of politics in the civil rights movement, it is easy to forget that experience in general is not an undifferentiated thing and also to assume that the experiencing self is a unitary entity, separate from and somehow prior to its experience. Most accounts of participation in movement activities as collected in numerous published oral histories or unpublished archival sources are retrospective. Thus the person responding to an interviewer's questions will tend to give his or her experience more coherence than is perhaps justified. Because the self's experience is retrospectively shaped by implicit narrative conventions, it is important not to consider the experiencing self as a fixed entity, but as the central figure in an ongoing narrative of events and context, one moreover for whom experience is not a matter of passive "exposure" but a "complex learning process or a process of seasoning."[11]

Additionally, experience is mediated by all sorts of other factors. There were significant divisions within the movement between middle- and lower-class black people, between the educated and the uneducated, the employed and the unemployed, those who lived in urban areas and those who lived on the land or in small towns. The purpose and style of political engagement could vary widely among these different groups. In addition, some understood and expressed their experience in religious terms while others were palpably impatient with the religious ethos particularly prevalent among black participants in the Southern movement. This latter division often coincided with generational differences: younger black people tended to be less religious and more militant, at least rhetorically, than their elders. These differences in age, religious commitment, and educational background also tended to demarcate Northern from Southern blacks in leadership positions. SNCC was originally a student movement, and several of its most prominent figures—Stokely Carmichael, Robert Moses, and James Forman—were from the North. Over time SNCC also grew increasingly secular. SCLC remained dominated by somewhat older black ministers who were generally Southern-born or had congregations in the region. As Alabama-born and religiously trained John Lewis remembered, there were "black northerners who really didn't understand the psyche of the black southerner . . ."[12] Finally, of course, there were racial divisions within the movement, with both Southern and Northern whites participating until 1965–66.

The other matter that needs brief discussion here concerns the disproportionate presence and importance of women in the Southern movement. As already mentioned, Septima Clark and Bernice Robinson helped start and run the citizenship schools. Even though Rosa

Parks role in Montgomery is well-known, Jo Ann Robinson's is just now receiving the attention it deserves. The NAACP's Daisy Bates was a powerful force during the Little Rock crisis in 1957, while we will later look more closely at Ella Baker's fundamental role in the founding of SNCC which, despite its later reputation for male chauvinism, gave younger women such as Ruby Doris Smith Robinson, Diane Nash, Cynthia Washington, Gwen Patton, and Bernice Reagon major roles to play.

Northern participants in the movement often recorded surprise, even puzzlement, at the enlivening presence of black women in the movement and the relative absence of black men who, according to one observer, "are often so pitifully weak—unable to decide or do anything." In the 1930s white anthropologist Hortense Powdermaker conducted a community study of Indianola, Mississippi and found black women "more buoyant and helpful than their menfolk," a phenomenon she explained by women's investment of hope in their children's futures. A local leader in Canton, Mississippi in the 1960s, Annie Devine, claimed that "The Negro woman does not in many cases have to go through all the things that men go through," while Marion Page of Albany, Georgia explained that her participation in the movement was motivated by concern for the children but also for black men so that they could be "master of [his] house the way [he] should . . ."[13] While none of this is conclusive, it does need some sort of explanation.

The beginning of an answer might lie in the hypothesis that, in the notionally patriarchal culture of the South, black men felt the emotional and psychological force of oppression and exclusion more directly than did black women. That is, the experience of black men contrasted more starkly with the dominant ideology of gender relationships than did that of black women who still had their traditional roles in the family to fill and whose entrance into the world of work outside their own homes (often as domestics) did not conflict sharply with existing white or black (male) assumptions about their proper role.[14] Though black men were expected to support their families economically and protect them from outside harm, they often found themselves unable to do either. Related to this might also be the fact that Southern black men had internalized the "honor/shame" culture Bertram Wyatt-Brown has described as so pervasive in Southern history and culture.[15] Because violent retaliation was seen as the appropriate remedy for being "dishonored," many black men would not participate in the non-violent activities of the movement. Thus it was not just street toughs who hung out in pool halls and juke joints who, feeling psychologically estranged from the non-violent ethos of the movement, kept their distance from it.

Jacqueline Jones has pointed to other factors determining the higher participation of women, among which she notes the greater number of women than men in the black population in general as well as the tradition in black culture of the feisty and verbally aggressive black woman. Furthermore, the black church's crucial role in the movement and its emphasis upon non-violence found a more willing audience among women since they traditionally participated more readily in the life of the church, finding it easier than the men to enter into the practice of public testifying and emotional expressiveness prevalent in the mass meetings. The traditional relationship between the male minister as leader and a largely female congregation reflected traditional roles of male dominance, but also placed women in positions of prominence in terms of movement activities. Moreover, the fact that the movement was not focused on the workplace, traditionally a male domain, meant that women had greater potential access to the movement than they would have had in a more conventional setting. That said, however, black women were as subject to onslaughts from whites as were men and were of course also subject to sexual derogation and violation. As one woman said, "I ain't no Negro. I'm a nigger. The Boss man, he don't say nothing but nigger girl to me."[16]

Overall, certain experiences in the movement constituted the basis of a new way for participants of all descriptions to think and talk about themselves. First, for many black people, particularly living in the rural and small-town South, to live in the region was to live at close quarters with fear. As one black mother observed, "So if you want your kids to live long they have to grow up scared of whites . . ." In *Coming of Age in Mississippi,* Anne Moody remembers that, after the Emmett Till affair in the mid-1950s, she was haunted by "the fear of being killed just because I was black." Middle-class and urban blacks were less exposed to direct threats from whites, but journalist Louis Lomax remembered that in his native Valdosta, Georgia "[n]ot even Southern Negro professionals were exempted from the excruciating humiliations. . . . I once attended the church of a Negro minister who had been cornered by a group of young white hoodlums and made to dance in the street" because he was dressed better than most whites. [17] The cushion of status and class aside, to participate publicly in civil rights demonstrations, even in larger cities, made participants feel distinctly vulnerable to verbal, not to mention physical, abuse from angry whites. But what was different about risking such vulnerability was that it was chosen rather than experienced as a fate; moreover, it was generally a collective rather than just an individual action.

From this it follows that the first, indeed the main, task of movement organizers was to help potential participants (and themselves) overcome often paralyzing fear and its displaced expression, apathy. As one SNCC worker learned, organizing was not exhausting because of the necessity for door-to-door canvassing but because of the hard work involved in "convincing them that being a citizen is worth risking one's life." "How," wondered another organizer, "can you tell a man he is afraid?"[18] Some found that participation in mass meetings gave them courage. Others placed their faith in God or trusted leaders such as Martin Luther King or Robert Moses or Stokely Carmichael to help them master their fears. A black man named Square Mormon in Fayette County later remembered that he was given courage by "what Martin Luther King said—'A person that haven't seen nothin worth dyin for, he's not fit to live anyhow.'"[19]

A particularly powerful and moving expression of one man's effort to contain and explore his fear is contained in a letter from jail written by an unknown black minister in the early 1960s. Under the title "I Only W̶a̶n̶t̶e̶d̶ Want To Be Free," it is comprised of an unfinished 195-line poem divided into eleven sections.[20] The letter/poem is eloquent in its stark, terse revelation of courage and fear, strength and vulnerability, anger and sadness. In contrast with King's at times stilted prose in "Letter from Birmingham Jail," "I Only W̶a̶n̶t̶e̶d̶ Want To Be Free" records and reflects upon the frightening experience of being arrested at 3:00 AM and jailed for thirty-six hours. Taken to jail where he awaits his fate, the minister writes that the deputies who arrested him showed up "in the doom of night."

But the poem is not just a meditation on present, inner fear; it also moves outward periodically to the public world and backward in time to World War II when the narrator was injured in combat "because / I want̶e̶d̶ America to be Free." Striking out the -ed has the effect of both linking past and present and making that link problematic. In addition, the retention of typos and crossed-out revisions, probably unintended given the circumstances of its composition, makes palpable the urgency and immediacy of the situation.

The backbone of the poem, what makes it cohere, is the repetition at intervals of the phrase "I want to be free" or "I just want to be free." This refrain serves to remind the reader—and perhaps the author—of why he has been incarcerated and for what purpose he has acted. A particularly powerful section illustrates the cumulative effect of repetition as it punctuates and counterpoints with the narrator's fear and resolve:

> . . . As I went out the
> front door I realize, I could have
> been going to meet death. This has
> happen to many Negroes. I got into
> the car with these two unknown
> white men as if they were my friends.
> I made up my mind, if I must
> die, I will die like a man. I knew
> they were taking me some where, be-
> cause I want to be free.
> As they drove back toward town, I said
> to myself I am glad I decided to come
> 7
> peaceful. If they are going to do any
> thing to me, I would rather it not
> be done in the presence of my wife
> & children. I thought about the murder
> of Meger Everets in Mississippi. He was
> shot in the back and killed because he
> wanted to be free. I said to myself,
> if they kill me it will be because
> I want to be free. I wondered how
> many Negroes will the federal govern-
> ment allow the white folk kill just
> because we want to be free.

In these lines the recurrent reference to the desire to be free creates the poem's substantive and formal focus, which is reenforced by the internal rhyming of "Mississippi," "free," and "be free" in the last eight lines. The poem's strength is augmented here by evoking one of the archetypal situations of danger for rebellious Southern blacks—the long, uncertain ride to jail, not knowing whether what would happen on the way or what would happen in the cell was more to be dreaded.[21] And while the reference to Medgar Evers, the Jackson, Mississippi NAACP leader who was murdered in June 1963, conjures up an actual murder, the locution "going to meet death" (rather than "my death") lends to death a strangely allegorical resonance.

Besides the freedom motif, this passage also thematizes the problem of how to face death. In a situation of almost total helplessness, it seems to be crucial to die with some dignity intact. The ironies proliferate in these lines, since the narrator first imagines that the white deputies look like friends—which no white deputies in those times could be—and ends the section with "I am glad I decided to come." This is a shock until we pick up the first word in the next section—"peaceful." Still the question of what it means to "die like a man" is uppermost, though again ironically, no one except his murderers, particularly not his wife and children, whom he has wanted to protect, will ever know the manner in which he confronted death. Evers was ambushed; and the narrator insists several lines later that "if they shoot me it will/have to be from the front."

What does it mean to die facing one's murderers? Having decided not to resist in front of his family, the minister-narrator feels it necessary to "face" them in private. At one level the desire to confront one's murderers may express the hope that, if the killers can see that the threatened person is human, if some literal (or metaphorical) contact can be made, then they will not be able to perform the deed. Yet "looking back" is also a profoundly defiant, even aggressive action. It is a refusal to be ashamed at one's helplessness and a readying of oneself for the end. It expresses courage, even contempt, and says that nothing really bad can be done to me. Finally, it fixes the killers in their own eyes as killers from then on.

It is important here to mention that James Lawson, one of the early movement's mentors in non-violence, felt that the technique of curling up in a foetal position actually provoked those wanting to do violence to the protesters; rather, Lawson contended, eye contact should be maintained with attackers. Whatever the case, there is no better example of the fact that King's philosophy of confrontation, with the spirit of *agape* at its center, was built on the sublimation of profoundly hostile impulses. This is not, of course, to denigrate but to show the momentousness—and fragility—of that achievement.[22]

The third thematic focus of the composition concerns the movement of the narrator's consciousness from isolation to solidarity with others and communion with God. To reenforce this concern, the poem is subtly organized around alternating movements between dark and light, down and up, the repulsive and the natural:

> My cell is down in the hole. Its damp,
> dingey, with out light except ~~that~~ the
> little natural light . . .
> The odor is most foul ~~but~~ ~~you~~ foul enough
> that my smelling senses have not
> sensitize after 36 hours. All of this, just
> because I want to be free.

But the isolation is broken near the end of the poem when the narrator sees the name of a notorious rapist and murderer scratched on the wall: "I can glimpse/a figure in the shape of a cross and/beneath it is scratched GOD IS GOOD." Shortly thereafter he adds, "In the top of this cell is a figure/like a heart" which threatens but does not succumb to bathos, since the fragment breaks off:

> . . . Looks like it was drawn
> with a shoe heel. Inscribe with what
> probably was a hard match stick is,

Though we expect a minister to find solace in prayer and from God's presence, the jail experience leads the narrator to sympathize and even feel solidarity with the criminal he had once scorned (he does remember that Jesus died between two thieves). And he begins to: ". . . wonder was he [the rapist] guilty?" Even if he

> executed the acts, who was guilty? Could
> ~~it have been a case where this man have~~
> ~~been denied~~ the American way of life
> that jailed me because I want to be
> 11
> free, be guilty.

Like Thoreau, but in a much more exigent situation and less able to entertain ironic reflections about the superiority of society in jail to that on the outside, the minister/narrator comes to see the world, and hence his life and actions, from a different angle. In Emily Dickinson's words, he now sees it "slant."

All this suggests that some participants did not just have to overcome fear and decide to risk their lives in a specific instance. It was also a matter of overcoming a whole sense of self organized around that fear. "Nothing out there now but white hate and nigger fear," pronounces Ernest Gaines's Miss Jane Pittman, "and the fear is the only way to keep going. One day they must realize fear is worse than any death. When that time come they will be ready to move . . ." Later she adds to herself: "You talk of freedom Jimmy. Freedom here is able to make a little living and have the white folks say you is good."[23] In the face of such obdurate circumstances, such a transformation of self, however exhilarating, could be a daunting thing. A civil rights worker in southwest Georgia put it this way: "When you ask a man to join you, you are asking for a confession that his life up until now has been lived upside down." What made the decision easier was that it arose in and was maintained by a sense of collective, public action. This sense of solidarity was mediated through a figure such as Martin Luther King, about whom John Lewis was later to reflect that he "destroyed a sense of being alone or a sense of alienation."[24]

Two anonymous poems written during Freedom Summer of 1964 voice this preoccupation with courage and solidarity.[25] Less introspective and personal than the minister's letter-poem, they make use of two canonical Old Testament stories to mediate the personal and the political. The first poem is a meditation upon the account in Genesis of Jacob's struggle with the Angel, a story with a long history in black American experience. In *There Is a River*, Vincent Harding cites the story of a slave named Jacob who killed his master and also a song derived from the biblical account:

Rassal Jacob, rassal
  as you did in the days of old,
Gonna rassal all night
  till broad day light
And ask God to bless my soul.[26]

In addition there were numerous stories of slaves who refused to back down from their masters and fought them to the death (or were sold down the river) or even, as in the case of Frederick Douglass, survived. Such stories took on archetypal status in the history of Afro-American resistance to slavery and echoed the biblical account of Jacob and the Angel as a "scene of confrontation." This canonical story of the risk of life and confrontation with someone or something more powerful is clearly one of the "master" stories, along with the Exodus story, which punctuate the narrative of slavery and freedom. Thus it is not surprising that we find it turning up in the 1960s.[27]

Indeed, in certain ways the Jacob story is more immediately powerful and cogent than the Exodus story in Afro-American history. In the latter story God delivers the children of Israel from bondage; in the former Jacob triumphs and wrests a blessing from whomever it is he wrestles with: he takes the initiative.[28] The story of Jacob and the Angel also lends itself more readily to a secular, political reading, since it hints that God or his emissary is the adversary rather than the accomplice of freedom. Generally the story might be read to suggest that not God but human beings are the agents of their own deliverance and must win the blessing rather than having it granted to them. Indeed, the Jacob and the Angel story potentially subverts the relationship between God and the children of Israel established in the Exodus story.[29]

The untitled Mississippi poem offers an ethical (rather than figural or anagogic) gloss on the biblical story.[30] It understands Jacob as exemplary for the civil rights struggle:

> And we like Jacob
> have to find ways to say to the problem
> to say to our fear
> I will not let you go
> except that you bless me.

Here the ethical relationship between Jacob and "us" in the present is made explicit through the simile. The first few verses concentrate on establishing the "problem"—the associative links run from "fear" to "life" and then to more concrete political referents drawn from the contemporary world of work and politics:

> walk up to our registrar
> walk up to our mayor
> walk up to the boss man

The temptation is of course to avoid the confrontation, "passing off the struggle until another day . . . or saying / I don't want to have nothing to do / with that mess."

The reason or necessity for the confrontation is that the "blessing is in the struggle . . . for I have seen God in the struggle / and because I struggled, / my life is preserved." The powerful ambiguity/ ambivalence here arises from the fact that the poem can be read as saying that God blesses those who struggle with the obstacles *or* that because we struggle with all the obstacles, including God, we are blessed—not by God but by the struggle. This ambiguity emerges clearly in the following lines (which typically gain force through repetition):

> He said, "No more shall your name be called Jacob,
> But Israel, which means wrestler with God,
> wrestler with life,
> wrestler with evil,
> wrestler with segregation,
> wrestler with the problem.

Here we see the way God is associated with or at least inclusive of the negative forces to be overcome. Thus the theological explanation of the possibility of reconciliation between the wrestler and the problem remain ambiguous.

Indeed, the poem itself is conscious of the undecidability here. In an alternative stanza, the mood is more questioning and the ambiguity internalized and explicitly thematized:

> Who was the man?
> some say angel
> some say demon,
>
> Maybe it was Jacob wrestling with himself,
> with his conscince conscience
> maybe it was jacob wrestling with his weaknesses
> with his doubts
> maybe it was jacob wrestling with his fears.

But the final emphasis in both versions falls not on how to identify with whomever or whatever Jacob is wrestling, but with the necessity of struggle and confrontation in spite of and because of fear:

> You're wrong
> And I will not let you go
> I wont let you get away
>
> And if we do that
> we'll find that
> like Jacob
> we receive the bless
> . . . .
> But the blessing was in the struggle
> in the wrestling match itself.

The other poem is more straightforward and less ambiguous but also less interesting psychologically and aesthetically. It takes as its text the story of Joshua and the battle of Jericho found in Joshua 7:10–12. In it a more direct link is established between God and the civil rights struggle: God intervenes in history "now" as he did "then." Thus the poem takes the Bible not just as a repository of exemplary stories for ethical and political instruction but also as a kind of prefiguration of the civil rights movement. If God intervened in history then, he will intervene now:

> If we are really believers
> then we believe that God will do no more for
> Joshua at Jericho
> than he will do for us in
> Mississippi,
> Alabama,
> Georgia,
> Harlem
> Chicago
> or
> Detroit.

Still, the poem also wants to instruct and, as might be expected, the reason why Jericho, "the city of segregation / and mass murder / lynching / and terror bombings / and beatings," falls is because "He and his people were together." They possessed "discipline . . . There was unity. / The people were together." They also "had to make noise" rather than be "full of Toms" who "will keep quiet."

Thus where the poem about Jacob and the Angel speaks of conquering fear and thus receiving a blessing, the Jericho poem emphasizes the value of unity in action. And where in the former the relationship to God is ambiguous to the point of directly questioning the standard theological relationship of God to black people, the Joshua poem assumes that God intervenes with and for those who together fight injustice.

In retrospect, this shift from fear to courage, from individual courage to solidarity, may seem inevitable, given the burgeoning support for the movement in the South and throughout the nation. It is, however, easy to forget that, besides fear, there was also often a sense of shame and self-contempt, a certain nagging feeling of *nullity*, to be counteracted. A graphic example of one white man's attempt to negate a black self can be seen in the following exchange. A black man says to a white registrar: "I am a citizen and a Negro and I have every right to be here in this building." Whereupon the hostile white official answers: "You aint nothing." We may suppose that this particular black man was relatively impervious to such cancellation. But another example illustrates the possible outcome of a lifetime lived without recognition. An elderly but quite lively black lady is reported to have resisted efforts to persuade her to register to vote. When asked her name by civil rights workers urging her to register she responded that "she didn't have one."[31]

This last example brings home the way that to have a name is to locate oneself in the world. Besides receiving the blessing from the Angel, Jacob's name is also changed to Israel or "wrestler with God." His name reflects the action he has taken; it becomes his fate, his future. Indeed, the experience of having been named and then rejecting that name and choosing another has been a constant theme in Afro-American experience. From the newly freed slaves who chose their names to the literary examples of James Baldwin's *Nobody Knows My Name* and Ralph Ellison's nameless protagonist in *Invisible Man* and on to the name changes mandated by the Nation of Islam: choosing a name has been an act of profound personal, social, and political significance. It is a way of rejecting an imposed role or identity and making a claim on a new one.[32]

Some movement participants spoke openly of the transformation in self-conception they had undergone. According to an elderly man in Fayette County, his involvement in local civil rights activities "end me up for bein their nigger . . . I wasn't no longer me after I took part in this Movement." The context of the remark makes clear that the man was no longer "me" either to the whites who thought of him as their "nigger" or to himself. Fannie Lou Hamer's husband, Perry Hamer, answered the white mayor of Indianola, Mississippi's question "How do you feel havin' white men sleep in your house?" with "I feel like a man . . . because they treat me like a man." Wilola Mormon, Square Mormon's wife, spoke of how "people need to stand on their foot and as a man . . . it would give us lotta confidence through us discussin . . ." And Mary Lane of Greenwood, Mississippi, a much younger woman, echoed this when she asserted that ". . . the black man has got to realize you know that he is a man and he has a—he has to make a stand . . ."[33]

Civil rights workers and local leaders were of course well aware of this crucial transformation—from "nigger" to Negro, from "boy" to man and "gal" to woman, and from "child" to adult. Annie Devine, a woman in her late forties and resident of Canton, Mississippi, remembered that "People were talking about becoming free, free of mind, and free in spirit, not to riot, not to loot, not to burn . . . to become real men and real women·. . . We've really almost grown up." And John Hulett, one of the founders of the Lowndes County (Alabama) Freedom Organization—the original Black Panther Party—observed that some "felt that they were inferior to even their own people, and the white people. Now these people began to take on a new life and they see themselves as being men and women."[34]

In a particularly dramatic encounter, Charles McLaurin, a SNCC organizer in Mississippi, addressed himself to a group of black men who hesitated to join a group of demonstrators. Across the street stood a number of hostile whites. The tension created by standing almost literally between an old and new sense of self was nearly unbearable: "If you don't sign up to go down to register to vote in Indianola—you say to the white man, 'Don't treat me like a man. Treat me like a boy!' . . . We've got to stand up." On that occasion, none of the black men joined the protesters. Another prominent SNCC worker in southwest Georgia, Charles Sherrod, reported that it was not just a matter of how many registered to vote "but how many people we can get to begin initiating decisions solely on the basis of their personal opinion." Finally, then, the courage and solidarity that led to public action created a sense of self-respect. "What did we win?" asked A. C. Searles, a black newspaper editor in Albany, Georgia: "We won self-respect. It changed all my attitudes. This movement made me demand a semblance of first-class citizenship."[35]

Indeed the acquisition of self-respect was often expressed in the rhetoric of freedom and empowerment. One civil rights worker reported that many black people "have moved into freedom of the mind, and it is theirs for life . . . ," while Bernice Reagon remembered particularly the "sense of power . . . confronting the things that terrified you." She ceased to "respect boundaries that put me down . . . I was empowered by the civil rights movement." Besides the appeal to Old Testament stories of liberation, the movement also mined the shared New Testament tradition to great advantage. One of the basic documents of the Freedom Summer project stated the purpose of freedom schools as "implant[ing]

habits of free thinking and ideas of how a free society works . . ."
The last four points of a ten-point rationale were:

8. Fear—whatever the cause—produces lies.
9. Living lies bends and breaks us.
10. That is to say—keeps us from being whole.
11. That is to say—keeps us from being free.

And finally, "If lies enslave us, then truth will free us. What is the
truth? Or, the same question, what is freedom?"[36]
This unpacking of the New Testament's "You shall know the truth
and the truth shall make you free" along with the similar Jacob/Angel
theme we have explored of "You shall confront the oppressor and the
confrontation will make you free" reveals one crucial meaning of
freedom at the heart of the experience of politics in the movement.
For, freedom meant more than just acquiring certain legal and
political rights: it involved the assumption of new self-respect and
appropriation of truth about things. Further, as we have seen, this
new sense of self was more than just an internal state of mind or new
feeling about oneself; as James Bevel said, it involved not only
"picking up one's soul" but also "walking with one's soul." This new
sense of personhood emerged from the process of overcoming personal nullity and acting with others to create a political community.
According to John Lewis, "Being involved tended to free you
. . . you saw yourself as the free man, as the free agent, able to
act."[37]
Moreover, though the civil rights movement depended quite
heavily on outside (largely white) financial aid, to arrive at a sense of
self/community that could act was also to realize that this action was
up to oneself and not up to someone else. Anne Moody remembered
telling a group of Mississippi young people: "If you are depending on
the writing on the wall to free you, you'd better forget it . . . We've
gotta be the ones to give it meaning." For her and many other young
black people, "this meant that the power to change things was in
themselves. More so than in God or anyone else." Fayette County's
Maggie Mae Horton said much the same: "That's what we gonna
work forward to—tryin to get peoples to quit waitin for God to come
do somethin for me . . . Nobody can come here and get my rights
for me. I got to get it myself." Fannie Lou Hamer expressed it in the
language of the Exodus story when she said she hoped to see the black
clergy "Headin' your flock out of the chains and fetters of Egypt—

taken' them yourself to register—tomorra—in Indianola." The Mississippi Summer Project, she observed, ". . . taught us a lot about what we should do ourselves."[38]

Such testimony amounted to the realization that black people neither could nor should expect freedom to be given to them. To be free was to have won freedom. Moreover it implied that the self-respect achieved through political action came less from white recognition than from recognition by and among themselves of this new sense of empowerment. One of SNCC's early leaders, Charles McDew, expressed this (bitter) realization when he later observed that "when a person cannot recognize your humanity, you cannot appeal to him as another human being."[39] It was this achievement of self-respect and belief in self-determination, coupled with the white failure to respond with recognition, that linked the experience of politics in the movement with the black power/consciousness movement.

This last point about winning freedom indicates a final dimension of freedom implicit in the discussion up to now—freedom as participation in political debate and action. From this perspective, freedom was not just a legal-political status nor was it exhausted by the emergence of self-respect. Rather, it was engendered in public meetings and marches and confirmed in the act of voting, the mark of being a citizen in a political order. It is easy to emphasize the limited importance of the suffrage and to criticize the movement as essentially reformist rather than revolutionary. Yet this is to read back into the Southern context our own experience in which the vote has become a kind of civic duty at best and a bother at worst. If we think ourselves back into that situation and remember the history of black political life after slavery, we will see what was happening as a move from black "political death" to a claim on citizenship. "I don't know," says the eponymous heroine in Alice Walker's *Meridian*, "It [voting] may be useless. Or maybe it can be the beginning of the use of your voice."[40]

Thus the experience of politics in the civil rights movement helps us remember the rich meaning of the concept of citizenship. For, by the classical definition, a citizen was one who participated as an equal in the public affairs of the *polis*. Such was the main activity of a free person; indeed, to be free in this sense was to be a citizen-participant. This particular sense of being a free citizen is scarcely alive in American political culture; but it is one that students, even black students in segregated Southern schools, gleaned hints of in civics lessons (though for that reason it is usually wrongly dismissed as irrelevant). Yet in Tuskegee, Alabama, the home of Booker T. Washington's Tuskegee Institute, Charles Gomillion articulated such an idea as early as the 1940s when he defined "civic democracy" as a "way of life . . . in which all citizens have the opportunity to participate in societal affairs and benefit from or enjoy public services." This was the ideal informing Gomillion's efforts to bring about political equality in Tuskegee. Lillian McGill of neighboring Lowndes County, Alabama, deployed the language of civic democracy when she spoke of the need "to participate fully in order to get their particular share of the common good" in the 1960s. And Isaac Richmond of the Penn Center in South Carolina echoed this participatory impulse when he described his work "for people to participate in decision-making."[41]

Others also intuited, as it were, the close connection between voting, being a citizen, and being free. Said an 86-year-old man in Fayette County: "I thought I was a free voter. If I was capable of votin I'd come to be a citizen." A particularly moving example of genuine pride in voting can be detected in the following exchange between a friendly voter registrar (after passage of the Voting Rights Act in 1965) and an elderly black woman. When the registrar discovered how few organizations she belonged to, he asked, "You're just a member of the Church?" Her reply was: "I am a U.S. citizen too." Later when the registrar urged her not to lose her registration form, she replied: "I'm too proud of it to lose it."[42] Thus if discussions and debates, singing and preaching in countless mass meetings, attending citizenship schools, and participating in marches constituted the informal process of becoming a political being, the formal confirmation of citizenship for many lay in the act of voting which confirmed their inscription on the political order.

Besides official citizenship, there is another dimension to freedom as participation which transcends voting, since voting, however important, is one of the least public facets of political freedom. For if one sees political action not as just instrumental to some other goal— the protection of rights or interests, for example—but also as a "mode of experience" valuable in its own right, then political participation may cease to be simply a civic duty and reveal on occasion what Hannah Arendt called "public happiness."[43] Black men and women did come to see themselves as activists for whom political action was a good in itself. Aside from external goals participants also realized new powers and capacities, acquired self-respect as well as interests, through engaging in politics. Indeed one may be happy involved in the *res publica* because it implies a relationship to others, not encompassed in terms of dependence or competition.

But what could happiness have meant in a setting where lives were at risk and the threat of physical and mental humiliation omnipresent? First it could refer to the sense of shifting from being publicly passive and relatively invisible, from being "saints of endurance," to becoming men and women of action who found a straightforward sense of release in acting, singing, marching, and talking.[44] Rosa Parks was to remember later about Montgomery and the movement that "It was real new and refreshing to know that for once, then, the people could unite spontaneously on a single issue." And no one can have experienced the mass meetings or observed many of the marches without sensing, among both leaders and followers, an authentic joy, exuberance, and "lightness of being" that lifted participants out of the grinding dailiness of their lives. "What I remember so much about that," wrote a former participant in the Selma campaign, "was the happiness of the people. . . . We could get out in the sunshine and let everyone know that we were Americans too." Unita Blackwell, who got involved with the MFDP and then later became mayor of Mayersville, Mississippi, spoke of her involvement in politics this way: "We found ourselves involved in working in political work, and we still ain't figured all of it out yet, but its been just wonderful." And white journalist Pat Watters was profoundly moved by the "undeniable joy in the mighty doings of the movement" that he observed particularly in the early days of the Albany campaign.[45]

Still, happiness can refer not just to an immediate state of consciousness but also to the sense of becoming more fully human, of discovering that neither one's sense of significance nor the world's meaning is fully explained by private relationships, the satisfaction of needs, or the promise of life after death. The self-respect so ubiquitously mentioned could be shared with others rather than remaining a private fact of self-consciousness or apparent only to one's immediate circle of relatives and friends. Thus public happiness in this sense would be closer to the revelation of a fundamental possibility or state of being. Whatever one's immediate experience of joy or sadness, pleasure or pain, communion or anger: such experiences would issue from a new and different sense of the self and its world.

*

Among the black Southern population a new sense of self as a political actor and as a self-respecting citizen often appeared as a result of participation in movement activities. A white observer at one of the precinct meetings of the MFDP in the summer of 1964 talked of it this way:

> They were full-grown adults who were participating for the first time in their restricted lives in the basic process of a free society. The light of pride in their faces showed through their embarrassment.[46]

Though the description of the scene comes close to being patronizing, it does capture much that was inspiriting about the entrance of black Southerners onto the public scene. Ironically, the experience of politics they acquired, often at a risk to their lives and what little fortunes they had, was far deeper than most white Southerners had taken possession of.

CHAPTER 3

Self-interest and Self-respect

To be a voter with the rest is not so much
and this, like every other institute,
will have its imperfections. But to
become an enfranchised man
. . . that is something.

Walt Whitman

If the testimony of participants in the civil rights movement is
plausible at all, then the idea that self-interest, the pursuit of power
and advantage, does or should invariably inform political action must
be reassessed. The primacy of self-interest is often associated with,
and indeed considered one of the chief historical innovations of,
mainstream American political thought.[1] In this account, the canonical expression of politics as self-interest is James Madison's *Federalist*
#10, while the post–World War II hegemony of liberal pluralism or
interest-group liberalism among academics and intellectuals represents its most recent apotheosis. Historically, then, the civil rights
movement burst into view just as liberal pluralism had become the
regnant political ideology. For that reason, it is necessary to examine
liberal pluralism and its animating ideal, self-interest, in order to
understand the conception of politics that the civil rights movement
implicitly, and at times explicitly, challenged.

It would be a mistake, however, to see the defense of interest
politics in the post-war United States or earlier as grounded exclusively in a realistic/cynical recognition of the dominance of the
pursuit of the main chance in American life. Since its emergence in
the political culture of the eighteenth century, the politics of "interest," as A. O. Hirschman has pointed out, has been considered a
positive alternative to politics dominated by unreflecting passions,

i.e., lust for place and power, or ineffectually guided by reason. Capitalism and its accompanying politics of interest would, it was hoped, civilize and pacify those passions which threatened to disrupt a settled, decent society. In addition the pursuit of interest originally went along with the political enfranchisement of and assertion of equality by the middle class against the fixed prerogatives of aristocracy.[2]

Indeed, the idea that politics was to be viewed through the prism of self-interest, that the pursuit of interest was a positive political good, emerged clearly in post–World War II American liberalism. In the post-war ethos, haunted by the horrors of the "ideological" politics of Stalinist Russia and Hitler's Germany, any idea that politics was to be guided by "virtue" or the "public good" or "positive" freedom—as opposed to its being about the pursuit of discernible, economic interest and position, was considered a sure prescription for totalitarian rule. Recent history had shown that the masses were fair game for the demagogue who seduced them from their (real) interests by appealing to envy and playing on their insecurity. The dominant virtue of interest-group politics was civility not passion; its goal was a modicum of satisfaction not a maximum of participation.[3]

There were several ironies at work in post-war American political culture. First, the very success of the "new" capitalism in providing wider prosperity, as well as the much-touted pluralism of American life, helped create the social insecurity and cultural disorientation which Richard Hofstadter identified as the breeding ground of "status" as opposed to "interest" politics and that Daniel Bell claimed dangerously transformed "issues into ideologies."[4] A further irony was that liberal pluralists originally—and rightly—identified the radical Right, e.g., groups such as the John Birch Society, as the prime source of political irrationality and moralism in post-war politics. But the logic of their analysis both reflected and influenced the relative lack of involvement on the part of figures such as Bell and Hofstadter in the civil rights movement and the hypersensitivity, even hostility, of the anti-Communist Left in 1962 to the fledgling Students for a Democratic Society (SDS), and later to SNCC, as being insufficiently anti-Communist and hence soft on ideological politics.[5]

In this chapter, I will explore in more detail the concept of self-interest and its relevance for understanding political engagement in movements such as the civil rights movement. Then I will attempt to define self-respect as one of the forms of freedom among movement participants and examine its relation to self-interest. And finally I want to look at some of the accounts in black American writing of the achievement of self-respect and explore how these accounts shed light on the concern with self-respect in the civil rights movement. .

The Politics of Self-interest

In claiming that the way to understand political behavior is to understand the interests of those involved, the politics of interests conflates three claims. The first claim is an empirical/explanatory one to the effect that the pursuit of interests is the only, or overwhelmingly dominant, (conscious) reason or (unconscious) motivation for engaging in politics. The second claim is conceptual or definitional, according to which it is assumed that politics is solely the pursuit of self-interest: that self-interest is what it means to engage in politics. The third claim makes the normative judgment that pursuit of interests *should* be the motivation for political participation, all others being ineffective or, as mentioned previously, even dangerous.[6]

A critique of the politics of interest can take any number of directions. Leaving aside the explanatory claim to which I will return shortly, the second and third claims, though not empirically falsifiable, are too restrictive to be of much use. A classic example of the second claim can be found, for instance, in Bayard Rustin's "From Protest to Politics" (1965), an essay of seminal importance in both registering and widening the growing split within the civil rights movement at that time. There Rustin, one of King's closest advisers and also associated historically with CORE, advocated a new political strategy for the civil rights movement, though in fact what he proposed was a toned-down reprise of the type of political strategy suggested by Ralph Bunche in the 1930s—a black-white coalition for mutual economic and social progress. The problem was not with the wisdom of Rustin's proposal per se. There was a lot to be said for the idea that the Democratic Party was the logical site for progressive forces to gather and push for progressive legislation.

More dubious was the definition of politics implied by the following crucial statement by Rustin: ". . . all these interrelated problems, by their very nature, are not soluble by private, voluntary efforts but require government action—or politics." Rustin went on to suggest that the best way to get "government action" on these problems meant "political action within the Democratic party" which had just been returned to power in the landslide 1964 victory of President Johnson over Senator Barry Goldwater. It was not that Rustin thought that "protest"—sit-ins, demonstrations, and mass protests—had been unimportant; rather, he felt that protest had done its job but the time had become propitious for "politics" in the true meaning of the term.[7]

The third, or normative, view of the politics of interest is illustrated quite clearly in V. O. Key's *Southern Politics* (1949), a work of obvious importance for understanding what the civil rights movement was up against in its struggle against segregation and disfranchisement in the South. In his classic study Key assumed that interest politics, party coherence, and political responsibility are, or should be, linked together to constitute the preconditions for a rational or normal political culture. "Normally a political party," he wrote, "has its foundations in sectional, class or group interests." This implied, in turn, a "differentiation in the policies" between competing parties and a "fairly cohesive group of party leaders held together by the ambition to retain or win office." The effect of all this should be the establishment of "standards of permanence, cohesiveness and responsibility that characterize the political party." But because such a situation had not been the case in the South, the politics of interest had historically lost out to the politics of irrationality, irresponsibility, and particularly racial demagoguery as pursued covertly by "Bourbons" and "Big Mules" and overtly by populist-racist demagogues.

But, reasoned Key, if Southern politics could come to involve genuine competition among interests organized into parties, which for Key implied the entrance of blacks into Southern politics and their alliance with progressive white forces in a liberalized Democratic Party, then the political life of the region would be improved and would be, for the first time, genuinely rational. Again, as with Rustin, Key's specific historical-political proposals were not wrong—though they did prove to be overly optimistic and he failed, as did almost everyone else, to see that black Southerners would enter into and redefine Southern politics from outside the party structures.[8]

But the general claim that political behavior can be empirically explained by the pursuit of interests needs particularly close examination. For if politics can be explained as the pursuit of interests,

then any useful distinction between the definitional and the normative claim about what politics is or what politics should be disappears.
There is, however, a growing sense, now almost a consensus, that the
self-interest explanation (as opposed to definition or imperative) of
political behavior is woefully inadequate. This emerging consensus is
made up of several different claims and counter-claims. First, as
Robert Frank has recently asserted, empirical evidence fails to
support the self-interest thesis. It is not, says Frank, "that self-
interest is an unimportant human motive, but that material forces
allow room, apparently a great deal of room, for more noble motives
as well."[9] The pursuit of self-interest may be the driving force in
"normal" American politics. To move, however, from this arguable
truth to a claim about politics in general fails to take historical
differences into account and thus impoverishes historical and theoretical work alike.

In what situations might self-interest not be the only or even the
main motive or reasons for political action? One dramatic answer
would be a revolutionary situation or any situation in which people
risk their lives to revitalize an existing political order, one example of
which would be, of course, the civil rights movement. That is, if we
can identify political settings in which individuals or groups place
immediate survival or interests lower on their list of priorities than
such other goods as political, economic, or social change or less
tangible objectives such as dignity, honor, self-determination, or
liberation—or, it must be added, racial or ethnic solidarity—then we
have *prima facie* evidence that self-interest does not trump all other
motivations of political action.

Indeed, "normal" politics encompasses a host of political actions
which are at least as other-regarding as they are self-interested. The
core institutions of the welfare state are an example, as is the
progressively graduated income tax. A third, more surprising example is the individual act of voting, which, according to Jane Mansbridge, is useless when considered from the standpoint of individual
self-interest, but not when considered from the standpoint of political
duty or solidarity or keeping faith with one's own beliefs.[10]

Moreover, there is a deep conceptual paradox underlying what
might be called the "realist" or "inside dopester" version of the self-
interest thesis. According to one-dimensional hermeneuts of suspicion (as inspired by Freudian, Marxian and economic determinist, or
Nietzschean teachings), all political rhetoric and self-explanation is

ideological rationalization, a smokescreen for self-interested motives. As John Diggins has written:

> Such interpretations [virtue- or common good–talk] might be entertained if we accept rhetoric as reality and assume that what is presented in political language not only shapes the dimensions of discourse, but also illuminates the actual nature of historical events. If, however, truth and reality exist independently of how words are used, and if language merely serves a legitimating function, we can consider the possibility that what goes unsaid in overt political discourse might reveal even more than the content of public utterances.[11]

The problem is that, on this account, we should not only not trust high-minded idealists or sinister revolutionaries; we shouldn't trust Diggins or anyone else. Put another way, Diggins assumes that the realist, the tough-minded devotee of self-interest, tells the truth, and is thus exempt from the theory of the word-world relationship that tells the realist that others are misled by their own rhetoric and/or attempt to mislead with their rhetoric.

Yet another problem here is that many defenders of an interest theory of politics never stop to define or to determine what an interest is. William Connolly warns against taking the concept as unproblematic, identifying at least four different meanings of interest: 1) an explicit policy preference; 2) that which would satisfy a more or less conscious want; 3) that which would satisfy a need; or, for him the most satisfactory, 4) that which retrospectively would be chosen again or which one could imagine choosing again. This last, preferred notion of interest has two provisos: first, long- and short-term interests may collide and, second, the choice of an interest which forecloses future choices (e.g., taking drugs or, more to our point, support of dictators or authoritarian policies) is highly dubious. Connolly's more general point is that interest is an "essentially contested concept." Invoking it leaves unanswered questions such as: Is an individual or a group making the choice? Are we talking of conscious or unconscious interests? What contextual factors limit or expand the range and nature of our interests? Can we reconcile the pursuit of self-interest with the manifest existence of other-regarding impulses?[12]

But how might the proponents of the self-interest theory respond? One standard and often superficially persuasive response is to (re-)define interest so as to encompass what appears to be self-sacrifice or altruism. The proponent of interest politics could claim that, even though a black farmer in Lowndes County, Alabama might have risked his life by becoming politically involved in the Black Panther Party in 1965–66, such an action appealed to his sense of adventure or affirmed his sense of manhood and thus constituted a kind of pleasure, or want. Less perversely, the proponent of self-interest might speculate that, though the farmer risked his life, or at least his credit from the local bank, by attending mass meetings of the party, he assumed that he would survive his attempt to register to vote and that the exercise of the franchise might later pay off in terms of material possessions or power. That is, the black farmer will eventually be able to vote for politicians who will increase farm supports or include black farmers in agricultural demonstration projects that will in turn improve their life chances. Analogously, a civil rights worker who voluntarily risked his or her life might be said to make the same sort of calculation about the unlikelihood of death and thus be maximizing his/her pleasure or at least enhancing his/her moral self-image. Though probably bewildered by the claim that someone might find political action a source of "public happiness," the proponent of interest politics could interpret both examples as illustrating the interest theory of politics, however we might define interest.

The response available to those skeptical of the interest theory would be to admit that the concept of self-interest *could* be expanded to include such examples. But they might also respond that to consider potential risk of life, for instance, as action from self-interest can hardly be reconciled with Connolly's preferred definition of interest or with any commonly accepted one. To do so strains, twists, and distends the notion of self-interest to the point that it becomes a "placeholder," an all-purpose category that, in doing whatever work we want it to, forfeits its explanatory power. If we can explain everything by self-interest, we haven't explained much at all. Explanation by self-interest becomes a "non-testable tautology."[13]

Finally the opponent of the self-interest theory might note that, though a political system as a whole may aim at the enhancement of self-interest, this does not preclude the possibility that specific political actions within the system might be motivated by any number of other concerns. As Frank has observed, "In many situations, the common pursuit of self-interest is incompatible with its attainment."[14] To enhance the self-interest of a group, some of its members must act or be treated in ways that do not enhance their individual self-interest or even immediate group interest. Thus the point or purpose of a system does not determine, nor is it reflected in, all the motivations of individuals or even institutional actions that are a part of it.[15]

Indeed these tortuous considerations suggest that the question about what really drives political action and engagement is incredibly complex. Alasdair MacIntyre has suggested that to separate self-interest from benevolence (and by extension from self-sacrifice) and then to make them opposing alternatives obscures the way most of us make decisions in these matters.[16] For the black farmer in Alabama or the civil rights worker, participation would not be a matter of explicitly calculating relative benefits (becoming more prosperous, feeling virtuous) and disadvantages (fear, anxiety, even death). Rather their participation in the movement would be a matter of keeping faith with a "way of life" or a way of being in the world. To have asked the minister whose poem we discussed in the previous chapter whether he was acting from self-interest or why he was acting as he did would have been impertinent and irrelevant. There is little moral or political sense to the question, "But *why* do you want to be free?"

In sum, then, the pursuit of self-interest is important but it constitutes only one dimension of political action. To place it at the center of the political experience of the civil rights movement, to imply that it should have been at the center, or to ignore the other sorts of motivations and reasons expressed by participants is to all but miss the point about the movement and to understand it as just another pressure group, concerned only with abolishing restrictions upon the pursuit of self-interest.

Self-respect

It is important to examine the concept of self-respect in relation to the political experience of movement participants since it was, I think, the form which freedom as autonomy, as the achievement of a new sense of self, assumed in the movement. Like self-interest, self-respect is more difficult to characterize than it first appears. Philosopher Bernard Williams suggests that it is a condition in which one is "identified with what one is doing" and "able to realize purposes of one's own, and not to be the instrument of another's will unless one has willingly accepted such a role," while psychologist Carol Gilligan has spoken of the necessity of recognizing "the psychological and moral necessity for an equation of worth between self and others," and Thomas Hill contrasts self-respect with "a failure to understand and acknowledge one's own moral rights." Laurence Thomas, one of the few ethicists or political philosophers who has tried to understand self-respect in relation to the black struggle for freedom, defines it as a state of mind analogous to "the sense of worth that is engendered by parental love." If self-respecting, we feel we deserve "full moral status" and the "basic rights of that status" by virtue of being a person. And Bernard Boxill, who has also related self-interest to political protest, claims that a self-respecting person will protest for his or her rights not so much to secure those rights, as to express his or her sense of worth.[17]

What is the relation between self-interest and self-respect? I would suggest that self-respect and self-interest are internally related and inseparable. This is implicit in the idea of self-interest preferred by Connolly and in Hill's notion of servility, for their positions suggest that to make a choice which bars future choices or to act so that one denies one's autonomy, "to lose one's sense of moral identity" or to violate one's sense of "integrity," as Williams puts it, is among other things to act against one's own interests. Neither an individual nor a group can act in its own self-interest without somehow taking its moral status into account, a position captured in civil rights worker Charles Sherrod's observation quoted in the previous chapter about the need to get people "to begin initiating decisions solely on the basis of their personal opinion."[18]

Another valuable point emerges from the philosophical discussions of self-respect: self-respect does not depend upon a person's specific capacities or concrete achievements. It is not, Thomas emphasizes, synonymous with "self-esteem" which does depend on capacity and accomplishment. Second, though self-respect is a traditional concern of moral philosophy, self-respect—or the lack thereof—is the particular problem of people who feel that they have been dishonored or shamed or made to act in a servile fashion. Thus those who have been sexually violated or tortured may have their self-respect damaged or nearly destroyed through what Michael Walzer refers to as a "denial of self-possession."[19] In this view, as novelist Salmon Rushdie or, earlier, historian Stanley Elkins has reminded us, shame, dishonor, and a lack of self-respect are states of mind to which groups who have been enslaved or politically and socially dominated are particularly liable. Individuals or groups in this situation may internalize their domination as a sense of injury to the self, though rarely in the total sense implied by Elkins.[20] To (re-)gain self-respect, in this view, one must assert his or her equality of moral worth or capacity; and one way of doing this may be to engage in public protest against the conditions producing this injured sense of self. To quote again A. C. Searles of Albany, Georgia: "What did we win? We won self-respect. It changed all my attitudes."

More recently, however, Orlando Patterson has challenged this "internalization" position by claiming that "There is absolutely no evidence from the long and dismal annals of slavery to suggest that any group of slaves ever internalized the conception of degradation held by their masters."[21] Patterson's is a remarkable claim and we will return to this issue several times throughout this book. Suffice it here to say that, though the Elkins thesis concerning the infantiliza- tion of slaves in North American slavery was way overstated, Patter- son's position, which is just as extreme in the other direction, is not the only alternative to it. Indeed it remains for Patterson to show why slaves, unlike other oppressed groups and individuals, never won- dered, in part of their psyches at least, if their oppressors weren't right about them.

Self-respect seems also to essentially entail equality of moral or human status. Philosophically, most notions of self-respect derive from the Kantian tradition of moral concern which is itself a secular version of the Christian teaching that we are all, as Martin Luther King asserted, "God's children." In Kantian terms we are to be treated as "ends" rather than merely as "means," as subjects who have a "free and rational will" not as objects.[22] In the Christian terminology of the civil rights movement we are infinitely precious in God's sight; in its secular language we are "somebody."

What most discussions of self-respect neglect, however, is that self-respect is not only concerned with establishing moral and psy- chological equality but also with asserting difference. It is not just that I/we are as good as you; but also that I am/we are in some sense unique and acknowledged as such, whether by a transcendent power, another person, or oneself. Such an assertion of difference need not be a way of claiming superiority over others. At best it is, as philosopher Stanley Cavell has suggested, "a continuing task not a property" in which it is a matter of "finding your own voice," even though that "voice" may only be found in and through the words of others.[23] Thus to assert a right, whether moral or legal, is a way of pointing to and asserting equality in difference. Most discussions of self-respect fail to pay sufficient attention to "otherness," not just as that which helps constitute what we are, but also as the source of constitutive acknowledgment (the ideal form of which King called *agape*) from an "other."[24]

Yet another important issue in thinking about self-respect is whether and the degree to which which self-respect is finally confirmed (or even may be engendered) through action with or before others. The importance of public action as a sign and confirmation of self-respect was illuminated by James Bevel's injunction to protesters not just to "pick up one's soul" but also to "walk with one's soul." Indeed it would be puzzling to claim to be self-respecting, and then never protest against the violation of one's rights. Self-respect is not just a state of mind; it implies some form of action which transforms self-respect from a subjective or private certainty into a public truth. This is not to deny Thomas's distinction between self-respect and self-esteem exactly, for what is at issue here is not tangible success so much as public affirmation of one's moral status through action. But it does mean that at some point self-respect must be shown rather than just asserted. In retrospect what was most striking about the situation of black people in the hard-core areas of the South, such as Mississippi, was not that their public protests were ineffective, but that there were hardly any such protests at all between the turn of the century and the 1960s.[25]

Yet another issue, as we shall see in later chapters, concerns the place or person(s) from whom one receives authorization to respect oneself. Indeed, are white people the "others" paradoxically necessary to confirm black people as worthy of respect? If so, does this not still leave black people dependent upon whites? Though the ultimate source of self-worth and -respect for Martin Luther King was God, King did, as we shall see, contend that one aim of non-violent direct action was to appeal to the conscience of white people and thus force them to recognize the humanity of black people. What is at issue is how much this desire for recognition was for whites to recognize what black people already realized and how much it was for whites to help black people come to the realization of their full humanity. King's enemies always suspected that it was more of the latter than was necessary.

Bernard Boxill fundamentally questions the wisdom of this impulse to "make others moral" and contends instead that respect from white people is elicited mainly by "fear." He also questions the propriety of making self-respect hinge on the "opinions of others," since belief about one's self thus derived would not be "rationally based." As Charles McDew said, "When a person cannot recognize your humanity, you cannot appeal to him as another human being." Seen in this light, public protests were a way for protesters to demonstrate and assert not win self-respect. "The self-respecting person," writes Boxill, "will protest. His protest affirms that he has rights. . . . His reassurance does not come from persuading others that he has self-respect. It comes from using his claim to self-respect as a challenge."[26]

Boxill's analysis of self-respect emphasizes the central role of public action as a sign and confirmation of self-respect. The problem is that Boxill seems to conceive of self-respect as a property of the self in opposition to everyone, friend or foe. It is true that no one else can be self-respecting for oneself, but Boxill underplays the importance of solidarity with one's allies in engendering or maintaining a sense of worth and respect. Nor does the fact that recognition must be wrested from one's oppressors mean that I, as oppressed, must come to share their views of me or their way of life as such. But it does mean that they must acknowledge my existence—Boxill's "fear" being one possible manifestation of this acknowledgment—and I must take their position, however hostile it may be, into account in thinking and acting. Yet Boxill does not really escape the problem of otherness, since his analysis implies a split self, one part of which becomes the source of acknowledgment, an internalized "other" whom I show that I am a person worthy of respect. Why this is more "rationally based" than an explanation of self-respect derived from acknowledgment by an actual "other" is not clear.

Finally, however, the issue is not just the definition of self-respect but the conditions under which it may emerge and be enhanced. Lawrence Thomas at least hints that self-respect is not a "given" of human existence but must be developed in relation to others. To make self-respect derivative of moral rights which are "given" (a modern version of natural rights theory)—as Hill and Boxill seem to—is acceptable as a kind of analytic model of moral and legal personhood. But such a position too easily suggests the idea of an hermetic self sealed off from other selves and engaged in a self-regarding quest for self-regard.

Winning (Self)-respect

Up to this point we have explored the part of the repertory of political thinking available to the civil rights movement derived directly from Christian notions of self-worth and analyzed it from a broadly Kantian perspective. But what is needed is an account that will envisage how self-respect and respect from others is gained rather than dwell on it as an already existing moral and psychological state. Though the Christian-Kantian tradition certainly never doubts the moral importance of other people—no cogent tradition of ethical thought could—it seems to see them primarily as limitations on the individual self rather than internally constitutive of it. [27]

To supplement this analysis of the static self, a socially based, dialectical account of self-formation can be found in and derived from the canonical account of the "master-slave" relationship in Hegel's *The Phenomenology of Spirit* (1807). Whatever its limitations, the master-slave analysis provides a paradigm (or model) for the emergence of self-consciousness and self-respect; it makes the existence of an other self-consciousness and the desire for recognition or acknowledgment from "it" necessary not just as a delimiting but also as a constitutive factor of the self; it acknowledges the role of force and the risk of life in the winning of a self; and finally it implies that self-formation (and by extension self-respect) is processual and that the self is not a fixed thing or entity, but a relationship arising from a process. [28]

Indeed there are powerful examples in Afro-American thought and writing of such dialectical accounts of self-formation. In this context Frederick Douglass's *Narrative of the Life of Frederick Douglass* (1845) and the first chapter of W. E. B. DuBois's *The Souls of Black Folk* (1903) stand out as canonical black American accounts of self-formation and self-respect. [29] They also anticipate the problem of the free, self-respecting self as it emerged in the civil rights movement and in the self-consciousness of black women in the 1960s and 1970s. The point here is not to trace the influence of Hegel on either man, or the influence of Douglass on DuBois, or that of both men on the civil rights movement. Rather it is to point to a common condition and a repertory of secular ideas about self–re-creation that runs throughout the history of black Americans.

It would certainly be a mistake to consider Frederick Douglass a typical escaped slave—or indeed a typical anything. Besides his superior intelligence, he was a skilled orator, a politician, a writer, and an editor. More to the point, his first account of life in slavery was atypically secular in its hostility to organized white Christianity and grudging in its enumeration of the benefits of Christianity to the slaves. To be sure Douglass considers the time that he used the Bible to teach other slaves to read and write his happiest time under slavery. But it seems to have been the acquiring of the ability to read rather than the content of what was read that was crucial for his students and for him. Indeed, the account of his closeness to these students—almost the only such instance Douglass records in his *Narrative*—moves him to question if "a righteous God governs the universe?" rather than to dilate upon the wonders of divine providence. More generally Douglass's world was not organized by the religious trope of "earthly/heavenly" life but the secular, Afro-American one of "South/North" marked out by the North Star, that great natural symbol of hope for the slaves. Moreover, as Robert Stepto has pointed out, Douglass's *Narrative* is paradigmatic for "the narrative of ascent to literacy and freedom" in later Afro-American writing such as Richard Wright's *Black Boy* and, in modified form, Anne Moody's *Coming of Age in Mississippi*.[30]

By no means does Douglass offer a full account of what it was like to be a slave in eastern Maryland in the 1820s and 1830s. Insofar as he dwells on details of situations or depicts personality, he is more concerned with the world of the masters than with slave life. Indeed, Douglass's narrative of ascent betrays a deep ambivalence toward black life and culture. Though acknowledging that his father was white, Douglass's account of family and kinship ties are spare to the point of non-existence; as we shall see, his attitude toward slave songs and celebrations was a skeptical one: they were symptoms of rather than antidotes to enslavement. In Stanley Elkins's formulation, then, *Narrative* belongs to the "literature of damage" about slavery.[31] And this should remind us that accounts of life under slavery and of the formation of self within that setting have less to do with how "things really were" than with the purposes of the author, the expectations of the audience (in this case, Douglass's abolitionist sponsors), and the constraints of the genre deployed.

More generally Douglass's *Narrative* reveals that at the heart of ascent narratives lies a deep ambivalence toward black as well as white culture and toward the selves produced under such circumstances, including oneself. Wright did not reject the white South alone; in *Black Boy* he also rejects what he takes to be his fate had he remained in Mississippi—to "become" his father, a black peasant trapped by the land and limited in his vision of possibility. To Wright black culture seems essentially limited and impoverished. Lest we see this as peculiar to Wright or perhaps an exclusively male reaction to lack of male prerogative, we should note Moody's quite similar fear in the early 1960s of being trapped by her mother's way of life in Mississippi:

> Mama and Raymond had been hooked to the soil since they were children, and I got the feeling, especially from Mama, that they were now trying to hook me . . . I saw how happy she was in her garden . . . She did have the most beautiful garden I'd seen . . . But it was the hardest way I knew of making a living."[32]

Though Moody's narrative traces no ascent to the North, only periodically her descent to New Orleans, it revoices Wright's doubts about Southern black culture and displays little or no recognition of what Alice Walker would later consider worth celebrating about her mother's garden.

On the other hand, like Douglass but unlike Wright in *American Hunger*, Moody arrives at a sense of purpose through involvement with a political movement: "I had found something outside myself that gave meaning to my life." This political involvement is important not because it reunites her with the adult black community, but because it establishes her difference from it and those habituations which have kept it subservient to the white world. She was fifteen years old when Emmett Till was murdered; and the impact of his murder, she remembers, not only increased her hatred of whites: "I hated Negroes. I hated them for not standing up and doing something about the murders." And Moody is less concerned with what black men have done to black women than with what black men have failed to do in response to the depredations of the white community: ". . . I began to look upon Negro men as cowards."[33] Moody's participation in the movement redeems her own self-respect and that of black people, though the concluding note of the book is highly tentative, even skeptical. Indeed political engagement in the civil rights movement may have given rise to a narrative pattern in black writing which would be an alternative to those of ascent or immersion—the narrative of political engagement, as exemplified in Moody's *Coming of Age* as well as Alice Walker's *Meridian*.

Returning to *Narrative*, a kind of *Bildungsroman* toward freedom, we can see how Douglass, as Ann Kibbey has observed, does not allegorize his progress toward freedom along the lines of *Pilgrim's Progress*. Instead, he creates a secular allegory of the path to freedom, the point of which is that freedom as a legal status is impossible, or at least empty, without autonomy or freedom of character, most centrally self-respect.[34]

Though Douglass rarely speaks of white masters and mistresses or overseers in terms of freedom, another lesson he wants to impart is that the unchecked power of whites over blacks corrupts the souls of whites. The members of the master class are slaves to slavery and to the emotions, including capriciousness and fear, that it generates. This lesson is made most poignantly specific in the corruption of Mrs. Auld, who teaches young Frederick to read. After having been berated by her husband for doing so, she succumbs to "irresponsible power."[35] This demonstrates to Douglass that the ameliorating effects of Christianity and the natural maternal kindness of women are easily undermined by the corrupting power of domination.

More interesting in *Narrative* is the way Douglass arrives at his decision to escape and how he finds the resources to persist in that determination. Above all, Douglass links learning to read and write with the formation of a "free" character. Only through words, he claims, can the natural desire for freedom be kept alive and nurtured. The "wild notes" of the slave songs are his "first glimmering conception of the dehumanizing character of slavery" rather than a sign of the persistence of the desire for freedom. And it is after surreptitiously reading several speeches against slavery and for Catholic emancipation in Ireland that he finds that they "gave tongue to interesting thoughts of my own soul, which had frequently flashed through my mind and died away for want of utterance . . . Freedom now appeared, to disappear no more forever . . . It was an ever present torment to me . . ."[36]

What we witness here is the first stage of Douglass's awareness that he might become a free man, that slavery is not a natural fact but a contingent fate. Learning to read is his "fall" into the world of possibility. Ironically this new awareness is brought home to him when he overhears Mr. Auld's railing against his wife for having taught Douglass to read. Through the "word" Douglass learns the meaning of slavery and freedom as concepts rather than experiencing them as conditions, a necessary first stage in differentiating himself from his "fellow slaves" and "their stupidity,"[37] the state of mind produced by an absence of possibility under slavery. At this stage, then, freedom is both more and less than the condition of not being legal chattel: it is a state of mind characterized by "hope" as opposed to a bestial state without past or future.

But such "inner" freedom is not enough either. Just as the power of the word was needed to deliver the slave from a pseudo-natural state into self-consciousness, from experience into conceptualization, so action is needed to translate/transform this sense of possibility into actuality, certainty of self, or as Hegel says, into truth of the self. What makes action possible is Douglass's overcoming of the fear of death. "I had," wrote Douglass later, "reached the point at which I was not afraid to die."[38] When the overseer Covey lays hands on Douglass one pre-dawn morning, Douglass finally decides to risk his life and fight back: "from whence came the spirit I don't know—I resolved to fight." After two hours of fighting until "the sun was almost shooting his beams over the eastern woods and we were still at it,"[39] a truce was called. Covey never beat him again. Douglass's account in *Narrative* (as opposed to the later account in *My Bondage and My Freedom* [1855]) is spare and strains for no grand rhetorical effects. But it is one of the most graphic set-pieces in the literature of slavery depicting the struggle for recognition conceptualized by Hegel in his *Phenomenology of Spirit*. Indeed, set as it is at dawn, Douglass's fight with Covey echoes the biblical account of Jacob's struggle with the Angel which enabled Jacob to win a blessing and change his name.

According to Hegel, the slave is the antagonist who concedes power over his or her life to another self-consciousness rather than risking that life. Freedom only comes through risking life, through putting one's body on the line. As though glossing Hegel, Douglass seems to believe that in refusing this risk the slave is shamed and dishonored, for as he writes in *My Bondage*, "Human nature is so constituted, that it cannot *honor* a helpless man, although it can pity him; and even this it cannot do long, if the signs of power do not arise."[40] In *Narrative* Douglass reflects on his fight with Covey:

This battle with Mr. Covey was the turning point of my career as a slave. It rekindled the few expiring embers of freedom and revived within me a sense of my own manhood . . . The gratification afforded by the triumph was a full compensation for whatever else might follow, even death itself.[41]

Thus the reward was "manhood," Douglass's gender-marked term for self-respect and indeed for freedom itself. Though Douglass often links manhood specifically with being male, it is not generally linked with biological maturity. Put abstractly, self-respect is an achievement which comes from wrenching oneself away from enslavement and by implication from biological creation altogether. The struggle is not for literal survival but one that puts literal survival at risk in the name of self-respect and honor. It is the way, in Elaine Scarry's terms, of re-creating one's self, one's voice, and one's world.[42]

Indeed this confontational model of freedom can be found in the writing of black women as well. In Harriet Wilson's *Our Nig* (1859), the central figure, Frado, appears for most of the book as a passive character, continually abused by the white mistress of the house and the mistress's daughter and generally defended by the sons and the master of the house. A female, class-marked version of the family romance, the Cinderella story provides a kind of template for the action. Yet the sympathetic sons never really confront their mother over her abusive treatment of their black servant ("our Nig") nor do they ever deliver her from her tormentor. As Henry Louis Gates notes, the novel ends ambiguously, sliding into a "realistic," novelistic register away from the romancelike quality of much of what precedes it.[43]

Our Nig also contains a scene of confrontation similar, though more muted in depiction and effect, to Douglass's fight with Covey. When pushed too far by the evil mistress Mrs. Bellmont, Frado stands firm and shouts:

> Stop! . . . strike me and I'll never work a mite more for you; and throwing down what she had gathered, stood like one who feels the stirring of free and independent thoughts . . . She remembered her victory at the wood-pile . . . She contemplated administering poison to her mistress . . .[44]

Moreover, the novel records, again in a less detailed and dramatic fashion, the awakening effect of the written word on Frado as well.

Much more dramatically stands the example of Sojourner Truth who confounded normal gender distinctions by engaging in a kind of one-woman guerrilla action against slavery. The result, however, was that some men doubted that she was a woman and at an anti-slavery meeting in 1852 she had to bare her breasts to the crowd to prove that she was a woman ("And ain't I a woman?"). She was, as she asserted at one point, "a self-made woman," a necessary process among black women which Hazel Carby has traced in some detail and labeled "reconstructing womanhood."[45] That Truth had to act and speak "like" a (white) man to help black people, only then to bare her breasts, a most "unladylike" thing to do, to prove herself a (black) woman shows the deep intertwining of race and gender and the difficulties that black men and women had in constructing a sense of self or a "voice," as opposed to having a self or voice constructed for them.

Another graphic example in black women's writing of the establishment of identity through confrontation, the willingness to risk one's reputation as a "woman" and even one's life, occurs in Zora Neale Hurston's *Their Eyes Were Watching God* (1937). There Janie finally defies her husband Jody by talking back to him and humiliating him in front of his friends. But it is in terms of voices rather than weapons that the conflict is joined and resolved. Says Jody at one point:

> Ah told you in de very first beginnin' dat Ah aimed tuh be uh big voice. You oughta be glad, 'cause dat makes a big woman outa you.[46]

Thus the scene of confrontation, involving risk and resulting in a transformed sense of self—indeed a sense that the self is contested and constructed rather than accepted as given—stands at the center of self-formation in much Afro-American writing.

Yet in both Douglass's fight with Covey and Frado's confrontation with Mrs. Bellmont, there is a departure from the Hegelian model, for both fail to win explicit acknowledgment that they are fully human and worthy of respect from their tormentors. To be sure Covey never flogs Douglass again and Mrs. Bellmont eases up on her abuse of Frado, but that is about all. This suggests that Bernard Boxill's claim that the most likely result of assertions of defiance and self-respect is "fear" in the mind of the oppressor has a certain cogency to it.

Significantly Douglass's story "The Heroic Slave" (1853) ends with an account of one Madison Washington's leadership of a successful shipboard slave revolt as told by the mate on the ship, a white man named Tom Grant. Twice, Grant relates how Washington had refused to kill and even "disarmed" him with his eloquence:

> The fellow loomed up before me. I forgot his blackness in the dignity of his manner, and the eloquence of his speech. It seemed as if the souls of both of the great dead (whose names he bore) had entered him . . . It was not that his principles were wrong in the abstract; for they are the principles of 1776.[47]

In this passage Douglass makes actual in fiction what seems not to have happened in his own life—explicit recognition of black humanity as a result of a direct confrontation. It was recognition from the white world that he hoped would result from black participation in the Civil War. As Douglass wrote during the war: "There is something ennobling in the possession of arms, and we of all other people in the world stand in need of their ennobling influence." To Douglass, military service would alleviate the stigma of a "lack of manly courage."[48] But it was respect, not love, that he seemed to desire from white people.

Still, Douglass's fight with Covey did not win him his literal freedom. He puns on the name of a later, kinder master, Mr. Freeland who was his "best master . . . until I became my own master . . . I began to want to live upon free land as well as with Freeland."[49] Legal freedom required and augmented self-respect and depended upon self-mastery. To triumph over the actual master was to replace him with oneself; it was to be self-determining. Finally, in contrast with self-mastery, Douglass mentions another sort of provisional freedom granted to the slaves by the masters. In the period around Christmas, slaves were often granted holidays to engage in dissipation and drunkenness. Douglass rightly sees such indulgence as a safety-valve for the master. Not only do these periods cause slaves to forget their oppression momentarily, they also have the effect, he speculates, of "disgust[ing] their slaves with freedom by plunging them into the lowest depths of dissipation." Once the period of besottedness is over, the slave returns to slavery with relief and finds "little to choose between liberty and slavery."[50] Thus this freedom as license and indulgence was a kind of repressive desublimation, a form of negative freedom within the prison house.

In sum, then, Douglass's allegory is an exploration of the nature of freedom. With Freeland as with Mr. Severe, the brutal overseer, the very names of the whites suggest allegorical qualities, markers in the passage from slavery to freedom and intended for ethical rather than theological edification. Douglass's *Narrative* escapes pious moralizing about the importance of inner or spiritual freedom by emphasizing the process of actualizing freedom and self-respect. Such "making real" (Scarry's term) derived not from a sense of religious acceptance or communal deliverance, not from a sense of having been liberated from this world for a reward in the next. Rather freedom in all its senses was ordered and preserved by the word, disciplined by work and planning, and actualized in (sometimes violent) action. If the "fear of the Lord [*Herr*] is the beginning of wisdom," as both the Bible and Hegel claim, then overcoming the fear of death, "the sovereign master [*Herr*]," is the beginning of freedom. Only then could the "flickering light of the north star" become an actual pointer toward freedom rather than a mere symbol of hope.[51]

With W. E. B. DuBois the dialectic of self-consciousness and self-respect encompasses the group as well as the individual. The contending self-consciousnesses are now two peoples—whites and blacks—rather than two social categories—masters and slaves. No evidence exists that Douglass had read or been influenced by Hegel. But DuBois, as Joel Williamson has documented, was profoundly influenced by late nineteenth-century Hegelianism while at Harvard and then in Berlin. According to Williamson, DuBois's language in *Souls of Black Folk* and specifically his view of history as the progressive emergence of *Geist* (spirit or mind) as embodied in "specific world historical peoples" is profoundly Hegelian. Williamson fails to mention—though it seems highly probable—that DuBois's theory of individual and collective self-formation must also have been shaped by Hegel's dialectic of self-consciousness.[52]

The crucial text in which DuBois sketches in his theory of black self-consciousness and self-respect is "Of Our Spiritual Strivings," the first chapter of *Souls*. There, the source of much twentieth-century black writing, DuBois offers his famous analysis of "double consciousness," an analysis grounded not only in DuBois's experience of being a black man in a white world but also in his experience of being a mulatto, like Douglass, somewhat estranged from both. DuBois begins with an incident from his own life—the rejection of his greeting card by one of his white schoolmates. This rejection constitutes his "fall" into racial awareness, analogous to Douglass's fall into his awareness of the full meaning of his enslavement.

> Then it dawned upon me with a certain suddenness that I was different from the others; or like, mayhap, in heart and life and longing, but shut out from their world by a vast veil. . . . The shades of the prison-house closed round about us all.[53]

The rest of the chapter and of *Souls* is devoted to exploring and working through the implications of this "difference." And DuBois's great cultural/political task will be to reverse the valorization of this difference.

Indeed such epiphanic episodes, in which the fundamental fact of the difference between white and black dawns on the subject, are rife in Afro-American writing. Hurston's *Their Eyes Were Watching God* locates Janie's realization at the age of six when she fails at first to recognize herself surrounded by a group of white children in a photograph:

> So when we looked at de picture and everybody got pointed out there wasn't nobody left except a real dark little girl . . . Dat's where Ah wuz s'posed to be, but Ah couldn't recognize dat dark chile as me. So Ah ast, 'where is me? Ah don't see me.'[54]

Just as debilitating but also potentially "enlightening" has been the realization that whites don't "see" black people. More accurately they see but fail to recognize them, "to recognize" here referring both to the failure of whites to understand the difference involved in being black and to an unwillingness to acknowledge the equal moral status of blacks. Ralph Ellison's trope of invisibility is a variation on the opening pages of *Souls*, particularly where DuBois asks what it means to be a "problem," even if there is sympathy for the "problem." And what DuBois suggests is that to know that one is recognized as a problem, particularly as a victim, can be deeply debilitating and infuriating.

According to DuBois, one fundamental implication of misrecognition by whites of blacks is that

> the Negro is . . . gifted with second sight in this American world—a world which yields him no true self-consciousness, but only lets him see himself through the revelation of the other world. It is a peculiar sensation, this double-consciousness . . . One ever feels his twoness . . . two warring ideals in one dark body, whose dogged strength alone keeps it from being torn asunder.[55]

Crucial here is DuBois's own ambivalence as to whether "twoness" is an advantage or a disability. On the one hand, black Americans implicitly know both worlds, as does the Hegelian slave, while whites know only their own, and then not fully. Moreover, from behind the "veil," black people learn to confront and articulate the reality of death, literally to make the music from it in the form of the sorrow songs that DuBois celebrates. By implication black people are beyond the "innocence" so often imputed to white American consciousness. For DuBois this double consciousness is the psychological and cultural precondition for the mutual enrichment of white and black cultures and thus the basis of his lifelong commitment to cultural pluralism.[56]

And yet, doubleness consumes vital energies and expresses itself through inner division and self-alienation as well:

> This waste of double aims, this seeking to satisfy two unreconciled ideals, has wrought sad havoc . . . has sent them wooing false gods and invoking false means of salvation and at times has even seemed about to make them ashamed of themselves . . . But the facing of so vast a prejudice could not but bring the inevitable self-questioning, self-disparagement, and lowering of ideals . . .[57]

Thus DuBois also recognizes an endemic tendency to shame and lack of self-respect in Afro-American life. What else could there be when the other (white) world only gives back to black people, in the manner of the distorting mirror, an "imaginary" image of themselves? The great task of the dominated is to find what *their* self-image might become.

There were two directions in which later thinkers concerned with black cultural consciousness could move with DuBois's analysis of black self-consciousness and pride. Shorn of its metaphysical scaffolding, the Hegelian dialectic of self-consciousness suggests that there is no essential self to be distorted by the dominant other. Rather the oppressed build up a sense of self within their oppressed condition until they realize that they can challenge their oppressors. From this perspective, black cultural characteristics are the outcome of historical experience; they can and indeed do change. Being black is a contingent factor; what is crucial is the possibility of transforming through political and cultural action the experience of domination and shame into freedom and self-respect.

On the other hand, DuBois was also taken by an Hegelian assumption of racial-*völkisch* essences. In every "people" there was an essential "self" or "identity" waiting to emerge under proper conditions. According to this view the dominant white world suppresses these racial-spiritual characteristics and engenders a false individual and group self which must be undermined and replaced by an authentic racial self. In this case being black is not a contingent but an essential fact about the experience and self-consciousness of Afro-Americans. Who and what you are is not just a matter of what is done to you and what you do; it also depends on an inherent potentiality waiting to be released. What remains central to both positions, however, is that self-respect depends on the recognition, acceptance, and articulation of the difference between the white and black experience (and/or essence): "he must be himself and not another."[58] Only if those differences are preserved, DuBois wants to assert, can there be some sort of cultural and political equality in America.

This DuBoisian concern with the politics of culture reemerged during and gathered strength in the wake of the civil rights movement. Unlike pluralists such as Ralph Ellison and Albert Murray who celebrated the multi-voiced nature of black culture, its inextricable involvement with European and Native American cultures, advocates of what was called the "black aesthetic" asserted that DuBois's "doubleness" reflected a stage of cultural awareness to be transcended. Indeed most of those articulating this position contended that the culture of black Americans was essentially African with a pernicious European overlay. Thus one destination of cultural self-respect was the assertion of a univocal black culture in which double-consciousness was finally overcome.[59]

But almost as soon as a black aesthetic and by extension a sense of black pride had been staked out, another sort of cultural pluralism was asserted, grounded in the difference between black men and women, a distinction all but lost in the pervasive male orientation of the black aesthetic. According to black feminists not only should a plurality of voices be encouraged, but the dichotomy in experience between male and female was just as important as racial difference in the self-formation of black women. Indeed Barbara Johnson was to suggest that "voice" arose from "self-difference" rather than "self-identity"; and both she and bell hooks stressed the effort needed to prevent the quadripolar nature of experience—black and white/ male and female—from collapsing back into the powerful bipolar model first conceptualized by DuBois.[60]

My concern in this chapter has not been to dismiss the importance of the pursuit of self-interest for politics in general or for the politics of the civil rights movement in particular. Rather I have attempted to establish the necessity of enriching our concept of politics by using the example of the civil rights movement to suggest that both other-regarding and self-sacrificing motives are present in and central to political action under certain conditions. Moreover, I have wanted to examine self-respect as a political phenomenon and suggest its importance in understanding the way the politics of movements such as the civil rights movement transcend the pursuit of self-interest as usually defined. Since the best way to understand the political importance of self-respect is to see it as an achievement rather than as something inherent or "given," the question of how self-respect is to be achieved also became important. And one answer, drawn from a close reading of Frederick Douglass and particularly W. E. B. DuBois, was that self-respect must be understood as necessarily collective and both political and cultural.

Indeed, this was where Booker T. Washington and DuBois ultimately disagreed. It was not that Washington denied the importance of self-respect; indeed his whole effort was to give to black people a sense of worth and importance. Rather it was that Washington saw such a state of mind as being achieved not through confrontation with but through the conciliation of the white world. It was not that Washington advocated passivity and quiescence; it was that action for him was limited almost exclusively to the economic sphere and implied an abdication of the political, at least in the present. Nor did Washington betray much awareness of the importance of black cultural identity for black self-respect. It was DuBois's great achievement to remind black and white people of the political importance inherent in the way a group understands and explains itself to others and to itself.

Thus finally the self-transformations undergone by participants in the civil rights movement were part of what they meant by freedom. Political change became a driving force behind a new cultural self-awareness and transformation. And these cultural transformations in turn took on political implications in the post–civil rights world, a world we still of necessity inhabit.

CHAPTER 4

Martin Luther King and the Meanings of Freedom

. . . King's life is the best and most important metaphor for American history in the watershed post-war years.

Taylor Branch

The movement made Martin rather than Martin making the movement.

Ella Baker

As the 1960s recede in time, the public stature of Martin Luther King has grown apace. The observance of his birthday as a national holiday (the first non-president so honored) and the presence of his bust in the U.S. Capitol (the first black person so honored) indicate the degree to which King has become a member in good standing of the American pantheon. While such monumentalization of King makes it more difficult to express blind hostility toward him, it also tends to blunt efforts to probe more deeply into his thought without being accused of outright hostility. As a result, King runs the risk of being "overpraised but undervalued." Indeed, what someone once said to Alice Walker—"You *Southern* black people . . . are very protective of Martin King and Coretta"—has the ring of truth, if "Southern black people" is expanded to include all those sympathetic to the movement. [1]

But the protective shield around Martin Luther King has already been penetrated. As historians and political scientists assess the civil rights movement in earnest, King's administrative abilities and his personal character have been subjected to intense scrutiny and no little criticism. Though King's thought has been examined, often fairly thoroughly from a religious and secular point of view, no one has yet explored his understanding of the term "freedom" and how we might understand the idea in light of King's example.[2]

In what follows I want to offer a specifically political reading of King's thought and life by focusing on the four meanings of freedom set forth earlier. While acknowledging the crucial importance of black religious and white theological sources to King, this political reading reflects my opinion that we must extract from King's thought what remains accessible and pertinent to those who do not share his religious faith or theological orientation. To do this I will examine, first, King's own conception of what he was about, of how he reconciled a sense of choosing his life with an equally strong feeling that he had been chosen for it. This is what I call King's "choice to be chosen." Then I will explore the way his political thinking reflects the four fundamental meanings of freedom I have identified and how his life as a political actor and speaker gave them new pertinence.

More generally, King articulated, and helped bring to articulation in others, much that was essential to the collective experiences of Southern black people of whatever class or station. To be "representative" in this way is neither to be typical nor is it to be superhuman. But King was able to capture the attention, even devotion, of black Southerners and then move them to a new place psychologically and politically because what he said and the way he said it resonated so powerfully with their own experience and aspirations. In focusing upon King's representative status, I hope to bypass the debate, then and now, as to whether King made the movement or the movement, as Ella Baker put it, made King.[3]

Here the testimony of those who experienced an often uncanny matching of mood between King, the people, and the times might be offered as provisional evidence. John Lewis's words cited earlier bear repeating. Being associated with Martin Luther King, claimed Lewis, gave "a sort of sense of somebodyness. Being involved tended to free you . . . you saw yourself as the free man, as the free agent, able to act." And in 1967 before she had become known as a writer, Alice Walker wrote, "I waited to be called to life . . . the face of Dr. Martin Luther King, Jr. was the first black face I saw on our television screen . . . I saw in him the hero for whom I had waited so long." It was, she remembered, like "being born again." Six years later Walker, who grew up in rural Georgia, placed this experience in a more collective perspective when she wrote of King that "He gave us back our heritage . . . He gave us home." King, she asserted, was "a man who truly had his tongue wrapped around the roots of Southern black religious consciousness." If Walker's reactions are at all typical, as I suspect they are, then Clayborne Carson's recent claim that

> If King had never lived, the black struggle would have followed a course of development similar to the one it did. The Montgomery bus boycott would have occurred, because King did not initiate it. Black students would probably have rebelled—even without him as a role model—for they had sources of tactical and ideological inspiration besides King . . .

should be seriously questioned.[4]

Walker's testimony also spoke to the issue of the movement's impact. Objecting to the widespread assumption circa 1967 that the movement had been a failure, she wrote:

> If knowledge of my condition is all the freedom I get from a "freedom movement," it is better than unawareness, forgottenness, and hopelessness, the existence that is like the existence of a beast.[5]

Though some older black intellectuals objected to such claims for historical uniqueness voiced by Walker's generation,[6] Walker was articulating an experience common to Southern black women and men involved in or touched by the movement. Indeed her claim makes clear the sheer cognitive, even revelatory nature of the movement's impact. Knowledge of one's condition itself foreshadows a kind of proto-political freedom, which raises individual and, by implication, collective life above the level of mere existence into the realm of self-awareness. It is a freedom tied closely both to a sense of the past (against "forgottenness") and to a sense of futurity (against "hopelessness") and thus reveals the possibility of political action for the first time.

I have cited Walker at some length for two reasons: first, to call attention to the powerful importance King—though not he alone— had in returning Southern black people to their history; and, second, to anticipate another objection to King—that he was not radical politically and that culturally he was somehow *both* an "integration-ist" who accepted "white" culture without question *and* limited by the Afro-American religious provenance of his vision. This line of criticism, most often coming from black radicals in the late 1960s and

particularly those living outside the South, has the virtue of raising
the question of whether King spoke to and for all black Americans or
just to and for black Southerners or just to and for black people who
wanted to assimilate.

Here it must be admitted that King's strength, one which Walker
pinpointed, was indeed a limitation in many ways. To scarred
survivors of ghettoes in the North and West, King's voice harkened
back to the Southern religious ethos they, or their parents, had
literally and sometimes psychologically abandoned. Here one thinks
of the tone-deafness of Malcolm X or Eldridge Cleaver to King's
rhetoric, a reaction powerfully echoed in John Edgar Wideman's
Brothers and Keepers (1984). Wideman's brother, Robert, is serving
time on a murder charge and remembers the reaction when he and
his friends in Pittsburgh got word of King's assassination:

> One of the older guys running the meeting look up and say, We don't
> care nothing bout that ass-kissing nigger, we got important business
> to take care of . . . Didn't nobody dig what King was putting down.
> We wasn't about begging whitey for nothing and we sure wasn't taking
> no knots without giving a whole bunch back.
>
> . . . this was when Rap Brown and Stokely and Bobby Seale and them
> on TV. I identified with those cats. Malcolm and Eldridge and George
> Jackson. I read their books.[7]

Clearly King did not evoke "home" for Robert Wideman; but
rather an alien territory long since fled. Such a reaction testifies to the
existence not just of different degrees of radicalism within the black
movement in the late 1960s, but also to the profound difference
separating Southern and Northern, rural and urban black people in
America.

Such reactions stemming from the immediacy of intense alienation
and anger were not the only criticism King received from Northern
black intellectuals and activists. In the late 1960s social critic Harold
Cruse offered a more sophisticated version of this rejectionist line.
Cruse's embattled radicalism was undoubtedly important in that
period; he gave the impression of a man who could not be intimidated
by anyone, black or white. Because "the Negro problem [is] primarily a cultural question," Cruse contended that an authentic black
radicalism had to marshall its intellectual energies to disseminate a
distinctive black cultural tradition by gaining control of the means of
cultural production, e.g., newspapers, radio, television, theater

groups, and the like. This would provide an institutional base for black liberation. Without cultural power, the political and legal gains made by the Southern movement were of relatively little importance.[8]

Cruse's distress at the lack of commitment to the political importance of black cultural consciousness was fed by the example of King whom he scored for advocating "cultural integration." King's formal education and his explicit intellectual allegiances were certainly shaped by the dominant European high culture. The leavening influence of or an articulated acquaintance with black history and Afro-American culture was not readily apparent. Only in *Where Do We Go From Here?* (1967) did King emphasize the importance of the black political or cultural tradition; and one suspects that this emphasis was primarily in response to the emerging black consciousness movement. Nor is there any doubt that King was an integrationist in the common meaning of the term. In these respects, Cruse was largely correct, just as those who search King's writings for awareness of the resentments or aspirations voiced by women in the civil rights movement find little aid or comfort.[9]

Yet Cruse's indictment missed a whole side of King's importance and that was the psychological and cultural resonances set up in the black population by King and the movement. Any political movement that energized the minds and mobilized the bodies of so many black Southerners (and some Northern blacks too) could scarcely be accused of insensitivity to the cultural traditions of black people. Though the legal and political goals of King and the mainstream of the movement may have been one with goals of the NAACP (or, for that matter, with the Communist Party), there was a vast difference between using the court system to gain equal rights and organizing, then mobilizing, masses of participants to engage in direct action to secure those rights. King's—and the movement's importance—in transforming the individual and collective self-image of black people was in its context the most radical "cultural" work imaginable. It was just as much—or more—of an example of cultural radicalism than anything Cruse could suggest.[10]

The Choice to Be Chosen

Martin Luther King's public life can be understood in terms of four fundamental choices, each a variation on the shifting relationship between activity and passivity, choosing and being chosen. These constitute what I call King's "choice to be chosen" as a public figure. I refer here not to clearly identifiable moments of choice, but rather to basic decisions that gradually emerged as having already been made and which gave shape to his life.

An essential indeterminacy lies at the core of the modern concern with identity. As discussed earlier, it is not clear whether there is a self "there" waiting to be discovered or whether such a self is constructed from the circumstances and choices confronting us. Indeed, as Hannah Arendt was fond of pointing out, it may make little sense to talk of identity at all, whether discovered or constructed, until the life in question is over and can be given narrative coherence.[11]

But whatever the metaphysical status of the self or the theoretical dangers of positing essentialist notions of identity, the language of identity has provided a vocabulary for talking about individual and group uniqueness and for arriving at and asserting self-consciousness and self-respect. The difficulties with "identity talk" are heightened considerably for black people in a white world, at least in the American context. As we have seen, such difficulties arise from the burden—or gift—of "double consciousness," a reverberating, ricocheting sense of self produced by the mirroring presence of the white "other," a presence that perpetually calls self-respect and -coherence into question. This precarious location of the self between paranoia and dissolution, a siting that Ellison's trope of invisibility captures deceptively well, is threatened as well as protected when the black person in question is a prominent figure such as Martin Luther King.

The question of what it means to become such a figure is pertinent to King's life. While studying philosophical theology at Boston University, King had taken enthusiastically to Hegel, particularly to *The Philosophy of History* and *The Phenomenology of Spirit* and was undoubtedly concerned with the Christian (and Hegelian) problem of how one arrives at one's calling.[12] An especially cogent example of "choosing to be chosen" came in November 1959 when King announced to his congregation in Montgomery that he was moving to Atlanta to continue his work there:

I can't stop now, History has thrust something upon me which I cannot turn away. I should free you now.[13]

Striking here is the ambiguous conjunction of freedom and necessity. In obeying "History," King says that he will free the congregation of his presence; yet "I should free you now" implies a deeper sense of mission to free them from old attitudes and an oppressive condition. King's reluctance to call attention to his own ambition should also be noted here. His statement to his congregation might also be read as a shrewd combination of high ambition—even hubris—and humility. Indeed this speech in Montgomery was the Emersonian moment in King's public life when freedom and necessity, choice and calling, seemed to coincide, when "causes" were penetrated by "intellect," "will," and "moral intention." It should be added that this sense of calling had to be continually reclaimed throughout his public life.[14]

Not long before his death King offered a less personal, more theological version of this same theme when he affirmed that the "essence of man is found in freedom" but that "Freedom is always within destiny. It is the fulfillment of our destined nature. We are always both free and destined." He also emphasized that he was speaking of freedom of the "whole man" and not just "freedom of the will." Thus freedom in this abstract metaphysical sense was more than an inner capacity; it was a condition of being in and making decisions about the world—"the capacity to deliberate, decide and respond."[15]

Though this choice to be chosen which he announced in Montgomery was fundamental, it was not the first crucial choice of King's life. Indeed David Garrow claims that the resolution of a deep crisis in his sense of calling in January 1956 was central to King's assumption of his vocation. His acceptance of a leadership role in the bus boycott despite the enormous danger it involved was essential to King the public figure—the commitment to risking his life and confronting death as a real and constant presence. This idea of the "risk of life" is central to any understanding of what it meant for King (and for many participants in the movement, as we have seen) to become political beings. And it caused King to make such assertions as the following: "No man is free if he fears death."[16] Thus we might say that King only felt free to act when he acknowledged the ultimate limitation upon his freedom.

In this connection we might consider King's two youthful suicide attempts less as attempts at self-destruction than as attempts to expiate guilt through pain, one possible source for the idea of "unearned suffering" which stood at the center of his political theology. After the assassination of President Kennedy in 1963, King told his wife Coretta that "This is going to happen to me also."[17] Premonitions of mortality were constantly in his mind, particularly near the end of his life; and some of his aides considered him excessively morbid on the subject. Still, King never actively challenged death and was in fact a quite reluctant martyr. In this sense his choice to risk his life by taking on a leadership role was grounded in the same mixture of activity and passivity found in so much of his life.

Questions of life and death lead inevitably to a third crucial choice in King's public life—his decision to embrace non-violent direct action as a way of life and as a mode of action. In this area he came closest to recognizing explicitly the complex mixture of activity and passivity in his own life and in the lives of black Southerners. In countering Reinhold Niebuhr's charge that passive resistance was just that—passive, King sought to transcend the violence yet mobilize the energy in the psyche of black Southerners, to replace their fear with civil courage, and to undermine their sense of being unfree by emphasizing that to be non-violent was a choice. Thus for King non-violent direct action issued from free men and women; it was certainly not the predictable response of oppressed people retaliating against their oppressors.

Whatever the general arguments for and against non-violence, King's choice of it as a philosophy and a tactic was a brilliantly creative response to a specific historical double-bind. Whatever way blacks chose to act, whites were sure to say "No, that's not the way" or "This is not the right time" or "Isn't that just like black people?" King sidestepped the double-bind by shifting the question from *whether* black people would take action to *how* they were going to act. To choose non-violence was a way of refusing to be the kind of people the culture had allegedly made them. In proving non-violence effective, at least up to a point, King also called into question Niebuhr's conventional assumption that while individuals could act morally based on love, groups were confined to acting "immorally" by employing power to secure justice. King showed, as did Gandhi, that groups could surpass their own past behavior and that individuals could be empowered by motives other than narrow self-interest.[18]

Finally, if this rejection of violence arose from King's "choosing actively and affirmatively what not to do," his fourth crucial choice— to become a black Baptist minister and to take a church in the South—reflected an affirmation of what, in Erik Erikson's words, "one is never not."[19] King's biographers tell us that he initially resisted becoming a minister at all. Once having decided to become a minister, he was intent on avoiding the emotionality of conventional black religion to the point that at Crozer Seminary he studiously tried to avoid seeming "black" at all. Indeed his decision to pursue a PhD at Boston University Divinity School reflected a long-term interest in teaching and writing.

Furthermore, like Gandhi, King was a colonial intellectual who left his homeland to further his formal education. While in the North he was required, again like Gandhi, to sort out his class and status as well as his racial and regional loyalties. Like Gandhi, King returned home to lead a movement drawn from all classes and potentially from all races. As Garry Wills has suggested, "By trying to run away from his destiny, he equipped himself for it." The appeal of a campaign to support the garbage workers in Memphis in 1968 may have been closely tied to the chance it gave King to return to the South and replenish his depleted resources, to reestablish his roots.[20] Thus in the process of choosing his vocation and location, King initially fought against the minister's role cut out for him. But once he accepted it, he used it as a lever against the conventional expectations associated with it. Again, in Emersonian fashion, King took the causes that shaped his life and transformed them into reasons for his task. He made them his own.

What did it mean to live a life organized around such choices, to be aware of one's public role and have it continually confirmed, even imposed, by others? My sense is less of a man who imposed himself upon events than of one who prepared himself for what history had in store for him. As with Lincoln, there was a certain aura of sadness and constraint around his public persona. Lacking Lincoln's public sense of humor, King created himself as a figure of gravity to the extent that one is brought up short by remembering how young he was (twenty-seven at the time of the bus boycott). Indeed it is still quite difficult to look through the prepared public face and catch a glimpse of the private man. There was a certain willed quality to his public demeanor. Like a finely-tuned string stretched to maximum tension, there was relatively little play in his public persona.

Yet such *gravitas* certainly masked inner conflicts, guilts, and desires. No strong-willed and high-spirited son of a father possessing the same qualities could have grown up without having to learn considerable self-control. The two suicide attempts, the constant

presence of guilt-feelings, and the later tendency to depression
bespeak considerable aggression turned upon the self. The creation
of Martin Luther King, the public persona, only exacerbated the gap
between his inner and outer, private and public self. One friend
reported his saying that "I am conscious of two Martin Luther Kings.
I'm a wonder to myself."[21] At times the costs of self-discipline,
ambition, and public visibility became apparent and the relentless
self-critic, spurred on by an overweening super-ego, emerged. As
one of his biographers wrote:

> When he did obey what seemed to be an occasional irresistible compul-
> sion, he said that he felt seriously called to be a martyr, a suffering
> servant, a disciple—but he found it extremely difficult to admit that he
> was worried about what he regarded as the destiny God had given
> him.[22]

His close friend and adviser, Stanley Levison, remembered that King
"could be described as an intensely guilt-ridden man . . . this kept
him a very restive man all his life."[23] It is difficult to think of other
public figures of whom anything similar could be said. But I take this
as a sign of strength not weakness, indicative of a man whose own
resources had not been depleted by the demands of his public role.

Occasionally we get a glimpse behind the mask. One segment of
Elie Landau's film *From Montgomery to Memphis* shows King
remembering ruefully how afraid he and his colleagues had been
when they found themselves conducting a mass meeting in Philadelphia, Mississippi with Sheriff Lawrence Raney standing ominously behind them. The scene is moving and poignant because it
forces us to see how young King was and hints at how scared he often
must have been. Also, his mellifluous public voice concealed a sharp
tongue. He once exploded at Urban League leader Whitney Young
for criticizing King's public opposition to the Vietnam War:
"Whitney, what you're saying may get you a foundation grant, but it
won't get you into the kingdom of heaven." Typically, King felt so
guilty at this outburst that he later apologized profusely to Young.[24]
Finally, there were those moments in his speeches—one thinks of
the concluding moments of the "I Have a Dream" speech in August
1963 or the last part of his final public address in Memphis in April
1968—when he broke through the measured public self to something
more fundamental and powerful. In those moments the role, the
circumstances, and the self seemed to come into congruence.

In general King's life displayed the pattern of ascent from the oppressive South to liberty and literacy and then to reimmersion in the black experience in the South which Robert Stepto identifies as paradigmatic in the canonical texts of black American writing.[25] In this sense, too, King's life took on a certain representative quality, unfolding entirely under the conditions of modern publicity and the vastly accelerated pace of twentieth-century public life in America. It is instructive to recall that Gandhi's public career lasted over half a century, while King's was compressed into just over twelve years. Though his career was made up of alternating periods of public involvement and private withdrawals, King's withdrawals were too brief to fully replenish his depleted emotional resources.[26] Once the favorite of the *Zeitgeist*—King's public career began in 1955, just a year and a half after the groundbreaking Supreme Court decision and in the same year as the Bandung Conference—he found himself working alone by 1968, out on a tight-rope without a safety net.

Yet King had entered onto his destiny willingly and *did* choose to be chosen. Perhaps he was most free in those last couple of years when the tides of history were tending in different directions, for then he chose against the *Zeitgeist*.[27] Finally he had the courage to keep on being the person he had become and to make choice and destiny indistinguishable. By speaking out forcefully against the Vietnam War and in searching for new ways to address the plight of poor Americans, he distanced himself from the white and black establishments; by rejecting the ideology of black power and the rhetoric of violence he distanced himself from black radicals. As he wrote in 1967, perhaps as an admonition to himself: "Ultimately a genuine leader is not a searcher for consensus, but a molder of consensus."[28]

The Political Meanings of Freedom

Though Martin Luther King tended to elide the distinction between freedom and destiny when he spoke of theological or personal matters, the various ways he acted upon freedom in a political context pointed to a greater complexity. This is fortunate, since the notion of freedom-as-destiny has an unhappy legacy as a political idea. If we understand freedom-as-destiny to mean that the goal of individual or group action is freedom, then such a meaning is defensible. But if the equation of freedom and destiny implies that freedom is whatever happens to that individual or group, then we are headed toward a justification of anything in the name of freedom. King certainly shied away from any resemblance to the latter equation in the political realm.

King's philosophy of non-violent direct action derived from his theological stance. It was based neither on Utilitarian nor Kantian grounds, for he made no claim that non-violent direct action maximized happiness or that it derived from adherence to a categorical imperative. (Undoubtedly he felt that it could also meet these criteria.) Rather, justification for non-violent direct action was grounded in a transcendent, yet personal power working in and through specific historical events and movements.

Specifically King's "evangelical liberalism" *cum* personalist theology implied that there were traces of God's presence in history and even in human action, "fallen" though human history might be. Neo-orthodox theologians held the distance between God and humanity to be so vast that only God's grace through faith in Christ could hope to bridge the chasm, while liberal theology assumed that there were other, albeit tenuous ways to span the gap. For theological liberals, the significance of Jesus was that he provided an ethically blameless life for human emulation. Despite their sinfulness, human beings were also created in God's image, while all human law was to be measured against God's moral law, i.e., natural law. In sum, for the evangelical liberal there were hints *in* the world of how to relate the Christian message to political, economic, and social realities.

For King—as for fellow Southerner Lillian Smith, whose views influenced him—segregation was not simply an unjust social and psychological reality; it also pointed to spiritual alienation from self, others, and God and ultimately to a denial of freedom.[29] To subvert the alienating power of segregation, King argued for the central importance of Christian love or *agape*. As he defined it, *agape* was:

> . . . understanding and creative, redemptive goodwill for all men . . . we love men not because we like them, not because their ways appeal to us, nor even because they possess some type of divine spark; we love every man because God loves him.

King went on to add:

> We should be happy that he [Jesus] did not say, "Like your enemies." It is almost impossible to like some people . . . But Jesus recognized that *love* is greater than *like* . . .[30]

It is important to note here that King's claim about *agape* did not deny that each person possesses a divine spark, only that the injunction to love one's enemies did not derive from that fact alone or from any merit one's enemies (or friends for that matter) might possess. That was the point of *agape*'s unconditional nature.[31]

More to our point, King felt that *agape* was directly applicable in the world as a political virtue. The goal of political action informed by *agape* was the creation of the "beloved community," both utopian ideal and actual possibility, the necessary context for full human freedom. Thus, what the freedom song "We Shall Overcome" meant was that we shall "come over" and close the gap between human beings, and not just that we shall "overpower" segregation. Finally, ratifying this action toward community, there is, wrote King, "some creative force that works for universal wholeness . . ." Echoing abolitionist Theodore Parker, King had faith that "Though the arc of the moral universe is long, it bends toward justice."[32] Such was King's way of describing the natural or moral law running throughout creation.

If we move from theological to biblical language, we find concrete expression of King's belief in a personal God at work in human affairs. He was particularly drawn to the "Exodus event," an historical example of God's intervention in history that prefigured the way God had delivered black Americans from slavery and then was aligned with them in their struggle against segregation. This is the context within which we can understand King's reference in 1957 to America as a "bewildering Egypt" and to himself as a Moses-figure ("I've been to the mountaintop") leading his people out of bondage to Pharaoh. "We too are in bondage," he wrote in 1963; and then proceeded to claim that the movement's freedom songs served the same purpose as the spirituals had in the time of slavery.[33] Thus one meaning of freedom in King's political thought derived from the corporate experience of deliverance from oppression by God's action in sacred and secular history.

Nor did King stop there. He also linked the biblical event and the aspirations of black Americans with the fate of the nation: "the sacred heritage of our nation and the eternal will of God" are consonant with "our echoing demands."[34] By implication black Americans had succeeded the Puritans as the chosen people in God's plan for redeeming secular history through the national community. It was as though only the Americans who were acquainted with systematic, historical oppression could be the bearers of liberation for the entire nation. As King wrote in *Where Do We Go From Here?*, black Americans were charged with "enlarging the whole society and giving it a new sense of values."[35] In this respect King's sermons and writings take on the tone and function of the jeremiad, but with a difference. Though they call America back to its founding principles, they tend to project the realization of these principles toward the future. Indeed, this future-orientation is implied by the rhetoric of deliverance and liberation and stands in tension with the nostalgic undertow found in the conventional Puritan jeremiad or the republican call for a return to first principles. From Martin Luther King, American civil religion received its most powerful contemporary black interpretation.

Though freedom as collective liberation was important for King, it did not convey the necessary transformation of the self experienced by those actively engaged in direct action. From this perspective, direct action might be seen as a form of preparation in the "wilderness" before the promised land was reached. Thus the second form of freedom had to do with liberation from an old self and formation of a new one. Political action became a kind of transformational exercise.

King described this self-transformation in several ways. In his early reflections on the bus boycott, he spoke of the "lack of self-respect among black people" and, using the (dubious) metaphor of maturation, asserted that the "Negro, once a helpless child, has grown up politically, culturally and economically."[36] In 1961 he identified "a new sense of dignity, a new self-respect, and a new determination among black Americans." Then after Birmingham he talked of a positive sense of being "somebody" and that the black man "had to win and to vindicate his dignity in order to merit and enjoy his self-esteem."[37] Later in response to the black power and black consciousness movements, he issued a "psychological call to manhood" and spoke of his "deep feeling of racial pride" and an "audacious appreciation of his [the Negro's] heritage." Echoing DuBois, he added that the "Negro's greatest dilemma is that in order to be healthy he must accept his own ambivalence."[38] This constant and increasingly militant emphasis upon pride and self-respect suggests that, for King, loving one's self as an individual and as a member of the race with a distinctive heritage was a prerequisite for, as well as a result of, demonstrating love for the oppressor.

Behind this emphasis upon a changed sense of the self was King's assumption that freedom was "never voluntarily given by the oppressor." To maintain otherwise would be a contradiction in terms, since "growth only comes through struggle."[39] Though the struggle need not be a violent one (in contrast with Hegel and, as we shall see, Frantz Fanon), this psychic freedom could only be purchased with a literal or figurative risk of life. Moreover, the motive force behind this risk of life was the wresting of recognition from the oppressor. But crucially, King translated the Hegelian theme of the desire for recognition into Christian terms: the power of *agape* aimed at winning recognition by appealing to the oppressor's conscience. The dialectic of power and recognition was moralized into the dialectic of love and mutuality. In Martin Buber's language, I–It was replaced by I–Thou; subject-object became subject-subject. As King described it:

One day we shall win freedom, but not only for ourselves. We shall so appeal to your heart and conscience that we shall win *you* in the process, and our victory will be a double victory.[40]

In keeping with this dialectical view of interpersonal relationships, King described the confrontation between police and protesters in terms of the trope of seeing and being seen so central to the oppressor/oppressed dialectic. The eyes stand metonymically for the self; the act of looking for confrontation. King's description of the scene in Birmingham illustrates this: there were "hundreds, sometimes thousands, of Negroes who for the first time dared look back at a white man, eye to eye." And he vividly conveys the reversal from passive to active, submissive to assertive, impotent to powerful when he writes:

Bull Connor's men, their deadly hoses poised for action stood facing the marchers. The marchers, many of them on their knees, stared back, unafraid and unmoving. Slowly the Negroes stood up and began to advance. Connor's men, as though hypnotized, fell back, their hoses sagging uselessly in their hands . . .[41]

It is also important to underline King's stress on the shared nature of such public action against segregation. The creation of a new free self was not the result of individual but of collective action. More immediately, solidarity was created among protesters and a sense of oneness was established in the "war for the transformation of a whole people."[42] Thus besides dignity and self-respect, the new free self was capable of courage and solidarity.

Though of the three modern masters of the "hermeneutics of

suspicion"—Marx, Nietzsche, and Freud—the latter figure had the least obvious influence on King, the vocabulary King used to describe self-transformation was as often a psychological/medical one as it was religious/moral. Similarly, he couched his diagnosis of American society in terms of its pathologies as often as he did its injustices. In *Where Do We Go From Here?* King described the "congenital deformity of racism" marring white society and added that "the preparation for the cure rests with the accurate diagnosis of the disease."[43] Indeed, King also applied the pathology model to the history of black America. "Pain" stood at its center and it had been "scarred by a history of slavery and family disorganization" which rendered the black family "psychopathic." King brought the two vocabularies of injustice and pathology together, however, when he identified the task to be "a battle against pathology within and a battle against oppression without."[44]

In keeping with the pathology model, King conceived of non-violent direct action as a way to expose the "dangerous cancer of hatred and racism in our society." The white liberal must see "the need for powerful antidotes to combat the disease of racism." Another favorite trope was the Socratic effort of bringing "tensions in the open."[45] Perhaps the missing figure implied by both the pathology and the Socratic gadfly metaphors is the psychoanalyst who combines Hippocratic and Socratic functions, albeit uneasily and somewhat confusedly. King's non-violent direct action, thus, exposed the sickness of the white part of the national psyche and revealed a complementary disorder in the black part. Yet both portions, he felt, contained a health and power to be nurtured and released as well.

Still both types of freedom—collective liberation and self-transformation—were ostensibly peripheral to the explicit goals of the movement: the liquidation of racial segregation and black disfranchisement in the South. As already mentioned, King assumed the existence of a natural law which was the source of "constitutional or God-given rights." In particular King frequently invoked the founding authority of the Declaration of Independence which, along with the Constitution, he identified as "the great wells of democracy."[46] He implicitly accepted the doctrine of "incorporation" according to which the Bill of Rights applied to state as well as federal actions by virtue of the Fourteenth Amendment. And his justification for violating the injunction against marching in Birmingham was that it was intended to stifle protest and thus violated the First Amendment guarantee of "peaceable assembly."[47]

In a broader sense King and the civil rights movement played a crucial role in translating constitutional argument into a moral discourse concerning just and unjust laws and thereby mobilizing people in a way that constitutional language did not. By echoing the abolitionist appeal to natural rights and higher law doctrines as the basis for civil disobedience, King carried on, whether consciously or not, the American tradition of radical liberalism. The wider significance of "Letter from Birmingham Jail," a document aimed primarily at a white, middle-class audience, lay in its function as a liberal *apologia* for civil disobedience and an indictment of white moderates, particularly the clergy of the South, for temporizing.[48]

Crucial here is the claim King first voiced in Montgomery in 1955 and last made in Memphis in 1968—"the great glory of American democracy is the right to protest for right."[49] Such a statement expressed his belief that Afro-Americans were part of the American polity as a matter of right rather than as a favor to be granted them as though they were aliens seeking naturalization. To protest publicly was itself to assume that one *already* belonged, that a space of public appearance waited to be rightfully occupied. To assert this was a kind of performative utterance, appropriating the right to protest in the act of asserting it.

The analysis of the difference between just and unjust laws in "Letter from Birmingham Jail" is crucial to comprehending King's understanding of liberal freedom as "equal protection of the law" based on one's status as a rights-bearer. In "Letter" King advanced two sets of criteria for judging a law just or unjust—one set was grounded in religious, metaphysical, or psychological teachings; the other was based on political-legal procedures. He began by citing Aquinas to the effect that "An unjust law is a code that is out of harmony with the moral law" and "not rooted in eternal law and natural law." Yet King realized that few people thought in such natural law terms and thus shifted to a psychological *cum* moral standard by claiming that an unjust law "degrades human personality." Still, this begged the question of what it was about an unjust law that was degrading. King's answer was that segregation "gives . . . the segregated a false sense of inferiority" and reduces them to the "status of things." He then reverted to theological language by agreeing with theologian Paul Tillich that "sin is separation." Thus if segregation is separation, segregation is sin. Though the logic is faulty, King felt justified in urging disobedience to laws preserving segregation.

Even then King was not satisfied. He shifted to procedural criteria by maintaining that an unjust law "is a code that a numerical or power majority group compels a minority group to obey but does not make binding on itself." In constitutional language such a law violates the guarantee to "equal protection of the law." He then added an explicitly political provision by claiming that no law is just if inflicted upon a minority who "had no part in enacting or devising the law."[50] Indeed if we take this participatory criterion as a necessary condition for calling a law just, King seems to imply a basic right to have an active voice in making the law. Such an inclusion of political participation among basic rights (whether "natural" or "human") has generally been absent from American (or European) natural rights thinking, for the reason that if a right is inherent, something one is born with, it is pre-social and pre-political. That is, there can't be a natural right to political participation if the polis is a human rather than a natural construct.

Finally King's criteria for what makes a law just or unjust implied not only the right to civil disobedience, the ultimate expression of the right to protest for right(s); it also posited the duty or "moral responsibility to disobey unjust laws." From this "liberal" point of view civil disobedience is, as John Rawls has emphasized, an attempt to rectify aberrations in fundamentally just institutions and is thus not revolutionary. Rather, in his/her willingness to suffer the consequences, the civil disobedient demonstrates the highest devotion to the spirit (as opposed to the letter) of the law. As King wrote, "One who breaks an unjust law must do so openly, lovingly, and with a willingness to accept the penalty."[51] Indeed, appeal to higher law/ natural rights doctrines can be understood as a way of reassuring fellow citizens that one is not aiming at anarchy or revolution. Though engaging in civil disobedience to ensure liberal freedoms may have seemed quite "radical" at the time, it is in fact a venerable part of the radical liberal tradition in American political culture.

The dividing line between liberal freedom and participatory freedom is a subtle but important one. Freedom as action or participation is everywhere implied in King's writings (and actions) but it is rarely spelled out in explicit terms. The closest he came to specifying this particular notion of freedom was when he quoted Cicero: "Freedom is the participation in power." We might grasp its elusive presence by suggesting that in every public protest *for* rights or justice or jobs there is an implied assertion that *by* protesting collectively people are claiming their status as citizens and aiming to revitalize the space of political speech and action. As stated previously, it is not that we are free and therefore can act politically or vice versa: political action already is a species of freedom. Citizen-participants *protest* for rights while rights-bearers have rights. As Wilson Cary McWilliams has written: "The citizen in the ideal sense remains a democratic goal; citizenship as a legal status is a necessary means to that end."[52]

A distinction made by Arendt is also relevant to our understanding of civil disobedience (as opposed to conscientious objection or what Thoreau called "action from principle") as a form of participatory freedom. In "Civil Disobedience" Arendt sharply distinguishes conscientious objection from civil disobedience and places the activities of the civil rights movement in the latter category, a distinction bearing directly on the question of the role of conscience in politics and particularly on King's elevation of Thoreau and Socrates to canonical status in the history of civil disobedience. Arendt points out that in appealing to individual conscience both Socrates and Thoreau were engaged in a negative action against something; their appeal to conscience was a solitary one and thus not generalizable, and they were acting essentially from self-interest, albeit of the highest sort in that they could not live with themselves if they continued to obey the law. By way of contrast, for those engaged in civil disobedience "concerted action springs from an agreement with each other, and it is this agreement that lends credence and conviction to their opinion, no matter how they may have arrived at it." Although Arendt has been criticized—unfairly I think—for excluding moral concerns from political action, especially from civil disobedience, her larger point is that appeal to conscience is individual and hence apolitical, while a decision to break the law as a group is arrived at collectively, whatever the motives of the individuals concerned might be.[53]

Here Arendt also puts us onto something important about King's philosophy of non-violent direct action *cum* civil disobedience. First, the motives among participants in the movement included both King's principled philosophy of non-violence and a tactical, pragmatic decision to be non-violent on the part of many participants. But what counts, if we follow Arendt, is the decision to act collectively. Moreover, white participants may have broken the law for reasons of conscience. To them segregation laws seemed both constitutionally and morally wrong and they did not wish to be complicit with unjust laws. But it is not quite correct to say that black people in the movement acted from conscience, not, at least, in the same sense as whites. For blacks, it was not primarily a question of deciding that segregation and disfranchisement were unjust, but rather a matter of acting upon some primordial sense of self-respect. In other words the disquietude they might have felt from obeying unjust laws arose not from a violation of someone else's rights but from a violation of their own.

King's more general attempt to widen the horizons of participants in the movement, to link the cause of black Southerners with the implementation of the republic's founding principles, involved an attempt to link the self-interest and self-respect of black Americans with the public interest and moral coherence of the nation. This was the political meaning of King's claim that "the Negro" was acting not only "to free himself" but also "to free his oppressor from his sins."[54] Again, King did not see the movement as aiming only at giving black people self-respect and helping them act on their own interests; its larger purpose, its service to the public interest, was to make the nation see that national interest and self-respect hinged on the success of the civil rights movement.

Finally, freedom as public action can be interpreted not just as a protest against specific unjust laws but also as a massive effort to illuminate or enlarge the public realm of freedom in the South and in the nation as a whole. As McWilliams has written, "A defensible concept of civil disobedience in our times is based on a claim to act not for the public but for access to it." King captured something of this capacity of public action to illuminate the dark corners of domination when he wrote on the effect of the Birmingham campaign: "It [the power structure] was imprisoned in a luminous glare revealing the naked truth to the whole world."[55] In illuminating the way things were in Birmingham, movement participants were also illuminated and revealed to be citizens. They emerged from obscurity into the public gaze of those authorities whom they "dared look back at" and into the gaze of the nation. Obtaining political power was not only a way of protecting one's rights and interests; it was a way to "keep on keeping on" being citizens.

Thus as a representative man, King's public words and actions revealed something essential about himself and about the movement generally—the possession of and willingness to display those crucial political virtues which Arendt identified as "virtuosity" and "courage." King and the movement taught the South, and the entire country, to be political again.

CHAPTER 5

Martin Luther King: Authorship and Ideas

What matter who's speaking?

Samuel Beckett

Nice as it would be to argue otherwise, Martin Luther King was not a political thinker of any great distinction. As mentioned, King at one time considered a career in teaching and writing, but once he became the public figure he felt called to be, he lacked, above all, the time to explore and meditate upon the political events he helped to precipitate and then shape. For this reason alone, his thought lacked the depth or complexity we expect from a thinker of the first order.

But there was more at issue. Though King's PhD thesis demonstrated that he could handle abstract ideas quite competently, it was conventional in approach and narrow in focus. On the evidence of the books and articles written later, King lacked W. E. B. DuBois's scholarly erudition, imaginative reach, or diversity of talents; nor did he have the training and patience (much less the time) to produce the detailed sociological probings of a Charles Johnson or an E. Franklin Frazier. And placed beside Frantz Fanon's razor-sharp incisiveness, King seems lacking in nimbleness or the ability to dramatize his ideas. Where, for instance, King was influenced by Hegel's thought in a fairly conventional way, Fanon took his place within a modern Hegelian tradition of social and political analysis and broadened its purview. Perhaps more surprisingly, King's texts did not come close to conveying the distinctive style and tone or the richness and power of his public voice. In sum though King used ideas, he never really extended their reach.

That having been said, King was still one of the best educated and most intellectually open of public figures, at least in the United States. He was conversant with many of the central philosophical and theoretical movements and concerns of his time. When he was sent to jail in Georgia in late October 1960, the occasion from which presidential candidate John Kennedy would reap much benefit for having phoned Coretta Scott King to offer his sympathy, King asked his wife to send him two volumes of Paul Tillich's *Systematic Theology* and a book on Gandhi among other things; and he managed to read two books while he was in the Birmingham jail in the spring of 1963— DuBois's *Souls of Black Folk* and Ralph McGill's *The South and the Southerner.*[1] Not only is it difficult to imagine John Kennedy or Lyndon Johnson in anything approaching a similar situation; it is just as difficult to imagine either of them choosing to read anything of comparable importance. One of Kennedy's favorite writers was Ian Fleming and he was reported to have displayed some knowledge of the work of James Mitchener and Norman Mailer upon being introduced to them. It is hard to find a record of Johnson's having read anything much at all beyond government reports and briefing papers.

King was, then, a political orator and leader with considerable intellectual ambitions and interests. What he did best was "retail" the ideas of others, dramatizing and even exploring them most cogently in action rather than in writing. Indeed, his political thinking was inseparable from his involvement in political action. The writings were, as Hannah Arendt said of Jefferson's Declaration of Independence, the way "for an action to appear in words."[2]

But no analysis of King's intellectual standing can remain content even with such a judgment. A half-way attentive reading of the recent works focusing on King and the articles analyzing his writing forces us to look more closely at the relationship between King and the texts appearing under his name.[3] We must now ask two questions: Did Martin Luther King write the books and articles attributed to him? and, second, Does this question matter?

When questioning King's authorship of the texts attributed to him one must first deal with the issue of (unacknowledged) multiple authorship in the form of ghost-writing. From *Stride Toward Freedom* through *Where Do We Go From Here?* King had plenty of help in his writing. Bayard Rustin and Stanley Levison were important from the start, while others such as lawyer Harris Wofford and professional writers Hermine Pepper and Al Duckett were instrumental in getting various texts completed. King drafted chapters; King worked closely with Pepper or Duckett or Levison; and King went over materials written by them. Sometimes King seems the author; at others a kind of co-worker; and sometimes a kind of supervisor of textual production.

The problems raised by ghosting and multiple authorship are myriad and rarely fully examined. Jefferson, for instance, wrote the first draft of the Declaration and then suffered corrections from a committee that included Benjamin Franklin and John Adams, not to mention the excision of passages by the Continental Congress. The *Federalist Papers* were written by three different men under one pseudonym; even then the opinions expressed in the various papers did not always tally with what Madison, Hamilton, or Jay had expressed in the debates at Philadelphia. Political writings of a polemical and declamatory nature, manifestos, pamphlets, and posters are often presented as anonymous or of disguised authorship.

But what differentiates modern "ghosting" from these activities is that King, like other public figures such as recent American presidents, signed the published texts as though they were his alone. Moreover, what differentiates King's writings, particularly his books, from official presidential papers, is that King's books not only expressed his views but were intended to generate publicity and money for the cause and organization, SCLC, that he served. Thus King's case resembled John Kennedy's in the instance of *Profiles in Courage* where Kennedy was not the primary author and prefigured Ralph Nader, whose mid-1970s columns on consumer issues, including truth-in-packaging, were ghosted by someone else.[4]

No doubt by now we have become accustomed, however reluctantly, to the phenomenon of ghostwriting. We know how to recognize the signals of its presence—from thanks for editorial help in the acknowledgments to explicit mention in phrases such as "as told to" or "with the help of." Nor generally is there a question as to whether the ideas or positions expressed in a ghosted book are those of the ostensible author. Bayard Rustin's observation about his and Stanley Levison's relationship to King was probably quite accurate: "It was not we directing him so much as we working with him and giving expression to ideals we knew he had or would quickly accept." But what is at issue in ghosting is the absence of the "author's" own singular and unique voice. Lacking the author's own voice, the name of the author, in this case Martin Luther King, Jr., denotes what Michel Foucault calls the "author-function."[5]

There is yet another matter to consider concerning King's authorship—the issue of plagiarism. In *Bearing the Cross* David Garrow reports that Ira Zepp discovered passages in King's work "that reflect 'exact reproduction or paraphrasing'" from several clearly identifiable texts by other authors.[6] And more recently Keith Miller has expanded the number of passages fitting Zepp's description and then tried to explain and defend this practice of King's.

Claiming that the most immediate sources of King's ideas were not Gandhi and Marx or Niebuhr and Hegel but less well-known writers who themselves simplified and popularized the ideas of these better-known thinkers, Miller suggests that in fact King didn't need the exposure to or the influence of these ideas to become the leader or thinker he became. A typical passage along these lines runs as follows:

> Had King lacked the benefit of his father's preaching, he would hardly have needed to read Niebuhr to grasp humanity's immense potential for evil. All he would have had to do was glance at the system of segregation.[7]

Thus, for Miller, King's experience rather than specific theories or ideas to which he was exposed in his education and reading was crucial in his intellectual and political self-formation.

Finally, expanding the examples of King's plagiarism from the books and sermons of others, Miller explains (and defends) the practice as a function of the particular culture King was brought up in—the oral folk tradition of the black church:

> His socialization in the folk tradition led him to ignore the bedrock rhetorical assumption of print culture, namely, that publication spells ownership.

And more generally:

> oral culture fails to define the word as commodity and instead assumes everyone creates language and that no one owns it . . . the rhetorical issue is always authority not originality.[8]

All this, concludes Miller, sheds light on the way King created and assumed for himself the role of a "masterful public intellectual" and a "magisterial public persona."[9]

How then do we take Miller's analysis/defense of King on this issue of plagiarism and related matters? On the first part of Miller's thesis, there is little cause for argument or alarm. King, that is, King and his writers, could very well have used secondary works and popularizations to bolster his points, though unless King was diabolically dishonest, there seems to be no reason to doubt that he did in fact read Marx and Hegel, Tillich and Niebuhr, DuBois and Gandhi at some point in his life.

The "experience over ideas" part of Miller's thesis seems to me much more dubious, for it misunderstands the ways ideas relate to experience. First, Miller too rigidly separates the two; on his account, there are experiences, then orally received themes and ideas (say, from sermons), and then ideas derived from texts. More important, he neglects to account for the way ideas consolidate or crystallize and then enrich and expand the reach of particular experiences. No doubt King responded to Niebuhr's writings on human finitude and sinfulness because of his experience of segregation and because he had been imbued with fundamentalist Christianity. But King also needed Niebuhr to generalize and make more nuanced the notion of sin and its political implications. Yet the inevitability of human sinfulness was not all that obvious to King himself, for he was also powerfully attracted to the more optimistic vision of individual and social possibility derived from the Social Gospel and liberal Christianity. The way Miller rather flat-footedly characterizes the nature of King's experience means that he can not explain why this latter position seemed so powerfully tempting to King. On Miller's account, people, including King, are never ambivalent or divided within themselves, nor can an idea have influence unless it fits exactly with the dominant influence on their lives.

Finally, the nub of the issue is the contrast Miller sets up between an oral, rhetorical culture and a written, analytical culture and between the rival claims of authority and originality. Miller's claim here isn't so much wrong as limited; it again presents a truncated view of King's experience and intelligence. First, Miller's King seems to have been influenced not at all by the dominant ethos of print culture; otherwise how could he have continued to compose and borrow the way he did? Did King never register the conflict between the two sorts of cultures? How did he ingest sophisticated ideas yet never be touched by the idea of originality or property? He did and he was, of course; for one thing his books appeared under his own name and he presented them as his own. It is one thing to incorporate other people's material in an oral presentation without acknowledgment; it is another to do so in a written presentation. Finally, the issue is not only or primarily one of authority versus originality but one of good faith and acknowledgment. By publishing his books, King was entering into another "language game," the rules of which King was hardly ignorant.

Moreover, there is here a barely disguised assumption in Miller's article that originality and property are pretty disreputable notions, having little or no justification since they form the underpinnings of individualism and capitalism. Yet it would be possible to see them as important, complex, but, on balance, positive achievements of modern Western culture. Indeed, defenders of Afro-American cultural distinctiveness have appealed to these very notions when questioning the position that black culture is a derivative form of European culture and when questioning the right of white people to write about the Afro-American experience.

Finally, King cannot escape criticism for his carelessness and intellectual bad faith in including whole passages from someone else's work as his own without acknowledgment. (Miller is very scrupulous about acknowledging the sources of his own information and support for his argument.) Of course King was in a hurry and under intense pressure; but there is finally no moral imperative for a political leader to write or go through the pretense of writing books or articles. Ironically, King's borrowing of passages not only casts doubt on his originality but also on his intellectual authority, a possession never in plentiful supply among politicians of any persuasion or color, but particularly lacking among black leaders. King did, as Miller says, create a "magisterial public persona," a public and rhetorical self of impressive magnitude and considerable positive influence. But he did not finally create an intellectual self of the same stature. By overriding intellect with rhetoric, by preferring to deploy ideas for their effects rather than to analyze ideas for their plausibility, King prefigured and helped perpetuate the development of a type of black leader who all too often substitutes rhetoric for ideas, repetition of phrases for analysis of situations.

Finally what is at issue in all this is not originality of ideas but authenticity of voice, specifically regarding the degree to which King distanced himself from his own existential voice and became an "author-function," the name attached to a set of evolving ideas and positions roughly representative of the thinking of the mainstream civil rights movement in the 1950s and 1960s—a kind of collective assessment of where the movement stood at various points. Indeed, this is the way I will treat King the writer and thinker in these pages. That King the man agreed with "King" the author-function is not at issue. But the fact that we need to make such a sharp distinction between voice and ideas should be a matter of considerable regret.

A standard criticism of King has always been that he failed to articulate a vision of or propose a program for the radical structural transformation of the American economy or society. One can grant the point provisionally by noting that after the mid-1960s King himself came to speak of the need for transformation, not just in the hearts and minds of Americans but also in the nation's social and economic institutions. The order of emergence of this concern is crucial, however, since King implicitly (and rightly) recognized that the "spirit of the times," as well as the requirements of the Southern black community, converged on the need for a psychological and political awakening before economic and social issues could be confronted directly.

This criticism can also be thrown back at King's critics with the question: what were King's ideological options? King first emerged as a public figure in the mid-1950s, the nadir, by most reckoning, of the American Left. And whatever the general validity or exact meaning of Daniel Bell's claim concerning the "end of ideology" advanced in 1960, there was a pervasive feeling circa 1955–65 that Marxism in general and socialist movements in particular had lost whatever appeal they may once have possessed. Though one might dream socialist dreams of some sort, an open proclamation of them was a one-way ticket to obscurity. Indeed radical publicist and activist Michael Harrington later confessed that he had deliberately omitted any mention of socialism from his influential *The Other America* (1962) because he felt that identification of his book with socialism would consign it to oblivion. Harrington was to later regret his own hostility to the early SDS for being insufficiently anti-Communist.[10]

Within this context, it is surely significant that though three of King's closest advisers in those early years—Rustin, Baker, and Levison—were veteran leftists, their influence on King and the movement fell much more in the areas of political organizing and strategy than it did in theoretical tutelage or the intricacies of socialism. Rustin for instance introduced King to the theory and practice of non-violence rather than trying to convert him to socialism. Even if we grant that King, according to Adam Fairclough, was "an advocate . . . of democratic socialism" by 1966, it would be much harder to argue that King ever considered placing socialism as such at the center of his ideological or organizational efforts. [11] It is the sheerest implausibility to conceive of a black minister in the South rallying the black community there around Marxism or socialism of any sort. The failure of King to think socialist thoughts very often or very consistently or very openly can be attributed not only to the lingering after-effects of McCarthyism or to a monolithic ideological hegemony that stifled radical thinking altogether but also to what seemed the grand irrelevance of Marxism or socialism itself and to King's commitment to Christianity.

But if King the black Marxist-Leninist seems farfetched, from where else might the coherent discipline, program, ideology, and institution have come, the lack of which Vincent Harding has claimed contributed so much to the collapse of the movement?[12] What could have carried the movement past its triumphs and frustrations and enabled it to gather its resources for a second stage? The only alternative seems to have been some sort of black nationalist ideology. And King was far from inclined toward that direction. Most varieties of black nationalism had little interest in non-violence and found it difficult to avoid a programmatic hostility to whites. But King's commitment to non-violence increased rather than slackened as the war in Vietnam grew apace and the appeal of black nationalism had never been very great south of the Mason-Dixon line or to King personally. Indeed, after Malcolm X's break with the Nation of Islam and his assassination in early 1965, the momentum behind the Black Muslims subsided considerably even in the North.

All this is to say two things. First, the ideological and institutional weakness of the American Left dictated that King in a real sense had to make up—or at least put together—his strategy, programs, and even ideology from disparate elements. This was a strength for a time, and his genius was to use the American political tradition—the civic culture defined by the Declaration of Independence and the Bill of Rights—against itself, while drawing upon unexpected political and cultural resources from the Southern black community. But it also meant that once certain ideological, demographic, and institutional limits were reached, there were few if any resources he could call upon to expand his political vision or modify his organizational strategy.

The Rhetoric of Freedom

What then about King's own sense of the conjunction of freedom and "messianic destiny" in his own life? What of his sense of chosenness?[13] Unless we believe that there is some perduring, constituting meaning to history or that God intervenes in human affairs, then we must understand King's religiously based vocation for political leadership as his way of explaining himself to himself and to others, of giving coherence and resolve to his life. All of us need some sort of larger framework or narrative to fit our lives into, but if we cannot accept the metaphysical or religious assumptions informing a life story such as King's, it is difficult to know what to do except translate them into other terms and judge their effects rather than pass on their truth-value.

King's sense of chosenness did, however, express itself in specific political form as the strong, charismatic figure sent to mobilize the Southern black population for freedom. But a long-standing criticism, expressed by activists such as Ella Baker with SCLC and under her influence in SNCC, was that King's charismatic "Moses-type" leadership actually hindered the emergence of political independence and autonomy in the black communities where he conducted campaigns.[14]

This line of criticism can be extended to the notion of black "chosenness" based on the Exodus analogy and its assumption that black people have a unique role in the "redemption" of America. One danger of King's version of black chosenness lies in its resemblance, ironically, to the myth of American exceptionalism and the centrality of its existence to the furtherance of freedom. It is easy to move from black chosenness to claims for Afro-American virtue and innocence, according to which innocence becomes the concomitant of historical oppression and victimization. But it is no more plausible to link oppression with superior virtue than to assert the connection between (white) American chosenness and innocence. Such a move merely inverts the claim that black people have nothing essential to offer the nation and are outside the founding consensus. More plausible is the claim that the civil rights movement of the 1950s and 1960s was the "carrier" of certain political practices and moral values that the nation as a whole had repressed and/or failed to implement. Only in that sense does it make sense to say that black people for a time had some special role in contemporary America.

Nor is the emphasis on King's deep roots in Afro-American Christianity and the black church without ambiguity. To stress too strongly that King was, as Cornel West has asserted, primarily a "product of the black church" is to risk making his, and the movement's, relevance to freedom struggles in which similar historical and cultural conditions do not obtain, seem pretty tenuous.[15] Indeed King's own ambivalence toward traditional black Christianity should not be considered a sign of cultural faintheartedness or an unseemly desire to deny his "blackness." Rather it should be seen as part of King's quite tenable suspicion of certain shortcomings in black Christianity. As Clayborne Carson has written:

> King's search for an intellectually satisfying religious faith stemmed from his reaction against the emphasis on emotional assertiveness that he saw in Christian evangelicism. . . . A religious liberal and pioneering proponent of what is now called liberation theology, King carried on a long and determined—though unsuccessful—struggle against the conservative leadership of the National Baptist Convention.[16]

A problem also arises with the idea of group liberation on the biblical model when it is combined with the language of anti-colonial, national liberation struggles. King was certainly aware of the differences between the situation of black Americans and oppressed people of the Third World. He did emphasize his solidarity with liberation struggles, particularly African, when he said in 1965 that the American Negro had a "deepening sense of identification with his black African brothers . . . Our heritage is Africa. We should never seek to break the ties nor should the Africans." Yet he added that "the Negro revolution is seeking integration not independence . . . here in America we've got to live together."[17] Thus in a sense King recognized that black liberation and self-determination must refer to new forms of individual and group consciousness, i.e., to freedom as a change in the sense of self and culture rather than to political liberation as such. For in America it has been necessary to sublimate and internalize, as it were, black self-determination, thus transforming dreams of political autonomy into plans for cultural and psychic autonomy.[18]

As an evangelical Christian, King placed considerable emphasis upon the personal experience of salvation and the great change wrought by this experience in a person's life. The emphasis upon personal experience undoubtedly stood behind the close connection he drew between direct action and a transformation of the self. Thus the moral and political implications of a therapeutics of political action and its link with political action as a form of freedom need discussing. In the classical (republican) conception of politics, civic freedom is closely tied to the assumption that citizens are expected to subordinate self-interest to the common good. Indeed acting for the common good is the definition of political virtue, a quality both presupposed and strengthened by participation in the political life of the community. Thus to be politically free may involve a restriction upon fulfilling personal wishes and desires, a check on (negative) freedom to do as one wishes. Self-determination refers to self-government in both a psychological and political sense.

Did King have anything that looked like this concept of political virtue? The answer would be a qualified affirmative. King and his followers were willing to risk their lives for a political cause transcending immediate self-interest. Specifically, despite its religious provenance, the notion of *agape* did play a role somewhat analogous to the classical idea of civic virtue. As a principle *agape* was a prerequisite for public action and was supposed to suffuse the protester's attitude during his or her political confrontation with the oppressor. Though not, as we have seen, an injunction exactly to establish a personal relationship with one's adversary, the institutionalization of *agape* was to be the foundation of the "beloved community."

But there is a problem with political action informed by *agape*. It is difficult to see how *agape* can suggest any very positive imperative to create a common secular world with one's enemies, since it so resolutely resists considering the "other" in any sort of "interested" fashion. Indeed, a minimal interpretation of *agape* would see it as a rough equivalent of the liberal value of toleration, and from that perspective, King's beloved community would amount to a kind of non-discriminatory community of individuals bound by little more than respect for one another as children of God. In the context of traditional Southern and American race relations, this would have been no mean achievement. But by the same token, it doesn't imply a very robust notion of community. To have made his vision of the beloved community more powerful, if less "liberal," King might also have emphasized the necessity of "interested" forms of love such as *philia* and even *eros* to bind individuals to each other and to the community. Though often seen as an impossibly demanding attitude, *agape* is at the same time hardly strong enough to provide a convincing conceptual foundation for a political community of any sort.

Moreover, as the momentum of public protest and mass mobilization (as well as white resistance) increased between 1962 and 1965, it was easy to forget that *agape* was a prerequisite for action, as King and his assistants emphasized in the training of marchers for confrontation, rather than public action being a means of transforming the self. The problem is that if participatory action becomes a means to change the self, we enter the dangerous but familiar ground of twentieth-century politics of which Max Weber so presciently warned when he wrote: "He who seeks the salvation of the soul, of his own and others, should not seek it along the avenue of politics."[19] Therapeutic or transformational politics is dangerous because once self-transformation is the goal, self-interest and self-respect are combined without the mediating or bridging power of an impersonal, other-regarding virtue such as *agape* to keep them in check. One destination of this politics may be something like Frantz Fanon's therapeutics of violence. Though I will return to this theme in the last chapter, suffice it to say here that the risk of life and the desire for recognition tend to degenerate into self-proving (and self-defeating) macho confrontations with the enemy, while solidarity tends to congeal into a stifling ideological conformity that makes thought and debate all but impossible.

King never succumbed to the despair of such a position, but his belief in the possibility of changing the self—that a sense of "somebodyness" was linked with political protest—was easily overemphasized. Still, insofar as King's philosophy of direct action acknowledged the importance of a changed sense of self, as well as insisted upon a change in attitude toward the adversary as a *prerequisite* for appropriate action, that philosophy, along with Gandhi's, was the most creative revisioning of political action in this century. It provided an alternative to visions of armed struggle and violent revolution which increasingly seemed to promise not a transformed humanity but the recrudescence of age-old cycles of revenge through violence.

Another problematic aspect of King's emphasis upon freedom as self-transformation emerged in the sometimes contradictory tropes and analogies he used to describe such a transformation. As we have seen he spoke of a shift from child to adult, from boy to man, and from nobody to somebody. But in what sense and for whom did black people seem children at one point and adults later on? If black men achieved manhood, what did black women aim at? The nobody/ somebody figure was less fraught with worrisome connotations, but it implied a strangely ahistorical view of the black past. It is hard to know where the answer lies, but King might have avoided some of · these conceptual/metaphorical problems by describing self-transformation more in terms of a shift from private to public involvements and from a passive, private self to an active, public one. In retrospect, such an explicitly political language might have allowed him to speak of change in the self without implying that black men had in some sense been boys or were the chief beneficiaries of self-transformation or that black people were actually childlike (as the language of the white family romance had always maintained). Indeed the implicit claim that only in the 1960s had black people escaped a sense of "nobodyness" could have been modified to emphasize the specifically political dimension of self-respect that emerged so clearly in that decade.

Related to this concern with freedom as self-transformation are the issues raised by King's resort to psychological/medical analogies to describe American and Afro-American society. Part of the problem was, as we have seen, that King deployed three separate languages of description and evaluation: a moral discourse focusing on justice and oppression; a political discourse concerned with unfreedom and freedom; and a medical discourse with health and pathology at its center.[20] From one perspective, King's mix of language games gave him considerable flexibility and enriched his analysis of the situation confronting the movement. Provisionally, the various discourses might be reconciled in the following manner: a sick white society had created unjust and oppressive conditions for black Americans which had rendered some Afro-Americans and the situations they lived in pathological. Freedom—the ability to "deliberate, decide and respond"—was the chief casualty of a segregated society.

The problem was (and is) that modern moral discourse implies a basic (Kantian) assumption of responsibility for conditions and actions; and this in turn implies a freedom to make choices. But to take the medical terminology seriously would absolve white Americans of their responsibility and make black Americans victims with whom to sympathize, dependent on someone else for cure. As Jennifer Radden has noted about the medical model: "sufferers are rightfully seen as victims of their condition and as blameless for having it."[21] It becomes difficult to see how either oppressors or oppressed can be considered free agents.

We are confronted here with what Foucault has called the "empirico-transcendental doublet," the self-contradictory view that human beings are both free and determined, capable of transcendence and a function of their surroundings.[22] When either position—that we are completely free agents or that we are totally determined—is stated in bald form we react uneasily. To excuse the actions or attitudes of a Klansman or to exculpate a restaurant owner for refusing to serve black people because of historical traditions and customary racial practices contradicts our strong suspicion that someone must be held responsible if we are to think of human actions and institutions in a coherent way.

On the other hand, to attribute total responsibility (and hence freedom) to black ghetto residents and thus to blame them for failure to maintain a family, hold a job, or commit themselves to some long-term goals willfully ignores the extent to which their attitudes and behavior are powerfully shaped by the "pathological" conditions of their world. Similarly, it is questionable whether hard-core white racists, particularly if they are poor or unschooled, can be held responsible in a strong sense for their attitudes either. And yet we do punish lawbreaking by both types of people and thus assume that they are responsible for their actions. This confirms Radden's further observation that being blameless for a condition "does not generally entail being blameless in acting from it."[23] It is necessary that we do hold people responsible; but in doing so we are not acting entirely consistently.

One temptation is to pretend that we can solve the matter empirically by gathering more or better evidence for freedom or determinism. Yet historians and sociologists of the black American experience have, making use of the same evidence, come to quite different conclusions concerning the relative freedom or unfreedom of black Americans. One group, which reached prominence in the 1960s and included sociologist E. Franklin Frazier, sociologist Gunnar Myrdal, historian Stanley Elkins, policy intellectual Daniel Patrick Moynihan, journalist Charles Silberman, and psychologist Kenneth Clark, make up the "damage-pathology" school. The work of this group stresses the degree to which the black family structure and hence black personality have been damaged by slavery and the subsequent history of discrimination and hold that, by extension, black Americans have relatively little control over their lives. On the other hand historians John Blassingame, Vincent Harding, Sterling Stuckey, and Herbert Gutman and writer Ralph Ellison have come, using the same data, to conclusions about black family structure, culture, autonomy, and agency quite at variance with the damage-pathology school. Clearly what is at issue here can not be resolved by appeal to evidence, since that evidence is so obviously subject to the weight of presupposition brought to it by both sides.

Thus it is a further temptation to say that we can no more solve this problem of mixed discourses and conflicting interpretations than we can pull ourselves up by our own bootstraps. Still, there are perhaps several provisional ways to consider the problem and thus avoid some of the rhetorical and conceptual dilemmas King, who belongs quite clearly with the damage-pathology group, landed in. (Though here it should be said that King was no more confused than most social analysts, then or now.) First, in the matter of white racism (provisionally, the term we give to systematic racial prejudice expressed by individuals and institutions), it is more helpful to say that racism is like alcoholism or drug addiction than to say that it is like cancer, one of King's favorite metaphors. Unlike the person suffering from cancer, or at least from forms of cancer not strongly related to personal choice such as smoking, the alcoholic has at some point chosen and continues to choose to drink; the addict to ingest drugs.[24]

Similarly, though born into a racist society, white people do have a certain latitude in accepting or acting on racist tenets or attitudes. The *akratic* or conformist racist may realize that it is wrong to act in a racist manner, but may continue to act against his or her better judgment out of habit or even self-interest. For this sort of racist, Gunnar Myrdal's assumption of a conflict between the American Creed and racist beliefs and practices has a rough cogency. But it should be noted that the *akratic* is not making an unfree choice just because he or she does not make the right or best choice. Being sick and being wrong are two different things.[25]

This line of analysis should cause us to reflect upon whether racism always, or very often, is a pathological symptom rather than a "normal" response to environmental cues and incentives. Unless the quality of being free of racist feelings or of feelings that devalue differences in other people is built into the definition of psychic or social health—and if it is, no "healthy" person or society has probably ever existed—it is far from obvious that most racists are psychologically disturbed. There are pathological racists for whom racist beliefs resonate with deep unconscious needs and fantasies and who hold their beliefs sincerely and "rationally," i.e., without any conscious sense of self-contradiction. But such people were (and are) not the main problem in the South or anywhere else. Racism is precisely so powerful because it does not depend on mentally disturbed people to perpetuate it.

Conceptually and practically, then, it makes more sense to treat racism as a "moral problem with psychological dimensions" than as purely a psychological or medical problem.[26] In the context of the 1960s, the rabid Southern racist or the snarling whites who hurled abusive obscenities at black marchers in Cicero, Illinois were much less culpable than white businessmen or politicians who supported or tolerated discriminatory hiring practices because to do otherwise would have endangered their profits or their positions of power. But to point to economic self-interest as the "reason" for adopting racist practices is also to consider matters too narrowly. The usefulness of Arendt's notion of the "banality of evil"—and where it is cogent in the case of white Americans—lies in its attribution to Adolph Eichmann of an essential failure "to think what he was doing." In using the phrase Arendt did not refer to some cognitive or intellectual failure on Eichmann's part but to a failure of Eichmann's moral reach and imagination. As Pat Watters put it in reference to the white South: "Eichmann, not Simon Legree, was the villain."[27] In this context, we might see King's choice of the pathology metaphor as a rather shrewd strategic choice, the way a Christian in a secular society could "hate the sin but love the sinner" and thus not needlessly alienate whites by attacking them in moral terms. But King also recognized that changing a racism-driven social and political system was a moral problem and thus he appealed to his adversaries' capacity to make moral choices.

King's characterization of parts of black society as pathological raises some similar problems. If the black family is pathological, are the people who inhabit it also sick? If so, are they capable of taking responsibility for their individual lives or of being political in a strong sense? As mentioned, King saw himself functioning as a catalyst or kind of therapist. Where his role was that of the moral gadfly vis-à-vis white America, though blunting that indictment through the medical metaphor, King's role in relation to black America was to be, as Vincent Harding has suggested, a "wounded healer." Black America was afflicted with a "psychological [and sociological] problem with a moral dimension." King's "cure" centered on a message of self-respect and love toward one's enemies. But no more (and no less) than Malcolm X was King thereby advocating a kind of sophisticated version of Booker T. Washington's self-help message. Where King differed from both men was in linking his message of self-respect specifically to political action. In the process of acting non-violently, participants, according to King, "become, for the first time, somebody and they have, for the first time, the courage to be free."[28]

Thus King threaded his way through the ethical and conceptual antinomies of freedom and determinism, responsibility and exonerability, action and passivity. In the process he sought to avoid the great weakness of the Right—its failure to believe that institutional or social conditions really affect our choices and life chances—and the analogous failure of the Left to imagine how people living under conditions of great adversity and oppression can nevertheless create a space of freedom within which they act to change their lives. Finally it was action that solved, or dissolved, the theoretical conundrums raised by the various explanatory models King employed. As with Marx and Freud, freedom was as much an achievement as an assumption, something that was inseparable from action taken in concrete situations.

Civil Disobedience and Liberal Freedom

What is the relationship between King's substantive, metaphysical criteria and his procedural, political criteria in determining whether a law or system of laws is just? Which set of criteria should take precedence? If faced directly with the question, King would have probably argued that since the American political and constitutional order derived from natural law, the procedural criteria for a just law were the legal-constitutional expressions of the substantive criteria. For instance, equal applicability, his first procedural criterion, is also a substantive criterion, since it implies that no one is treated as an object, i.e., with less respect than anyone else, though distinctions such as age may be legalized if they are relevant concerning an activity such as voting. Thus the two sets of criteria are the same thing expressed in two different conceptual idioms.

Still, objections can be raised to the belief that the two sets of criteria are reconcilable in all cases. It would not be incoherent theoretically nor inconceivable historically that a law or system of laws could meet the criteria set forth by Aquinas, Augustine, Tillich, or whomever else without having been adopted by democratic participation, King's second procedural criterion. Indeed, the classical liberal position, emphasizing negative freedom and the protection granted by rights, neither implies nor requires that those affected have a hand in the establishment of just laws.

But King moves beyond traditional liberal political thought here, for his second procedural rule is an independent criterion rather than one implied by or derivative of equal applicability. He asks rhetorically (and thereby answers in the negative): "Can any law enacted under such circumstances [without participation by the group affected] be considered democratically structured?"[29] One could object that this question is irrelevant since being just and being democratic are not the same thing. But King's rhetorical question implies that one of the characteristics of just laws is that they are arrived at democratically.

But the question should also be turned around—can the procedural criteria be fulfilled but the substantive criteria violated by a law? One situation where this might be the case occurs when a law, though adopted by democratic procedures, discriminates against citizens of another country or of a certain race or religion but does not bear on citizens of the United States, whatever their race and religion. More importantly, one can imagine a category of citizens who agree to laws that discriminate against themselves. Women who vote against measures guaranteeing women equal rights might be such a case. King doesn't give us any guidance here, but the equal applicability criterion should, I think, override the participatory criterion. Human (or transnational) rights are needed as protection against unjust laws, even if the latter have been democratically arrived at.

King's assertion that civil disobedients should accept the penalty for their actions by going to jail has also been challenged in a slightly different context by Ronald Dworkin. For Dworkin such a position entails the belief that the quasi-Kantian question "what if everyone does it?" clinches the matter and that civil disobedients or conscientious objectors should accept their legal deserts, even if we agree that they have a strong moral justification for refusing to suffer the penalty of disobedience. But, according to Dworkin, a person has "strong rights . . . whenever the law wrongly invades his rights against the government." If someone asserts such a strong right by disobeying a controversial law he or she thinks violates that right, then there is no moral reason for that person to go to jail for disobeying it. Punishing a person in such circumstances is the last thing a government should consider, given the various contested aspects of the law and the circumstances of its violation. Indeed the moral/constitutional-legal distinction is a specious one, according to Dworkin, since it is just the constitutionality and hence legality of the law that is at issue in the first place.[30]

But King's position allows a quite convincing counter-argument. First, King did not contend that the willingness to go to jail was the primary justification for civil disobedience. Rather it was the failure of conventional approaches that pointed up the need for civil disobedience; and he repeatedly stressed the obligation to work within the existing political institutions before engaging in civil disobedience. But the Southern context had a lot to do with King's emphasis upon accepting the consequences of lawbreaking, for King wanted to distinguish the actions of people engaged in principled civil disobedience from those of segregationists who defied federal and sometimes state law. King was less concerned with the "contagion" effect of civil disobedience, i. e., "what if everyone did it," than he was with appearing to advocate disobedience based on nothing better than subjective preference or self-interest.

This suggests, in turn, another reason for King's belief in suffering the consequences of civil disobedience—the publicity value. Such would visibly demonstrate what John Rawls refers to as the civil disobedient's "fidelity to law."[31] King and the movement understood that how they appeared in the eyes of the nation and the world was crucial to their success. But he might have more clearly avoided the implication that a civil disobedient was morally (as opposed to politically) obliged to suffer the consequences of lawbreaking. Still, King was more realistic, more "political," here than he has often been given credit for. By suffering the consequences, as well as insisting that protesters manifest a certain demeanor, King was trying to present the best possible case for and by the civil rights movement. Fairly or unfairly, he recognized that it fell upon black people to be better than their opponents and that the movement could hardly risk alienating Northern public opinion or losing potential support from the federal government.

All this might be granted without quieting another sort of objection that came from critics to King's left. Their objection was that black people had burdened themselves with a moral obligation that no whites were ready to assume. Indeed, such a position implied that black people must somehow earn their rights. And "unearned suffering" was demeaning not redemptive. Again we have a conflict over what constitutes self-respect. But two qualifications should be kept in mind here. First, the behavior that seemed demeaning to King's critics was not intended to avoid conflict but to acknowledge and confront it. Second, and most important, suffering was undergone proudly and in public. It was a way of *showing* spiritual superiority, of marshaling "soul force" against "physical force," rather than asserting it verbally. And finally it didn't look demeaning or cringing.

There is a third contested area of King's theory and practice of civil disobedience. Some have noted that King never disobeyed federal laws (as opponents of the Fugitive Slave Law had done in the 1850s) or federal court injunctions (such as Judge Frank Johnson's temporary injunction against a march from Selma to Montgomery) and that his action fell short of civil disobedience "in the stricter, traditional and more serious sense."[32] Others have noted that because participants in the sit-ins and freedom rides felt the laws they violated were unconstitutional anyway, they were appealing to constitutional standards and thus not engaged in civil disobedience strictly speaking. In other words King knew that ultimately the Kennedy and Johnson administrations, as well as Northern public opinion and the Supreme Court, were on the side of the movement. Protesting for rights, up to and including civil disobedience, was an appeal within the federal system of laws to federal power against the power of various Southern states. Thus the issue was really about federalism versus states' rights not individual rights versus legal obligations or state power.[33]

There is something to be said for this cluster of charges, but not a great deal. As mentioned before, it was one of King's great achievements to turn dry, though important constitutional issues such as states' rights into vital moral concerns about individual (and ultimately) group rights. Though strictly speaking it was often a matter of federal law versus states' rights, Hugo Bedeau rightly asserted at the time that "it seems irrelevant that his [the protester's] dispute with the government takes the form of a dispute over the legitimacy of a certain policy or of the authority of a certain government agency" if the activity is considered illegal by some authority.[34]

Specifically, such charges ignored the constant danger that participants in the movement risked from private citizens and state or local authorities in the South. The Supreme Court never offered clear-cut constitutional protection for the sit-ins and perhaps could not in the nature of the case directly recognize civil disobedience, however defined, as constitutionally protected. Only the Civil Rights Act of 1964 spared the Court this onerous task. Indeed, as Fred Berger has observed, "there is still no clearcut jurisprudence of civil disobedience to which the American legal system is committed."[35] It was this situation Hannah Arendt addressed in the concluding pages of her "Civil Disobedience" essay in which she called for some sort of constitutional protection of civil disobedience.[36] Nor was it obvious that the national administration, the Congress, or the FBI would intervene on behalf of protesters in any given case. One of the horrors of the situation in the South was that civil rights workers needed the initial refusal of federal protection against violence directed at them in order to attract national and world attention to their cause and thus eventually force some sort of federal protection. Indeed civil rights workers engaged in voter registration work for the VEP felt justifiably betrayed by the lack of federal protection, since such protection had been promised when the voter-registration project began. A kind of symbiosis did exist between the movement and the federal government, but it was a tortured rather than harmonious one. Therefore, it distorts matters considerably to see the struggle for social and political rights as already settled before it began. Such a view assumes a misplaced trust in the inevitable triumph of worthy causes and in the operation of power in America.

Civil Disobedience and Participatory Freedom

There are generally three justifications for free expression—as a way of arriving at the truth and exemplified by intellectual or academic freedom; as a means of self-expression and self-development, expressed in commitment to artistic or personal freedom; and as one of the prerequisites for self-government.[37] In the liberal tradition emphasis falls upon the first two; in the republican tradition, it falls upon the latter justification. From this latter point of view, King's emphasis upon direct action, including civil disobedience, can be seen as a way of reasserting and maintaining what Harry Kalven has called the "public forum," the virtual space of political debate and action created by the First Amendment but not coincident with any one of the branches of government or with the "State" generally.[38] It is the American version of the *res publica*. The crucial constitutional foundation of the public realm is not the "equal protection" clause of the Fourteenth Amendment but freedom of speech and the right "peaceably to assemble" of the First Amendment.

The question that emerged during and after the civil rights movement and the anti-war movement was, how was one to speak and act within the public forum and under what conditions? It was impossible for King and the civil rights movement to separate the articulation of their political beliefs from action embodying those beliefs. In constitutional terms they were implicitly asserting that the right "peaceably to assemble" should enjoy the same protected status as free speech.

The problem was that, again, there was (and is) no constitutional jurisprudence approving civil disobedience. No one was more disturbed by direct action and civil disobedience than Alabama-born Hugo Black, the one figure who did more than any other on the Supreme Court to revitalize the First Amendment as well as generally siding with the civil rights movement. Indeed in *A Constitutional Faith* (1968) he asserted that the right to assembly did not "guarantee that people will be supplied by government or by private parties with a place to assemble even though their assembly is peaceful."[39] Interpreted loosely such a statement merely acknowledged the power of legal authorities to regulate the context (as opposed to the content) of the exercise of First Amendment rights. Yet read with Black's animus in mind, animus that had grown considerably over the years, the statement seemed to make public protesters unreasonably dependent upon public authorities and/or private individuals for permission to exercise their rights to assemble peaceably. As commentator Eric Severeid responded to Black in a television interview in 1968, protesters, whether involved in civil disobedience or not, can hardly "assemble in air."[40]

Broadly, at issue between Black and the movement were two different understandings of what was properly said and done in the

public forum and generally whether there was a constitutional distinction to be made between speech and action. In certain obvious
cases, there is a clear difference between speech and action. Speaking in support of a group advocating armed revolution or even
advocating revolution is clearly different from commiting a violent or
illegal revolutionary action. But in reference to King's involvement
with the movement, where violence was neither advocated nor
planned, a valid distinction between speech and action seems much
more problematic.

Here, it is not just that speaking may imply a form of action, e.g.,
the performative utterance "I now pronounce you husband and
wife," it is also that acts of civil disobedience are intended to
communicate ideas about the unjustness of the law. They are,
according to Berger, "statute-violating acts that demonstrate, in their
commission, the protested injustice or policy." Indeed Berger has
argued that the First Amendment should protect such conduct if
conventional channels are blocked, if the purpose is to "foster open,
unfettered, informed debate" by, for instance, revealing conditions
about which the public may not be informed or which they do not
wish to confront, and if we take "persons as a value." Surely, he
argues, we can distinguish types of conduct that "infringe no basic
political or moral rights from those that do," while granting that
"there must be some limits, but they are not marked by what is a
'normal' matter of expression."[41]

Thus, in constitutional terms, Berger suggests that the right
peaceably to assemble should assume equal status with free speech.
In both cases, a distinction should be made between abridgment and
regulation, the former being unconstitutional, the latter constitutional. The larger point is that the same sort of criteria must be
applied to non-violent political action as to speech, since there is no
important distinction to be made between political speech and non-
violent political action. Considered in the light of this discussion,
King's exercise in non-violent direct action, including civil disobedience, served not only to assert and to vindicate rights but, by
appealing to the First Amendment, it asserted the existence of a
public forum in which individuals could be citizens and appear as free
men and women. By engaging in such action, King was reasserting
the political freedom which lay at the core of the classical conception
of politics.

Violence and Non-violence

Considerations of the theoretical possibility, the practicality, or the desirability of non-violence encompass such a vast range of concerns that to begin to consider them in any depth would involve writing another book. There are, however, more "local" aspects of the debate about violence and non-violence bearing upon the meanings of freedom and to those I would like to turn.

One central question concerning non-violent direct action turns the focus back upon those engaged in "free" public action. It asks whether and to what extent such action restricts the freedom, i.e., coerces, its opponents and in what the differences between non-violent and violent coercion consist. The modern American thinker who raised these questions most cogently was theologian Reinhold Niebuhr who claimed in *Moral Man and Immoral Society* (1932) that non-violence depended more on coercion than persuasion for its effectiveness. "We cannot," wrote Niebuhr, "draw any absolute line of demarcation between violent and non-violent coercion" for "coercion [is] a necessary instrument of social cohesion." According to Niebuhr the difference between violence and non-violence was not the presence or absence of coercion, but that "destruction is not the intended but the inevitable consequence of non-violent coercion."[42] Indeed, even education, the attempt to enlighten the conscience of one's opponent, involved an element of coercion. Niebuhr's broader justification for his position was that achieving justice was more important than preserving freedom through persuasion. Violence was justifiable if it promoted justice. Though Niebuhr agreed with Gandhi and, by extension, King, that non-violent resistance was usually the better method, it was not, according to Niebuhr, always or obviously morally preferable.

As a theology student, King had wrestled with the Niebuhrian critique of non-violence. But as a movement leader he had to confront similar but more specific criticism to the effect that non-violent direct action was a form of blackmail, the subtext of which was that "if we moderates are not allowed to march, extremists will resort to violence." Indeed several times King described direct action as a kind of safety valve, as a "creative force" diverting black anger and frustration into constructive channels.[43] And it is hard to see the objection to such a warning as long as King did not control those who were bent on violence and set them loose as a way of fulfilling his own prophecy. By 1967 he had come to admit that "ethical appeals" and "persuasion" had to be "undergirded by some form of constructive coercive power."[44] King had backed into agreement with Niebuhr insofar as he admitted that persuasion and appeals to conscience were not always effective by themselves and that America was not a fundamentally just society in which segregation was an unfortunate aberration.[45]

Indeed one might claim that King was engaged in (the quasi-Rousseauean) activity of forcing his opponents to be free. By assuming that racism was a form of irrationality, a kind of psychic pathology and hence a restriction on the racist's full potential, appeal to conscience was a way of forcing opponents to confront their attitudes and hopefully to abandon them. But King never abandoned the idea that non-violent coercion was qualitatively different from violent coercion. While Niebuhr considered coercion the crucial issue, for King it was violence. Moreover, where Niebuhr saw non-violence as a means or technique, King took it to be an end in itself. For all his self-described Christian realism, Niebuhr's position was a strangely purist one reminiscent of the Christian idea that there is no spiritual difference between desiring and acting upon that desire. Such a position is "otherworldly" not because it is naive—indeed it expresses a certain realism and psychological sophistication—but because it fails to take into account the seriousness of action on another person's body. And it tends to elevate motive over deed.

In fact coercion had always been part of direct action insofar as sit-ins, boycotts, picketings, and mass marches threatened to disrupt the normality of a community life, confronting people and institutions. Such direct and indirect coercion set the scene for movement appeals to white conscience or even white self-interest. Thus David Garrow's thesis that after Albany, when Sheriff Laurie Pritchett generally refused to be provoked into violence against marchers and protesters, King and SCLC shifted from "non-violent persuasion" to "non-violent provocation" is broadly tenable.[46] But in some ways the charge is less damning that it seems—the shift represents an example of shrewdness not cynicism. It signified that having resisted obvious verbal taunting, protesters and civil disobedients were not responsible for their opponents' conduct.

Yet another argument directed against King's philosophy of non-violence is that it was unrealistic, even inappropriate, in cultural-historical terms. According to this argument, American culture in general and (black and white) Southern culture in particular have historically glorified and encouraged violence. Non-violence on this view has "no real cultural or social underpinning in American society,"[47] an academic view anticipated by H. Rap Brown's less scholarly judgment in the 1960s that "violence is as American as apple pie."

It is hard to know what to make of this apparently clear-eyed contention. First, it implies that there are or have been cultures where non-violence has secure underpinnings, though evidence for such a sweeping judgment about any culture is hard to come by. More importantly, it implies that cultural traditions are monolithic, that cultures are *this* way rather than *that* in some deterministic way. A much more complex view would be Erik Erikson's view that cultural traits are always paired with their opposites in a dialectical relationship.[48] The importance of King's position was that it did not stress metaphysical, biological, or cultural/social determinism. It rather emphasized, as mentioned earlier, the existence of the choice to be non-violent.[49] King obviously knew that he was not operating in a cultural or historical vacuum, but wagered, as it were, that the experience of Southern black people had in fact equipped them for a non-violent struggle. Finally, the point about the inability of black or white Southern culture to provide firm grounding for non-violent struggle could just as cogently—or irrelevantly—be made about the possibility of democratic politics or "the rule of law." That is, any theory of change that aims for some ideal state is underdetermined by the facts. There is simply no knock-down evidence on either side of these issues.

If all this were not complicated enough, there is a related, in some ways more compelling, group of objections to non-violence. For some, it is not that non-violence is impossible per se but that it has psychologically undesirable effects on its practitioners. (In practice this position tends to move back and forth between the undesirability and the impossibility of non-violence.) The classic statement of this argument came from psychologist Kenneth Clark in his *Dark Ghetto* (1965).[50] King's approach, admitted Clark, had been of considerable effectiveness as a tactic in the South. But Clark's position was that:

> A deeper analysis, however, might reveal an unrealistic, if not pathological, basis in King's doctrine as well . . . the natural reactions to

injustice, oppression, and humiliation are bitterness and resentment. The form which such bitterness takes need not be overtly violent, but the corrosion of the human spirit which is involved is inevitable. It would appear, then, that any demand that the victim love his oppressor . . . imposes an additional and probably intolerable psychological burden. . . . The very attempt to cope with this type of philosophical abstraction [i.e., *agape*] in the face of the concrete injustices which dominate their daily lives can only lead to deep and disturbing conflicts and guilt . . .

In addition, Clark suggested that one reason for King's popularity among whites was that his philosophy was:

[n]ot inconsistent with the stereotype of the Negro as a meek long-suffering creature who prays for deliverance but who rarely acts decisively against injustices.[51]

Here we have the language of pathology, the triumph of the therapeutic, hurled back at King with a vengeance. For Clark there is such a thing as the "natural," the failure to act according to which is not only "unrealistic" but leads to psychic conflicts and burdens.

One immediate objection to Clark's position is that Clark himself failed to understand that *agape* does not, as King repeatedly insisted, enjoin people to "like" or to desire their enemies. Besides, as King responded to Clark in a 1963 interview, Clark's position confuses "nonresistance with nonviolent resistance." Ralph Ellison also shrewdly pinpointed the way Clark "misses the heroic side of things" and betrayed his regional provincialism in "reveal[ing] how much he doesn't know about Southern Negroes." Southern and Northern black people, continues Ellison, are different in that black Southerners have learned ways of "mastering the psychological pressures of which Clark speaks. . . . Southern Negroes learned about violence in a very tough school."[52]

Though Clark offered no explicit theoretical grounding for his position, it was broadly psychoanalytic of the Adlerian variety in assuming that repression of impulses does not abolish but displaces their force onto other "objects," including the self. But Clark ignored the possibility that impulses can be sublimated as well as repressed or displaced; more importantly his position ignored the fact that it is precisely the function of direct action to release those conflicted impulses in other forms, for instance as "soul force," a clear example of what Erikson called the necessary "ritualization" of aggression.[53]

Thus Clark missed the importance of direct action as part of the philosophy of non-violence, a much more sophisticated position than his crude frustration-aggression model allowed. In doing so, he implied that the alternative to King's position was the kind of therapeutics of violence which was in fact to have great appeal to certain segments of the movement even as he was writing in the mid-1960s. Such is the destination of repression models of impulse "management" which offer no complementary theory of the way aggressive impulses can be translated into or ritualized as symbolic actions rather than just "acted out" in the form of retaliation.

Clark's second charge against King also reflected an historical blindspot about the ways white and black people understood each other. Clark got only part of the story right, for it was as easy to argue that whites perceived blacks as violent and disruptive people who acted solely upon impulse rather than as "meek, long-suffering creature[s]" who always turned the other cheek. Like many white critics, Clark placed King and the non-violent movement in the double-bind I mentioned previously—any way black people presented themselves—whether it was as peaceful or violent—confirmed a negative stereotype. The only creative response to judgments like Clark's was to do as King did and act in accordance with his own vision rather than trying to figure out what white people expected—and then do the opposite.

Finally Clark's claim that non-violence reenforced the impression that blacks were people "who rarely act decisively against injustices" was obtuse, particularly in relation to the civil rights movement. Whatever the difficulties with applying Southern methods in a Northern context or the psychic burdens of non-violence, it is hard to take seriously a position which saw only indecision in the first mass movement of Afro-Americans against injustice since Reconstruction. Such a position was simply not tenable.

But there is considerable truth to the retrospective judgment voiced by Vincent Harding, for instance, that King's non-violent philosophy raised hopes too high. Among black people King's advocacy of non-violence fed hopes that whites would respond to calls to conscience; and his message did perhaps encourage white people to think that the costs of changing the conditions of black Americans would be relatively easily defrayed, that it would be a matter of changing laws, making institutions more accessible, and assuming a new, more tolerant attitude on racial matters. When whites did not

respond more readily to black calls for freedom and justice, then, as
James Farmer has suggested, the rejection of the philosophy of non-
violence may have also made it easier to abandon the tactic of non-
violence.[54] Similarly when whites perceived that blacks were still not
satisfied after "all" that had been done for them, a kind of emotional
backlash and exhaustion with the whole issue began to set in.

Coda: Forgiving and Forgetting

In *The Human Condition* Arendt describes the great power of love
but also the way it eradicates the distance between people, a distance
which is necessary for judgment and action. In this sense love is anti-
political since it leaves no "world" in which to act. Yet she did suggest
that a political expression of this power, what she called "respect" or
"friendship" could be said to exist. It is:

> a regard for the person from the distance which the space of the world
> puts between us, and this regard is independent of qualities which we
> may admire or of achievements which we may highly esteem.[55]

Though Arendt may have misunderstood the nature of *agape* and
confused it with *eros,* her characterization of friendship is remarkably
like King's concept of *agape.* Both imply an impersonal attitude,
detached from any merit or quality the other person may possess.
Because King enjoined it as an attitude toward enemies as well as
friends, *agape* is an attitude that not only preserves a space between
allies, but also closes some of the distance between enemies. As a
political force it recommends an impersonal regard for their persons
and imagines, at least implicitly, a future when all citizens can inhabit
a common world.

Furthermore, such an attitude presupposes "forgiveness," one of
the two qualities (keeping promises is the other) that Arendt claimed
was so necessary for the survival of any political order. Forgiveness is
needed to break the cycle of vengeance endemic to politics. But
forgiveness in turn depends upon a kind of forgetting, what Nietzsche
referred to as "learning to forget," the prerequisite for creative action
in history.[56] It is not that the oppressed should literally forget what
they have suffered. That would neither be possible nor desirable.
Rather, as King wrote, "we forget in the sense that the evil deed is no
longer a mental block impeding a new relationship."[57]

Forgiving and forgetting, then, would not be ways for black

Americans to excuse white America for what it has perpetrated. Rather, through such actions black Americans might free themselves from the embittering force of remembered suffering. From this point of view, King's ultimate significance, one which has yet to be fully appreciated or absorbed, lies in his effort to incorporate the complex dialectic of forgiving and forgetting into (American) politics. Through that effort King suggested a way of beginning things anew, of taking action to rectify yet transcend the history of vengeance, and of transforming the compulsion to repeat into the capacity to act.

CHAPTER 6

SNCC, Participatory Politics, and the People

There's a street in Itta Bena called FREEDOM
There's a town in Mississippi called LIBERTY
There's a department in Washington called JUSTICE

When David Halberstam was a young journalist on the Nashville *Tennesseean* in the late 1950s and early 1960s, Richard Whalen, then a *Time* magazine correspondent, came to Nashville to gather material for a cover story about the civil rights activists there. Whalen contacted Halberstam to see if a meeting could be arranged with the young students, whose names are now familiar—James Lawson, John Lewis, Diane Nash, and others. After checking, Halberstam reported that the students were reluctant and also very busy but that they could meet Whalen at 6:00 A.M. the next morning. Whalen, according to Halberstam, did a double-take, then fell silent. After a few seconds, his response was, "They're going to win, aren't they."[1]

That was at the beginning, and for a time it looked as though they might win. But the fate of the Student Nonviolent Coordinating Committee shows the destination of courage, energy, commitment, and hope in an historical situation that ultimately would not yield to these qualities. If Socrates' equanimity in the face of death and Jesus's message of forgiveness informed King's vision of politics, it is Antigone's uncompromising claim against Creon and the established political order, the politics of indignation and even rage, that foreshadowed the destination of SNCC. In its short and unhappy life, SNCC as an organization moved from utopian hopes to an almost nihilistic despair, from militant interracialism to black separatism, and from a commitment to radical reform of the Southern racial order to advocacy of revolution.[2]

138

Viewed against the backdrop of American radicalism, not to mention the somnolence of Cold War domestic politics, SNCC was an aberration in American political history. Its dilemmas were more reminiscent of those faced by radicals in nineteenth-century Russia or in national liberation struggles of the Third World than those of the first American revolutionaries or the populists or even the abolitionists. The most apt historical analogy probably would be the *narodniki* in Russia who went *en masse* to the people in the "mad summer" of 1874. The Russian students were a diverse lot, traversing the political spectrum from earnest reformers to violent revolutionaries, from anarchists to socialists. What they shared was an ethical as opposed to dogmatic theoretical orientation. Though their goal was "to live in complete accordance with the idea of duty to the people," the *narodniki* did divide over whether they, as Isaiah Berlin expressed it, "had come to teach or to learn." They were also intellectual heirs of Rousseau and felt that the "greatest of all evils was inequality." They hated the Tsarist state and the bourgeoisie, and their first commitment was to rectifying social and economic disparities rather than securing political and legal rights. Differences there certainly were between the young Russians of the 1860s and 1870s and the American civil rights workers of a century later, but the similarities are nonetheless quite striking.[3]

And yet the American political culture can generally incorporate radical individuals and movements with little difficulty. For instance the Thoreau memorialized in American thinking is the Thoreau of non-violent civil disobedience not the fervent supporter of John Brown and his vision of redemption through the shedding of blood. The story of abolitionism is usually part of the subplot intersecting with the dominant narrative of national progress leading to the destruction of slavery *or* it is read as an object lesson in the practical ineffectuality of moralizing fanaticism. Similarly, Populism is understood as an interesting third-party movement which in time-honored fashion enriched the two mainstream parties *or* as an object lesson in the politics of irrationality and anti-modernity. One lesson to be drawn from these examples is the tragic nature of American politics, the presence at certain historical junctures of democratic demands which the political order cannot or will not accommodate and that are subsequently usually tidied up in standard accounts of our political history.

I want to emphasize this tragic dimension of American politics. My sense is that the history of SNCC was genuinely tragic and arose from an irreconcilable conflict between the goals of the SNCC workers and the mounting evidence of their experience, between the level of political awareness they achieved and generated in others and the degree of change allowed by the "system." To begin to penetrate the SNCC experience requires an acquaintance with writers, usually disillusioned revolutionaries or mordant conservatives—Dostoevski through Conrad to Koestler and Camus and on down to Naipaul— who have explored the pathos (and pathology) of failed revolutions. In contemporary American fiction, the closest thing we have to such fictional explorations of the psychology of failed radical hopes are Alice Walker's *Meridian* (1976) and Rosellen Brown's *Civil Wars* (1984).[4]

What happened in the course of SNCC's history (roughly 1960–1968) was that the interaction of white resistance and internal organizational experiences produced a vision of politics which resembled what SNCC had originally most disliked about the charismatic approach of Martin Luther King and the demagoguery of the movement's white Southern enemies. And while it seems inevitable that SNCC would become intellectually and emotionally taken with the colonial analogy as the best way of understanding the plight of black Americans; that it would embrace the political and cultural vision of black power; and that it would flirt with the doctrine of the therapeutics of violence, each of these notions was either so misleading or so self-contradictory as to undermine SNCC's political effectiveness or long-term viability. Throughout it all was the attempt to come to grips with the meanings of freedom at work in the movement.

Several difficulties with my view of SNCC should be mentioned. Any critique of SNCC runs the risk of blaming the victim. When individuals work over months and years under something approaching the conditions of an underground resistance movement, as SNCC workers did in Mississippi, Black Belt Alabama, and South Georgia, it is difficult to be critical of theoretical weaknesses or intemperate political judgments. Still, SNCC insisted that the people they organized were not just victims and that they could take control of their lives against what seemed insuperable odds. For that reason, if no other, we must take SNCC seriously enough to pass judgment upon, as well as simply describe, the choices it made in the face of what were often insoluble dilemmas.

Finally, there was something inexorable about SNCC's fate. Immoderate in its hopes, one could almost predict that its reaction to frustration would be extreme. But to speak of frustration powerfully understates the case. One also gets the feeling from the accounts of younger civil rights workers that the fundamental failure of white liberal and moderate forces to fully grasp the nature of the situation in the South made the actual physical hardships even worse. Most white Americans simply wanted to deny that things could be *that* bad in Mississippi or Alabama or Georgia or West Tennessee. Missing was the realization of how central racial discrimination and racism were to the Southern (and ultimately to the Northern) way of life and how vulnerable to terror and intimidation black people were in many parts of the South.

As with Martin Luther King, the weakness of the white and black Left at the beginning of the 1960s cannot be overemphasized. Decimated in the anti-radical ethos of the 1950s, the older American Left offered little or no help to the young SNCC workers. To be sure there were exceptions. Bayard Rustin was not only an important influence on Martin Luther King, he exerted considerable influence on a contingent of future SNCC workers from Howard University, including Stokely Carmichael. Still, Rustin was always closer to SCLC and he moved rightward politically just as SNCC was headed toward black power. Ella Baker, a veteran organizer from the 1930s, was also invaluable in shaping the original SNCC vision. A friend of Rustin and King intimate, Stanley Levison, she became the driving force behind the mid-April 1960 meeting in Raleigh, North Carolina at which SNCC was founded. As Julian Bond remembered, "She was a tremendous force"; she "didn't patronize us" and "was more militant, if anything, than we were. . . ." John Lewis echoed Bond when he remembered that Baker was "in the real sense of the word . . . our personal Gandhi. The spiritual mother. . . ."[5]

Aside from such black radicals, the largely white social democratic Left in the early 1960s seemed more concerned with whether New Left organizations such as SDS and SNCC allowed Communists into their ranks and refused Communist support on every possible occasion than with sympathetic criticism or advice to either group. Indeed various anarchists, pacifists, and independent radicals— David Dellinger, Barbara Deming, A. J. Muste, and Paul Goodman—often associated with *Liberation* magazine, gave more moral support than the social democratic Left. Younger white leftists such as Michael Walzer, Tom Kahn, Staughton Lynd, Howard Zinn, and

Richard Flacks contributed to the early debate within the Left about the theory and strategy of the black movement. (It should be said that Irving Howe's journal *Dissent* covered the civil rights movement from the beginning and published many of the semi-theoretical debates just referred to.) This is not to say that it would have been better had the Old Left exercised control over SNCC (and by extension the white New Left); only that the experience of the Old Left, so crucially forged in the anti-Stalinist struggles of the 1930s and 1940s, seemed inevitably to dictate caution rather than daring and to offer carping criticism rather than critical encouragement. There was simply too great a discontinuity between the two generations of radicals.[6]

Thus unimpressed by old shibboleths, particularly what C. Wright Mills called the "labor metaphysic," SNCC, even more than Martin Luther King, worked out its vision as it went along.[7] Most refreshing was its insistence on bypassing established organizations and encouraging communities themselves to take charge of their own institutions. On the other hand, lacking organizational stability or much of a theoretical framework, and often hostile to just such provisions (the half-baked Marxism which surfaced in the late 1960s among some black radicals was a symptom of exhaustion not rejuvenation), SNCC had to deal with defeats as though they were personal shortcomings or the result of a conscious conspiracy directed at them by a highly coordinated enemy. With the exception of figures such as John Lewis and Charles Sherrod, most SNCC workers lacked a sustaining religious faith and thus had no way to forgive their enemies, their friends, or themselves for their defeats. Personal commitment and the solidarity generated by shared adversity had to do the work of ideology and organization. Fairly soon, a certain brittle quality began to creep in. Burn-out, as we shall see, would be the result for many.

Nor were SNCC workers oblivious to such problems. James Forman, who was older than most of his fellow SNCC workers, read constantly; and in the mid-1960s, he searched for a way to spark some sort of intellectual renewal within the organization. Gandhi, Thoreau, and Camus had been early influences, but they gradually gave way to Malcolm X, Mao Zedong, Kwame Nkrumah, Che Guevara, and Frantz Fanon.[8] Also like King, most of the original SNCC workers were scarcely better acquainted with black American history or literature than were their white compatriots. They rediscovered the black American experience (and its connections with Africa) in the 1960s; it was the outgrowth of rather than the impetus for their political activity.

In sum the core of SNCC activists, whether from the North or South, whether from black middle-class or lower-class backgrounds, were bright but not well-educated, intelligent but lacking perspective or wisdom, courageous but lacking in judgment, radical but wanting a theoretical vision, and moral without the capacity to absorb the white world's inability to recognize their moral claim.

Practice into Theory: Political Organizing

Nothing more distinguished SCLC from SNCC than their conflicting visions of political organizing. Where King's approach was to mobilize the community by mass meetings and marches, conducted by himself and his staff, SNCC developed a theory of organizing that stressed the way in which a sense of community self-respect and self-determination grew from the community's efforts to generate its own programs and leaders. Rather than appearing suddenly on the scene and then leaving once a campaign was finished, SNCC workers lived and worked within the communities they attempted to organize. Theoretically, they were enablers rather than leaders. Like all organizers, they were there to make themselves superfluous.

If there is one figure who was responsible for this theory of organizing, it was Ella Baker. Though in *"Democracy Is in the Streets"* James Miller tries to scotch the notion that "the idea of participatory democracy was a product of the movement," and certainly the rudiments of the idea of participatory democracy had a wide variety of sources, the one person most responsible for its dissemination well before the emergence of SDS was Baker.[9] Born in Norfolk, Virginia in 1903, Baker grew up in North Carolina and in the late 1920s moved to New York where she organized co-ops during the Depression, worked for various black publications, and was a recruiter and field organizer for the NAACP until the early 1950s. Executive secretary of SCLC when SNCC was organized in April 1960, she left SCLC for SNCC with no little bitterness when Wyatt Tee Walker was named executive director of SCLC in August of 1960. Above all Baker wanted the fledgling student organization to avoid SCLC's emphasis upon a "leader-centered group" and rather to emphasize a "group-centered leader." People, she claimed, should be organized to be "self-sufficient rather than to be dependent upon the charismatic leader, or the Moses-type leader." "One of the major emphases of SNCC, from the beginning," she later remembered, "was that of working with indigenous people, not working for them, but trying to develop their capacity for leadership." Once people developed a sense of themselves, they could then "understand where their interest really was and the relationship to their own capacity to do something about it." "My theory is," she said, "strong people don't need strong leaders. As an organizer you start where the people are."[10]

In other words, by attacking the dependence upon charismatic leadership so engrained within the Southern black religious community and by linking action with self-awareness and self-interest, Baker provided SNCC with the proto-theoretical rationale for its growing differences with King's SCLC. Indeed the important distinction Miller makes between participatory democracy as face-to-face debate about community policies and participatory democracy as direct action in public, usually in mass form, would become the major theoretical difference between the two organizations and eventually a source of tension within the SNCC itself.[11]

In the early 1960s, Charles Sherrod, a former theology student turned organizer in Southwest Georgia, elaborated upon the early SNCC vision in philosophical/religious terms. Sherrod insisted on the close connection between freedom and recognition of the self when he wrote: "The threads of freedom form the basic pattern in man's struggle to know himself and to live in the assurance that other men will recognize the self." Clearly close to King's politics of recognition, Sherrod also claimed that the struggle in Albany for "the recognition of human dignity in all human beings" was a struggle in which "the philosophy of non-violence was without rival." Finally Sherrod yoked the philosophical and political vision of the community together with the role of the organizer: "We must forever be under the judgement of the community in which we live . . . whatever we do or propose must be executed after careful consideration of the people." The rationale for all this was community control of its common life and interests. As he wrote sometime after 1963, "That's what freedom means, having the power in the system and over how the system is styled."[12] With Sherrod's position in mind, we can say that early SNCC thinking sought to tie together self-respect and self-determination within the community. Freedom as self-transformation and freedom as action taken together in public were thus closely linked to self-determination.

Mississippi—the place, the experience, and the point in time—was crucial in the history of SNCC. The summer of 1964 marked the high tide of SNCC involvement there and the maturation of its vision. Central to SNCC's activities—its attempts at voter registration and then organization of the Freedom Democratic Party (FDP) under the aegis of COFO—was Robert Parris Moses. If any one individual embodied the public image of SNCC in the years up to 1965, it was Moses. A former philosophy student, Moses's quiet manner and almost religious devotion to the people were legendary. A reluctant public speaker and leader, Moses was fundamentally opposed to any cult of personality and was to withdraw from political activity when he saw that such a cult was growing up around him. It was Moses who was primarily responsible for the decision to bring white volunteers into Mississippi in the summer of 1964, over the opposition of many SNCC workers and local people, and he felt deeply the guilt involved in exposing them and black Mississippians to increased violence and even death.

Despite his insistent self-effacement, Moses exerted enormous influence and elicited deep loyalties. In many quarters he, not King, was the most admired civil rights activist. Unita Blackwell in Mississippi remembered that he was "just a light in my heart now," while Mary Booth of Greenwood said that "He really showed me the light . . . about being black without being ashamed of being black. . . . He was a leader not a speaker." Annie Devine of Canton emphasized the non-directive role he assumed, for Moses "didn't tell FDP anything . . . It wasn't his nature anyway." Another Greenwood woman, Mary Lane, spoke of how "I really admired Bob . . . if it was Bob who said it, you knew it had to be done. . . . And he would always say, we have to love one another." And fellow SNCC worker Julian Bond remembered that Moses was best as an "organizer and as a fellow who had the ability to completely empathize with people who were completely different from him."[13]

Moses first went to Mississippi in 1960 and contacted Ella Baker's friend Amzie Moore in Cleveland. At that time, as later, Mississippi was notorious even among Southern states for the depth and intensity of its racial feeling. It was, in the words of Ole Miss history professor, James Silver, a "closed society" even for its white citizens. Though things were changing, the pace was awfully slow. Two salient facts give a sense of the overpowering control whites exerted against blacks. Though in 1940, as historian Neil McMillen reports, a measure to delete "all reference to voting, elections and democracy" from civics books used by black children was narrowly defeated in the Mississippi Senate, a 1920 law forbade "advocacy of social equality" or "intermarriage" in printed form. More significantly, there was no "tradition of sustained, organized challenge to white dominance" in the state nor, except for a streetcar boycott in 1904, were there any public group protests or challenges to the Jim Crow system up to the 1960s.[14]

Moses's eventual purpose was to organize "young people . . . who had no economic ties" and were thus "able to act as free agents" to go into the black communities and register people to vote. For this task young blacks had to be convinced that "their job, and even their life's work, would be to work to make some sense out of living in Mississippi." The development of indigenous cadres implied the need for organizers, black and white, who "identif[ied] with these people." The role of outside organizers was thus a temporary one of training indigenous organizers, since "the roots of the party were in people and in units, organizations and neighborhoods," and, Moses was later to reflect, "could be" traced back to these small meetings and to the sense of identity which began to grow out of meetings . . ." One local organizer, Lawrence Guyot, specified the effects of this organizing when he spoke of the way in which the "freedom vote" conducted in the autumn of 1963 "crystallized and accelerated the whole activity of political participation" for "people who were frightened, 100 percent if that's possible," and who had a "history of political consciousness but certainly not political participation. . . ." Like Moses, Guyot emphasized the importance of grass-roots participation in meetings and the need to "make precinct meetings or some other political subdivision a functional entity" since black people in Mississippi and in much of the deep South were excluded from regular party organizations.[15]

Beyond that, organizing was clearly not just a means to some concrete end; it was a way of creating a new sense of self and community and of articulating the submerged interests of both. For Moses and his colleagues, the means were as important, if not more so, than the ends. To separate means and ends was specious, since each implied the other. As Edward Brown, one of the Howard

University group so influential in the history of SNCC (along with contingents from Nashville and Atlanta), asserted, there *was* an ideology at work, even in those years: "that ideology has to do with freedom and breaking of dependency; dependency of any kind." Brown spelled out this close connection between independence and participation when he added: "The ideology has to do with freedom, it has to do with democracy, in terms of people participating in decisions—it has to do with the whole rebuilding of the sense of community."[16]

The general purpose of such organizing was articulated by activist-historian Staughton Lynd when he wrote of the need to develop "parallel structures" to challenge existing political institutions. Such parallel institutions would provide the "experience of self-government"[17] so lacking in the lives of Mississippi black people. Two examples of the creation of parallel structures were the "freedom vote" in the autumn and winter of 1963–64 (an idea brought from South Africa by Allard Lowenstein) and the organization of the Mississippi Freedom Democratic Party which, through local meetings and then a state convention, chose an alternative Mississippi delegation to the Democratic Convention in Atlantic City in August 1964.

Besides these explicitly political innovations, the most interesting parallel institution to emerge in Mississippi was the "freedom school," a suggestion of SNCC worker Charles Cobb. These schools would begin remedying the grossly inadequate education received by black children in the state. Administered by Lynd during the summer of 1964, there were some 30 schools with between 3,000 and 3,400 students and 175 teachers participating.[18]

Like so much else undertaken by SNCC, the freedom schools helped shape innovative developments in educational thinking during the 1960s. They were not narrowly remedial in any straightforward way, since the assumption behind them was that what specific skills and general knowledge gave students was a new sense of confidence in their ability to deal with their world. In the broadest sense the purpose of the schools was political; but this new sense of self could be produced as much by acquiring competence in mathematics as through studying politics. As defined by one SNCC document, the schools were intended: "1) to provide remedial instruction in basic educational skills but more importantly 2) to implant habits of free thinking and ideas of how a free society works, and 3) to lay the

groundwork for a statewide youth movement."[19] The intimate connection between a "free" mind and "free" action was stressed in
another document which spoke of creating:

> an educational experience for students which will make it possible for
> them to challenge the myths of our society, to perceive more clearly its
> realities and to find alternatives—ultimately new directions for ac-
> tion.[20]

And volunteer Liz Fusco wrote that the "decision to set the people
free for politics is the only way that people really can become free,
and that is totally." She also emphasized that students were being
brought around to the view that escaping to the North, until then
conceived of in "the sense of 'go home to my Lord and be free,'" was
no answer in itself. Instead they were learning to see Mississippi as a
place that could be changed rather than "some vague white monster
doomed irrationally to crush them. Simultaneously they began to
discover that they themselves could take action against the injustice . . . ."[21] This was political education at its most fundamental—
education in the possibilities of action.

Many freedom schools published newsletters or short newspapers
in which young black people had the chance to express their views
about everything from national politics to events in the local community. One constant motif was a concern with the meaning of freedom.
Freedom's Journal in McComb returned repeatedly to the theme
through poems and contributions of the form derived from the comic
strip *Peanuts:* "Happiness is . . ." Definitions of freedom were
sometimes very specific ("going to public libraries") and at other
times were much more abstract ("standing up for your rights" or
"racial equality, justice, and fraternity," or "happiness for all").
Freedom was typically animated as when one contributor asserted
that "When we find Freedom we will not let it go."[22] The editor of the
Freedom Courier in Greenwood spoke of freedom in "negative"
terms when he/she said that "We feel free when we can do as we
please." What seemed at first a simple answer was made more subtle
when the editor added, "This is not exactly love of freedom . . . It
is more nearly hatred of restraint." Retha Barnes echoed the first part
of the characterization of freedom when she said "I want the right to
go any place and to do what I want. I want freedom." Others stressed
the indivisibility of freedom: ". . . no man is free until all men are
free," while a McComb contributor raised the level of the argument

by saying that "Freedom is as much a state of mind as it is a physical condition. . . . If this [the ability to go where you want] is given with reluctance and you are just put up with and not respected, you are not truly free."[23] If these samples are at all representative, they attest to the way the concern with freedom permeated the education offered by the freedom schools and that freedom as a concept tended to encompass a variety of "goods" sought by participants in the movement.

Besides offering training in practical skills such as typing and in relatively esoteric ones such as foreign languages, emphasis in the freedom schools also fell upon learning the rudiments of American history and government and, more importantly, the black American experience. As Fannie Lou Hamer said, "The purpose of being free is not to marry your son or daughter" but to acquire a "decent education, knowing something about their own heritage . . ."[24] Her assumption, of course, was that people are better able to think and act if they are aware of precursors and predecessors. Such knowledge would create an inner space of possibility from which an external space of action could be imagined.

Despite many difficulties—lack of adequate educational materials and equipment, racial and cultural tensions—the freedom schools were generally assessed enthusiastically. The author of a "Proposal for a Freedom Information Center" spoke in measured, even despairing, terms of the tendency to let someone else do the work, but then reaffirmed the rationale for the center:

> It is possible that this problem is insoluble, that a community of strong, independent, cooperating individuals cannot exist among human beings. But we believe that such a community can and in fact must begin to live before we can say that there can be any change here . . . We believe that there is a direct and significant relation between knowledge, sense of involvement and real power.[25]

Another assessment was more sanguine:

> The feeling that at least there is something they as individuals can do to better themselves and their lot in Mississippi has been created. Once this spirit has been aroused, change *has already begun to take place.* In a real sense, the Freedom School is attempting to spread this spirit to students who can gain from this a new sense of their identity and importance as people.[26]

Overall, SNCC's political vision, as it emerged by the summer of 1964, emphasized the interdependence, even interchangeability, of knowledge, self-respect, autonomy, power, and participation in community action. Emphasis fell upon achieving consensus rather than depending upon "mechanical" procedures such as voting to authorize decisions. Freedom meant not just release from white oppression and material impoverishment; it also implied a sense of a new acting self and a feeling of empowerment. Such a vision of politics was reminiscent not of Leninist theories of political mobilization guided by a party elite, but of the communitarian anarchism put forth by such thinkers as Paul Goodman and of C. Wright Mills's idea that "publics" were vital to the functioning of a genuine democracy.[27] More generally, it signaled the recrudescence of a kind of democratic republicanism in which political debate and action were assumed to be central to community- and self-determination. Freedom was the process as well as the prize.

The Colonial Analogy and Black Power

Yet Freedom Summer was the beginning of the end of SNCC. It marked the start of a process that saw SNCC change its nature drastically and all but disappear by 1968. Historians and participants have given full accounts of the crucial internal and external developments between August 1964 and June 1966 when the "black power" slogan was first proclaimed publicly by Willie Ricks and Stokely Carmichael on the march through Mississippi after James Meredith had been shot. Crucial in the shift to this racial populism was a series of developments—the failure of the Democratic Party to seat the MFDP delegation at Atlantic City or even offer an acceptable compromise to them; the visit by several SNCC workers to Africa in the fall of 1964 and an encounter there with Malcolm X; the growing urgency of the situation in Northern urban ghettos (there were major riots in Harlem and Bedford-Stuyvesant in summer 1964, then in Watts the next summer) and the obvious need for social and economic change in the cities; and finally the shift of attention and resources to the Vietnam War by the Johnson administration.[28]

The change was most obviously registered at the leadership level. Neither John Lewis, SNCC chairman from 1963–66, nor Robert Moses was a charismatic in any conventional sense. Nor did they want to be, since SNCC was in principle suspicious of charismatic leadership. But with Moses's abandonment of movement activities altogether and the election of Stokely Carmichael to replace John Lewis as chairman in May 1966, the way was open for Carmichael and his successor, H. Rap Brown, to assume or have thrust upon them—or both—the role of media celebrities. SNCC was becoming a "leadership" organization. Indeed the more the media focused on Carmichael as spokesman, the less political organizing went on. There was no follow-up campaign in Mississippi in the summer of 1965, while the organizing efforts spearheaded by Carmichael and the rest of the SNCC contingent in Lowndes County, Alabama in the fall and winter of 1965–66 faded after the Meredith March in June 1966. Moreover, as Doug McAdam has noted, just after SNCC had put nearly 1,000 mostly white workers through an intensive course in Southern racial history and politics, the move to exclude whites from the organization began to pick up momentum. Carmichael had been one of SNCC's most valuable organizers; his role in Mississippi a crucial one; and he was in fact opposed to excluding whites from SNCC. But as chairman of SNCC, he adopted a provocative, hit-and-run style which made good copy for the media but was a harsh exaggeration of the style of leadership about which SNCC had always been so withering when criticizing Dr. King and SCLC.[29]

The reorientation of SNCC was not just cosmetic nor purely media-induced. It also reflected a shift in the philosophy of organizing at work in SNCC and its attitude toward "the people." There were several temptations inherent in the organizer's role. An organizer ran the risk of reenforcing that dependence which the purpose of organizing sought to undermine. An organizer could also manipulate the community under the guise of letting it make its own choices. In the process he or she might also romanticize the people as sources of infallible wisdom and authenticity, what James Forman called "local people–itis."[30] Finally an organizer might begin, against all evidence, to treat the community as a unitary entity without diversity of opinions or interests.

All this happened in SNCC. On the one hand the rhetorical and emotional commitment to "the people" seemed stronger, if anything, than earlier. Rejecting the DuBoisian notion of elite guidance of the masses, Julius Lester wrote in 1966: "It was out of Mississippi that one of the most important concepts of the 'movement' came. Let the people lead themselves. . . . There would be no talented tenth. Only the community." But just as statements such as Lester's were

regularly appearing, the transformation in the role of SNCC chairman was proceeding apace. The more SNCC became identified with
its chairman, the more "the people" were to be roused to action from
the top down through public rhetoric. The more SNCC spoke *for* the
people, the more its roots in the Southern black communities
withered. As one black leader sardonically observed, "SNCC always
does what the poor people say to do . . . so long as the poor people
say what SNCC wants to do."[31]

In addition the nature of the "community" and "the people"
became much more explicit. Though SNCC was an interracial organization and notionally committed to a populist coalition of poor whites
and blacks, it had become abundantly clear, if there had ever been
any doubt, that no interracial coalition was in the offing. Many
Southern whites were either leaving the Democratic Party for the
Republican or were attracted by the politics of resentment offered by
Alabama Governor George Wallace. Indeed, there were more new
white Southern voters registered in the 1960s than there were new
black voters added to the roles. Thus the "community" and the
"people" in question were obviously black.

In this situation, though it is hard to be exact, there was increasing
reference to "the people," a locution implying a unified totality with a
single collective identity. "Identity has always been the key problem
for the Negroes," wrote Lester who proceeded to chart the emergence of the "black man" (in place of the "Negro") with "soul" and a
culture and language of his own.[32] A vision of a community of black
individuals, that is, a vision of plurality, was replaced by a vision of
black people, independent of specific gender, regional, or even
political traits, on the way to becoming a political/national entity.
SNCC personnel adopted a kind of "substitutionism," according to
which they implicitly claimed to speak for and to a unified community
of black people or "the black community." They became the embodiment of the will of the people rather than eliciting the various voices
from the community.

Or this change can be charted in terms of a subtle transformation in
the notion of consensus. When the focus shifted from a specific group
of black people in a Southern community deliberating on a particular
issue or set of issues to black people as a totality, then it was easy for
consensus to become reified into something akin to the "general will"
of all black people, a deep-structural set of common feelings, concerns, and interests that overrode superficial differences in interests

and existed apart from the conscious wishes that individual black people had—or thought they had. It was not, in other words, an empirical but something approaching a metaphysical concept. Individuals who dissented from the will of "the people" could then be branded as "bourgeois" or "Uncle Toms" and "Aunt Thomasinas." They had fallen prey to false, i.e., white, consciousness. This idea of something inherently and discoverably "black" is most apparent, for instance, in a 1967 SNCC pamphlet which urges "learning to think Black and remove white things from our minds."[33]

In terms of the history of political thought, these developments in SNCC reflected the emergence of certain quasi-mystical notions of popular sovereignty first articulated by Rousseau and found also in the Russian populism already mentioned. For Rousseau popular sovereignty was not just a contractual matter as it was in the Lockean tradition and as expressed in Jefferson's *Declaration*. Rather the idea was invested with an emotional and religious fervor and implied a discoverable general will or common interest. The great weakness of this Rousseauean version of popular sovereignty is that it glorifies the people as the source of political legitimacy without being very specific about the institutions through which the general will is to be expressed and/or protected. For instance, Rousseau distinguished quite clearly between sovereignty and government; where the former was derived from the people, the latter might assume any number of forms, including monarchy.[34] In twentieth-century terms, such a qualitative concept of popular sovereignty can allow a party or an individual leader to speak for the people and claim democratic legitimacy without actually ever being required to count heads (or hands). As was the case in nineteenth-century Russia, SNCC workers increasingly felt that the existing political ideologies, practices, and institutions were corrupted by white racist control and liberal indifference and thus hardly worth preserving. What remained was the people's will represented by and through SNCC.

From an historical-political perspective, the shift in SNCC thinking was reflected in its increasing reliance upon the colonial analogy to describe and explain the plight of black Americans. Nor was the colonial analogy confined to SNCC. James Bevel, who was in charge of planning SCLC's Chicago campaign, repeatedly described that city's slums as "internal colonies."[35] This analogy was central, for instance, in Stokely Carmichael and Charles Hamilton's *Black Power* (1967) and reflected the general influence of Third World liberation movements and the specific impact of Malcolm X and Frantz Fanon upon SNCC thinking by this time. In their book, Carmichael and Hamilton delineated three spheres in which black people stood in a colonial relationship to white America: the political, the economic, and the social. Political colonialism referred to everything from the way the white power structure directly controlled the political choices of the black community to the way it indirectly maintained control through black puppet-politicians. America's much touted pluralism seemed to vanish when racial issues were involved. Second, Carmichael and Hamilton claimed that the black community was economically exploited as a source of cheap labor and a captive market for overpriced goods. Finally, they contended that, with the exception of a few black bourgeoisie siphoned off by the system, black Americans were consigned to a permanently low social status and thus suffered individual and collective loss of esteem and respect.[36]

How plausible was this line of analysis comparing the position of Afro-Americans with people in colonial areas of Africa, Asia, and Latin America? In many ways it was quite compelling, taken as a first approximation of what it meant to be black in America; and some of its appeal undoubtedly lay in the way it was a variation on the Exodus dream, the first nationalist vision in the Western tradition, so crucial, as already mentioned, in the Afro-American tradition. However, critics such as Christopher Lasch soon identified problematic areas. First, it was doubtful that the economic importance of the urban ghettos to the dominant economy was as great as the colonies had been to the metropolitan colonizer. Though individual capitalists made profits in the ghettos, large national and multinational corporations could probably get along very well without them. Nor was it easy to imagine black ghettos developing economic independence, if and when this quasi-colonial economic domination was removed.

More interestingly, Lasch pointed to a conceptual incompatibility in *Black Power* between the conception of black Americans as an internal colony and the frequent comparison of black Americans with other ethnic groups such as the Irish, Jews, or Italians who through group solidarity and development of their own community institutions had acquired a place in the American system. The ethnic analogy was a prescription for incorporation into the economic and political system, while the colonial analogy certainly suggested the need to revolt and fight for collective liberation from the oppressors.[37]

But the most cogent objections to the colonial analogy, despite its pertinence in matters of culture and psychology, were demographics and geography. In this matter, Carmichael and Hamilton might have consulted Harold Cruse. In an essay "Revolutionary Nationalism and the Afro-American" (1962), Cruse scored Marxists for offering black Americans little more than "socialism plus integration" by failing to pay adequate attention to revolutions in the "underdeveloped world" and the plight of American blacks who were themselves "a Subject of Domestic Colonialism." Cruse advised that black intellectuals should also abandon the integrationist strategies of the "NAACP–Martin Luther King–student legalistic and 'passive resistance' tactics" and develop a nationalist position. But, Cruse emphasized, the problem with seeing American blacks as a colonial people was that they existed in "close proximity with the dominant racial group." As a result, the nationalist "rejection of white society is analogous to the colonial people's rejection of imperialist rule. The difference is *only* [emphasis added] that people in the colonies can succeed and Negro Nationalists cannot."[38] Taken literally the colonial analogy was a recipe for disaster.

What desperately needed clarification, even in Cruse's essay, was the nature of black nationalism implied by the colonial analogy. For Cruse the justification for the nationalist position seemed to lie primarily in its power to reveal the hollowness of conventional Marxist (not to mention liberal) dreams of integration. The integrationist position failed to address the cultural-psychological distinctiveness of Afro-Americans and thus left them with no option but to assimilate into the dominant culture. Though Cruse was also concerned to challenge the "facile equating" of nationalism with segregation or with "formal nationhood or geographical separation," the danger of the colonial analogy in Cruse's or later in Carmichael and Hamilton's less subtle account lay precisely in the equation of it with nationhood and separation, thus arousing hopes and expectations that could not be fulfilled.[39] Otherwise, the "nationalist" position was a form of ethnic politics with an overlay of radical racial rhetoric, pluralist politics plus soul food.

In other words black nationalism was only one destination of "black power," first deployed as a slogan in June of 1966 and fated to replace "freedom now." Again Julius Lester registered the mood underlying this change in slogans in the following sardonic comments on freedom: "Was it a place somewhere between Atlanta and Birmingham and you kept on missing it every time you drove that way? It was a street in Itta Bena, Mississippi. Ain't that a bitch?" Ricks explained the move in more abstract terms when he claimed that "We had moved to the level of verbalizing our drive for power—not merely for the vote, not for some kind of freedom, not for legal rights, but the basic force in any society—power."[40] When preceded by "black," the combination was predictably controversial, even explosive.

What did black power mean in the context of the mid-1960s? It was initially left ambiguous so as to alienate more conservative civil rights leaders such as Roy Wilkins.[41] Soon its various meanings were too many to track. For Lewis Black of Hale County, Alabama it meant "to respect their color . . . we are powerful people to protect ourselves . . . the courage to stand side by side with man . . ." For Paul Puryear, a black academic at Tuskegee Institute in Alabama, it meant something similar: "a movement for psychological redemption from the setters of racial superiority." For SNCC activist John Wilson "power means having the capability to force or to push and be able to fight for what you want, is developing enough power to fight for what you want and take it."[42] And for the authors of *Black Power*, it seemed to refer either to black political strength within a pluralist political framework or to the control by black people of their own institutions and ultimately their destiny. Black power tended to shift back and forth between a psychological and a political meaning and ultimately encompassed both as forms of self-determination.

Though much discussion of black power was hysterical, there were undeniable difficulties with the idea of black power and its deployment as a rallying cry. Most obviously, those SNCC spokespeople who used the slogan often coupled it with an explicit willingness to use violence, at least in self-defense, and thus were rightly seen as having abandoned the commitment of the civil rights movement to non-violence. But a far more important criticism, one advanced by Cruse, was that black power advocates tended to equate advocacy of violence, even in self-defense, with radical theory and practice, when in fact there was no necessary connection. In certain contexts, black power was thus premature and provocative.[43]

Put another way, the use of black power as a slogan made it easy for critics to equate power with, rather than distinguish it from, violence. This was an understandable confusion since black power advocates were generally guilty of that confusion as well. Indeed the conventional wisdom of political thought, radical or otherwise, has assumed that political power depends primarily upon disposal over and willingness to use instruments of violence. But again Arendt's work is relevant to this issue since she contended that power and violence are inversely related: to use or invoke violence reveals a lack of political power. For, to Arendt's way of thinking, power depends upon numbers, upon the amount of popular support a government or group can muster, while violence depends upon instruments and can never be more than a means to an end. Political rule founded on violence alone is terror and exceedingly unstable.[44]

Beyond the power/violence link and the equation of black power with a kind of self-respect (a matter to which I will return), black power tended to be identified with various forms of black nationalism. Clearly literal secession from the United States and establishment of a black state either in the continental United States or elsewhere were chimerae, fantasies substituting for political and social projects. Secessionist positions were usually amalgams of Garveyite dreams, biblical visions of deliverance and Nation of Islam-type social discipline. Moreover unless black political theorists seriously proposed changes in the Constitution to protect group as opposed to individual rights and powers—and Cruse did at least mention the need to "make the Constitution reflect the social reality of America as a nation of nations, or a nation of ethnic groups"[45]— black power in a political sense was, as already mentioned, just ethnic, interest-group politics with a bite. Even at that it seemed questionable to call it a form of nationalism.

The most coherent, if not very specific, form of nationalism was Cruse's "enclave" nationalism. Cruse suggested that since the political, economic, and cultural dimensions of black life were inseparable, it was crucial that black people control all of these dimensions. Indeed he tended to privilege the cultural: "As long as the Negro's cultural identity is in question, or open to self-doubts, there can be no positive identification with the real demands of his political and economic existence."[46] Such assertions were hard to disagree with by the end of the decade, and Cruse's position seems broadly compatible with the position of Carmichael and Hamilton. But the difficulties in implementing it were readily apparent in the unsuccessful attempt to gain community control of the public schools in the Ocean Hill–Brownsville district of Brooklyn in 1968.

But though the meaning of black power was politically and constitutionally hard to specify, after the mid-1960s the use of the slogans
"black power" and "black consciousness" did signal a clear emphasis
upon freedom as self-respect, psychological self-determination, and
the assertion of black identity. As Carmichael and Hamilton wrote:

> . . . We must first redefine ourselves . . . reclaim our history and
> our identity from what must be called cultural terrorism. . . . We
> shall have to struggle for the right to create our own terms through
> which to define ourselves and our relationship to the society, and have
> these terms recognized. This is the first necessity of a free peo-
> ple . . ."[47]

Indeed this concern with freedom as self-respect, as a prerequisite of
self-determination and recognition, was precisely the element of
continuity between the original SNCC and the post-1964 SNCC, as it
was between the non-violent wing of the movement and the emerging black radical movement. Whatever their other differences, and
they were considerable, the two positions remained close on this
matter, something that Cruse for instance never acknowledged.
What divided them, as we shall see, was the way to achieve this sense
of personal and political identity.

More broadly, the search for a black identity through politics
reflected a new emphasis within twentieth-century radical consciousness. If, as Arendt suggests in *On Revolution*, the significance of the
French Revolution (as opposed to the revolution in America) lay in its
abandonment of political freedom and its concentration upon the
"social question," i.e., the eradication of poverty, and its commitment to "the people rather than the republic,"[48] the twentieth
century has seen the "psychological" and "cultural" question emerge
as preeminent in the revolutionary fight against colonial rule in Asia,
Africa, and Latin America. That is, prior to solving the problems of
mass poverty and social wretchedness, most liberation struggles have
attempted to forge a new identity for "the people." Outside of
Europe, the proletariat envisaged by Marxism has been all but
absent, while at the same time the development of a unified, popular/
national consciousness, free of the values of the colonizing culture,
has become a necessary means and end of nation-building. It has, in
other words, been necessary to discover or create "the people" as the
source of cultural as well as political sovereignty and self-determination.

Of monumental significance in the emergence of this cultural and psychological question is the contingent fact that Western domination has been justified and explained by cultural and particularly racial differences (with the arguable exception Northern Ireland). As a result post–1945 liberation movements have eventually been driven to posit race and culture as the basis of collective identity, after having initially rejected race as a valid form of classification. That is, having defined the terms of domination as racial, "white" colonizers have then found their rule challenged by people who assert a counter-identity grounded in a celebration of race. A pattern has established itself: where grounds for liberation were initially made in universalist terms, they come to be reexpressed in particularist terms. This of course was the position SNCC had arrived at by the mid-1960s, thus recapitulating in America's "colonies," first the South and then the urban ghettos, the trajectory of revolutionary self-consciousness in this century. However misleading the colonial analogy was in certain respects, it was certainly compelling on this one matter—neither the individual nor class but race was the organizing category of consciousness and action. It was the master-trope of all liberation movements.

Using the term "trope" implies that "black" was not meant literally or not *just* literally. To be sure black referred to an actual color. But even movements such as Marcus Garvey's had differentiated among shades of blackness, as though such differences signified different properties or potentialities. By the mid-1960s, blackness had come to refer to a way of experiencing the world as a place of exclusion and oppression. It reflected a collective historical experience and distinctive cultural tradition. Thus race was an experiential and historical-cultural category more than a descriptive or biological one. As already seen, it was claimed that there was a way of "thinking black" as well as "looking black" and "acting black." A form of literal "appearance" implied a shared experience of the world.

There were several immediate implications of this valorization of blackness. First, it strongly implied, as we have seen, that blackness signified a unitary experience and shared set of interests and that individual black people were potentially unified selves. From this perspective, what DuBois called "doubleness" was a weakness rather than a strength. Second, all conceptual terminology such as self-respect, self-determination, and freedom were subsumed under the master-trope/concept of blackness. It became the central "virtue" term among black radicals. Finally, not only did black identity imply a natural solidarity among black people, it also implied a relationship of emotional, trans-historical solidarity with ancestors in America and Africa, thus lending a "vertical," temporal dimension to identity.

Equally important, the evolving SNCC position redefined the "other" from whom recognition of identity and moral status could be accepted. For Martin Luther King, as we have seen, white recognition of black worth and identity was important, since as oppressors white people had historically withheld that recognition. Moreover, recognition across racial lines was pragmatically desirable as long as black people could see no alternative to living in a predominantly white society. Though it did not imply obsequiousness toward whites, it did affirm the necessity of taking whites into account as the source of recognition. But SNCC came to reject whites as crucial "significant others" in the re-creation of a black identity. Again, Julius Lester expressed the shift clearly. "At one time," he wrote:

> black people desperately wanted to be American, to communicate with whites, to live in the Beloved Community. Now that is irrelevant. They know that it can't be until whites want it to be and it is obvious now that whites don't want it.[49]

Lester went on to admit that some blacks wanted to turn the tables and victimize whites, but added:

> For others it simply means the white man no longer exists. . . . he is simply to be ignored, because the time has come for the black man to control the things which effect [sic] his life. . . . For so long the black man lived his life in reaction to whites. Now he will live it only within the framework of his blackness . . .[50]

The crucial term here is "ignore," for it reflected a situation in which the only reality that counted was black reality. Instead of winning recognition from whites through struggle, black people would achieve a new sense of self through acting with other black people. The social origins of self-respect had been redefined.

Here it is again important to draw out the differences with King. In King's terms, SNCC had abandoned *agape* as the operative political virtue. It was not that black people were now encouraged to hate and do violence to whites, for that would imply that whites still controlled their psychic destinies, since to hate another is still to be under the control of that person. Rather whites had become non-subjects, a kind of natural "given" from whom one no more expected or wanted approval than from an animal or a stone. At best, like natural objects, whites were potential resources.

Nor is it quite correct to imply that the ideology of black identity lacked other-regarding political virtues. Rather, the other-regarding virtues—recognition, but also affection, pride, solidarity—were operative among black people alone. In particular, solidarity, the sense of brother- and sisterhood, derived from what Arendt referred to as the "great privilege of pariah peoples" to feel particularly "the warmth of human relationships" among themselves.[51] Using King's terminology, relationships of solidarity among black people could be characterized in terms of *philia* and especially *eros*. If *eros* is the desire to be united with or recuperate that which is lacking, this missing sense of wholeness could be created in and by mutual oppression and struggle. Whites, on the other hand, no matter how sympathetic with or supportive of the black struggle, could never share in this "warmth," even if like Robert Zellner they had been part of SNCC since its inception. They could never really know what it meant to be black.[52]

But was this a form of racism? The problem, then and now, is the slippery nature of the concept of racism itself. Strictly speaking, modern racism refers to a pseudo-scientific assumption that race is a "natural kind" implying essential genetic differences in capacities and that these differences signify an essential inferiority or superiority. (The move from difference to valorization of difference is a psychological not logical move.) If we accept this strict definition, then most of the philosophies of black power and black consciousness of the 1960s can not be called racist in this essentialist sense. Indeed, only the Black Muslims openly adopted a position which posited essential differences between whites and blacks.[53]

However, racism is sometimes also attributed to those who advocate or implement policies which establish institutional bias or exclusion based on unalterable (usually physical) characteristics. By definition society or any sort of group distributes membership and privilege differentially. Black separatist positions in the 1960s claimed to escape racism by asserting that separation did not imply subordination of the excluded (in this case white) group and that exclusion derived from a particular historical experience or ideological allegiance rather than from differences in essential capacity.

An example of this position can be found in *Black Power*. There Carmichael and Hamilton define racism in behavioral terms as "the

predication of decisions and policies on consideration of race for the
purpose of *subordinating* a racial group and maintaining control over
that group."[54] Their definition was a shrewd one, for by making
racism a matter of intention ("for the purpose of . . .") to subordinate, charges of racism could easily be diverted. Yet by emphasizing
intentions Carmichael and Hamilton ran into two sorts of problems. First, intellectual justifications—as opposed to the historical
reality—of the separate but equal principle (or enlightened *apartheid*) can meet the intentions criterion without much trouble by
simply maintaining that the separate facilities or institutions are not
intended to subordinate. Second, by stressing intentions, Carmichael and Hamilton weaken the force of their discussion of institutional racism. Assuming the primacy of intentions, they first claim
that the important distinction is between individual racism which is
"overt" and institutional racism which is "covert." However, as their
discussion proceeds, they lean more heavily on the distinction
between personal and impersonal forms of discrimination. Moreover, some of their examples of institutional racism—lack of provisions and hence a higher death rate for black babies, the stunting of
the development of black children—suggest that effects, perhaps
more than intentions, should be the primary criterion for determining institutional racism.[55] In their account, for instance, Southern
phenomena such as the white primary or the grandfather clause
would clearly exemplify policies that covertly and intentionally exclude blacks; but the underrepresentation of blacks in, say, medical
schools which have never had racially biased admission requirements, e.g., the Bakke case, would be hard to accommodate to their
view of institutional racism.

If we accept these latter examples as illustrative of a kind of
functional racial discrimination, apart from and even contradictory to
individual or institutional intentions, it is difficult to see how black
separatist organizations can be automatically eliminated from the
charge of institutional racism. (I should add that I am concerned here
with a descriptive not a constitutional judgment concerning racism.
Racial discrimination is a constitutional issue; racism as such is not.)
For even if the criteria of exclusion have to do with collective
experience rather than biologically determined skin color, it is
difficult to see how a white person or a Native American could ever
qualify, since the allegedly shared experience *is* a function of biological appearance.[56] Thus intention to subordinate is not really to the

point, since de facto exclusion may be tantamount to discrimination and a form of subordination. Whether we call it racism or not—and I think it should be called institutional or functional racism to distinguish it from "essentialist" racism—the definition offered by Carmichael and Hamilton would allow a form of racial discrimination. A third type of racism can be found in expressions of hatred and contempt directed against a group or members of a group, even if no theoretical basis or discriminatory intent stands behind that expression or action. Calling black people "niggers" and white people "honkeys" would exemplify this form of racism, as would the title of the SNCC pamphlet "We Must Fill Ourselves with Hatred for All White Things." Such a "situational" or "reactive" racism permeated much of the black power ideology. Indeed acting upon such totalizing judgments can potentially be as dehumanizing as essentialist racism or institutional racism. But expressions of immediate anger and insults are probably less serious in the long run than the other two forms of racism, since anger and insult are less easily theorized or institutionalized. As Albert Memmi summed it up, the racism of the oppressed is at worst "not aggressive but defensive . . . neither biological or metaphysical but social and historical," since it "fears and admires" the oppressor.[57] At worst the rhetoric of "whitey-baiting" was a way of getting even and, when directed against white supporters, a form of moral cowardice. Those who engaged in it put whites in a double bind; if they responded in kind, their racism was confirmed; but if they were silent, they acquiesced in a charge that was often not true.

There are two particularly significant implications in all this. First by the late 1960s, racism had lost much specific meaning and had become a way of attributing guilt by imprecation. Indeed the history of the term bears a certain resemblance to the histories of terms like "fascism" and "totalitarianism" which have been drained of meaning by misuse. The serious political and cultural-psychological issues raised by SNCC (and Martin Luther King increasingly after 1965)—the pervasiveness of all three sorts of racism in American society and the need to rediscover the historical and cultural roots of black life—were too often trivialized into intimidating slogans. All this having been said, the ideology of black power did not have to be racist in any of the senses mentioned, though it usually slid rather easily into either institutional racism or situational racism. Behind the popularity of black power as an ideal lay the colonial analogy, predicated upon the dream of somehow excluding whites from black life and institutions, a dream which in North America was precisely an impossibility.

Finally we need to explore the political implications of Arendt's claim about "warmth" among oppressed people, for it implies that the extreme closeness of pariah people, the ideal of unity, or the real experience of solidarity, leaves little room for diversity or plurality. Lacking what Arendt referred to as a space "in-between," individuals in the pariah group find it difficult to accurately assess their oppressors or to get any distance on their own world. Thus when black people—or any people—conceive of themselves as a unified oppressed group, private activities or feelings are scarcely tolerated and disagreement, should it arise, is easily branded as betrayal. A conformist cast of mind easily emerges.

Most important, this suggests that oppressed people, whether Afro-Americans or Jews (or Poles or Czechoslovaks) may find it difficult to imagine or establish "lasting institutions" which both preserve some group coherence and create the conditions for political freedom. Once the bonds of external control have been lifted, individuality will reassert itself and warmth will cool. Indeed this warmth "has never survived the hour of liberation."[58] There is no way to preserve this solidarity, claims Arendt, and it is a good thing that there is not. All attempts to preserve the (pseudo-organic) community of the oppressed lead to political authoritarianism, conformism, and intolerance of dissent. From this point of view, attacks by SNCC and black culture ideologists on "white" or "Western" or "bourgeois" forms of rationality represented more than just an assertion of new Afro-American consciousness or the desire to resurrect traditional African forms of thought and life. They were also warnings against the expression of a critical consciousness within the black community. In other words, communities in which political debate can take place are hardly compatible with communities of (erotic) solidarity. Among the oppressed *qua* oppressed, the tendency is for there to be no open, public debate, only agreement or exclusion.

What I am suggesting here via Arendt is not just another melancholy Weberian complaint about modernity's hostility to politics and the inevitability of the defeat of political solidarity by the forces of possessive individualism. No Weberian, Arendt hoped that it would be possible to establish a form of political life which was neither based on imposed solidarity nor on a political version of the "iron cage." For this she introduced the concept of "friendship" as an alternative to "fraternity" (or solidarity) to describe the ideal relationship among citizens. The purpose of law and the institutions of self-government is to preserve a space among individuals where political talk and action can be encouraged to flourish and where common interests can be achieved. But the result is something far different from Rousseau's general will, since this political space is grounded in plurality rather than unity of voices, depends upon face-to-face debate not mystical will, and is a result rather than a presupposition of the political process.[59]

Nor am I talking of something theoretical or purely utopian in nature. SNCC might have built such a political culture upon the experience of countless mass meetings held in towns and cities throughout the South in the civil rights years. Certainly Bob Moses's idea of small-group, grass-roots deliberation or the Lowndes County (Alabama) Freedom Organization would have been important touchstones of political community and political freedom. The freedom schools and SCLC's citizenship schools were also powerful models for more permanent structures of political education and mobilization. Each of these political phenomena pointed toward the development of the "habit of self-government" so important in the preservation of a space of political freedom. In such a political order, political identity or position would not be fixed once and for all. Though the decision to make policy or take action, based upon group deliberation, would presuppose some form of collective agreement, such agreement would have to be created rather than assumed. Loyalty would be to the institutions guaranteeing the space of debate and action rather than to "black people" per se whom a general will supposedly unites. This is is not to bemoan the fact, retrospectively, that exact plans or constitutions were not projected. Rather it is to regret that the political vision built upon the SNCC experience of political organizing was all but forgotten after 1965 and replaced by visions of black unity and totality.

The Band of Brothers

Though I have described the radical shift in the SNCC vision and what was lost in the process, it is still difficult to explain why, as

Vincent Harding wrote in 1968, SNCC "turned so fully from its former dreams." The dreams were not just deferred, they were disavowed. Part of the answer lies in what happened internally to SNCC as an organization between 1960 and 1966.[60]

Both SNCC's early vision of an interracial "beloved community" and its later vison of a racial totality were derived in large part from its own self-conception and the attempt, as James Forman later described it, to create in SNCC itself a model of the kind of society the SNCC workers wanted to bring into being. But the contrast between the two visions is a glaring one. In reminiscing about SNCC's early days, John Lewis compared it to a family:

> We were a circle of trust, a sort of band of brothers . . . We felt that the goal was an open community, a loving community in a redeemed society, and that the means must be in keeping with that. We felt that if the goal was integration, then we had to use an integrated means.[61]

And Forman was to remember that "our basic strength rested in the energy, love and warmth of the group." Though most of the field-workers in Mississippi, for instance, were black (35 of 41), the original commitment of SNCC to an interracial composition was clear. Writing in 1964, SNCC's first historian Howard Zinn acknowledged the tensions at work among an interracial cadre of organizers, but also optimistically (and all too prophetically) suggested that SNCC pointed the way for American society in general. Speaking in November 1963 in Mississippi, Bob Moses objected to keeping whites out of the movement: "otherwise we'll grow up and have a racist movement . . . the one thing we can do for the country that no one else can do is to be above the race issue." Thus SNCC saw itself as engaged in what Wini Breines later called "prefigurative politics."[62]

In retrospect, this prefigurative politics seems cruelly irrelevant to SNCC's fate as an organization. From embodying a vision of how society might ideally be constituted, SNCC came increasingly to reflect many of its more distressing aspects. The image of SNCC as, in Forman's words, a "band of brothers and sisters" increasingly was replaced by the realization that SNCC was a fighting unit in a "war zone." "I've heard of combat," said Fannie Lou Hamer, "but that's exactly what we was having here."[63] Along with this came mounting internal tensions over what the proper structure of the organization should be. In general, Moses and a faction called "freedom high" were opposed to discipline within SNCC or discipline exerted over the groups SNCC was organizing, while Forman became increasingly convinced that control over field-workers should be centralized in the Atlanta office. For Forman power was an undeniable fact of life; thus the uses of power had to be learned and applied. His approach increasingly emphasized the formation of a hard-core cadre and the need to "build structures" rather than depend upon "charismatic leadership" or anarchic self-direction.[64]

SNCC's most tragic figure was Moses. After the summer of 1964, Moses adopted his wife's surname "Parris" in an effort to forestall the cult of personality that had grown up around him. He withdrew from SNCC activities, broke ties with whites, and eventually spent time in Africa. At a SNCC meeting in Atlanta in 1965, Moses, in commemoration of his name change, passed around a bottle and some cheese, saying: "I want you to eat and drink." The bottle, remembered Cleveland Sellers, "was empty."[65] Lewis recalled this bizarre imitation of Christ slightly differently:

> This time this guy [Moses] stood up and took a soft drink bottle with water—he said it was wine but it was not wine—and started singing and marching around the room with a lot of people. It was like being in a revival where the minister saves the souls of the sick.
>
> He didn't want to emerge as the leader . . . He didn't want to become a symbol. He didn't want that responsibility and he felt that the only way to get away from that would be to leave.[66]

Whatever exactly happened at that meeting, Moses's behavior illustrates former SNCC worker Ivanhoe Donaldson's claim that the experience of organizing in the South "wiped out half the people who got involved . . . They went into shock . . . some of them are just barely functioning." "Look what it did to Bob Moses," suggested white SNCC worker Connie Curry, "It made him into a—it broke his heart . . . He used to get hurt every time anybody would look mean at him literally." Indeed the SNCC experience reminded Curry of the Irish proverb: "A heart broken too often turns to stone." Forman almost bled to death from an ulcer, while Stokely Carmichael had a kind of breakdown after seeing Alabama state troopers on horses "stomping on people, the troopers beating them down." Such intense pressure arose from a constant exposure to violence and from the constant temptation either to respond in kind or to cut and run. Charles Cobb recalled that "it was important for people to know that despite the physical violence . . . that we were prepared to stay and stick it out."[67]

But organizing also created the guilt of bringing down violence upon the community being organized: "It seemed," said Cobb, "as if there was some kind of relationship between your aggressiveness and the amount of terror, harassment, and so forth imposed on people who weren't directly related or involved in what you were doing." CORE's Dave Dennis also felt a version of survivor's guilt: ". . . but like as I've been cheated. I mean nothing ever happened. You begin to find that you feel guilty about it, because you want to know why him, or why her, and not me?" Of a group of freedom riders, he remembered that "they had been willing to give up their lives. . . . Now what that means and what it meant then and what does it mean to the individuals now, I don't know. But I know what I saw." Finally, Curry summed it up: "So I really do think that the toll that was taken in those early days was just tremendous . . . . those early sit-inners and SNCC people really believed that they were going to win."[68]

Making it even more difficult to maintain personal or political equilibrium was the difficulty of escaping the SNCC ethos itself. There was no time or space for a personal life independent of political identity. Cleveland Sellers claimed that during the 1960s "SNCC was my life," while John Lewis, one of the most fearless and dedicated, recalled that "for six years, 1960 to 1966, SNCC and my commitment to and involvement in the Civil Rights Movement were my life. I wasn't married; I just didn't have any outside life."[69]

If much of what I have written up to now has been in praise of the political life, these candid assessments may help bring things back into perspective. Against the unforgettable experience of participating in the political awakening of a people, this lack of personal life, the guilt of drawing suffering down on innocent people, the corrosive effect of stifled anger must be placed in the balance. Curry's two observations regarding the SNCC workers encapsulate the range of the SNCC experience: "they really believed that they were going to win" and "a heart broken too often turns to stone."

Not surprisingly, the greater the personal and organizational tensions, the more the feeling grew that "we in our own eyes became pure. The rest of the world was 'messed up' . . ." Where Mississippi had once seemed a special case, it was the SNCC view after the summer of 1964 that the Magnolia state was the nation writ small, that all America was Mississippi. Pat Watters and Reese Cleghorn described the change as follows in *Climbing Jacobs Ladder:* "What was new was the strident harshness, the racist overtones." And in *Down to Now* Watters described a "battle-weary SNCC . . . wanting to lose" with a "compulsion to prove to themselves and to others that nothing could work within the American system, the growing rationale of revolution in their minds." This new cast of mind reflected, as well as contributed to, what in Watters words became the "increasing unreality of [SNCC's] approaches to society and politics."[70]

Moreover, the more internal strife and disunity prevailed in SNCC, the more it proclaimed the unity of Afro-Americans. Indeed the more white society and culture were deemed irrelevant to the fate of black people, the more white America became an ideological obsession; the more white society was indicted for its racism, the more SNCC found black racist themes to its liking. Such denial/reversal was yet another indication that something like Kenneth Clark's thesis about the impossible demands made by non-violent direct action may have had some purchase on the truth when applied to the SNCC cadres. Indeed, the burnout, the moral and emotional exhaustion, seems to have been more widespread among SNCC workers than among SCLC leaders or, and one says this with caution, than among the Southern black population itself, the very people Clark implied were incapable of bearing such a burden. This suggests that Ellison's point about the resilience of Southern blacks has considerable merit to it. And, as already mentioned, black SNCC workers from the South and/or those possessing a religious commitment were best able to preserve their commitment to the original SNCC vision and resist the more extreme, often racist versions of black power. These workers possessed more sticking power, having been brought up in a black culture not simply of accommodation but also of flexibility, one that was more, as Ellison often said, than the sum of reactions to centuries of white oppression. Southern blacks had more experience with and, perhaps for that reason, a better grasp on the white Southerners' mentality. Black Southerners didn't expect so much so quickly and were perhaps more surprised at the amount of change that had taken place than their Northern counterparts. Thus their disillusionment and disappointment were neither so deep nor so thoroughgoing.[71]

Finally the organizational divisions within SNCC, represented broadly by Robert Moses and James Forman, were more than indices of internal tensions. They also had important theoretical implications. Indeed the dispute over whether SNCC would be a kind of launching pad, a "coordinating committee" for various decentralized local projects, or whether it should act as a leadership organization that formulated and supervised projects and exerted discipline over field-workers and affiliates echoed the history of revolutionary politics. Social theorists could recognize the *Gemeinschaft/Gesellschaft* and the charisma/routinization dichotomies, while political theorists cum historians could recognize the conflict between infantile leftism or communitarian anarchism and quasi-Leninist theories of political leadership. Indeed, for the political realist the SNCC experience seemed but another melancholic illustration of the lessons of theorists of elite hegemony such as Vilfredo Pareto.

The straightforward issue was that SNCC had placed itself in a kind of double-bind. On the one hand it wanted to be a radically different sort of political organization, an anti-organization as it were, in order to check the development of internal power struggles, bureaucratic rigidities, and authoritarian leadership. Yet it also wanted to be effective which some suggested implied unified authority within the organization. What was not clear in theory *or* in practice was that SNCC could be both. No wonder that SNCC was suspicious of its own successes, wanting at times to prove itself a failure. The contradictory impulses at the heart of its own self-conception suggested as much.

Yet the debate about the nature and purpose of SNCC was, ultimately, a debate about the nature and uses of power. Moses and Forman were in broad agreement that the essence of power was the imposition of restrictions. Where they differed was in seeing any alternative to this conception or use of power. For Moses the only legitimate power (though he probably would have resisted naming it power at all) was when plans, arrived at by people, were then put into effect by those people themselves. For Forman someone had initially to bring order to a situation, to clarify needs and goals, and then not simply throw plans out for consideration but be ready to argue for and even impose them. Indeed, for Forman, involving a community in making plans or in participating in marches was less important as a process in itself than as a "means of overcoming the lethargy and hopelessness of many black people."[72] For Moses on the other hand the whole point of participatory democracy was that the means entailed the ends, that the ways in which decisions were made determined the effects those decisions had—if you will the ends, you will the means. More generally, however, the distinction between means and ends was a pernicious one which led to manipulating people rather than enabling people to become self-determining or free.

The tragedy was that this "concluding" argument *within* SNCC was a repetition of the original challenge SNCC had presented to the dominant conception of power and politics at work within the larger society. But even more discouraging, neither Forman nor Moses won out. SNCC lost its organizational coherence *and* failed to build the grass-roots institutions to preserve the spirit of political freedom it had done so much to rekindle.

CHAPTER 7

Violence and Self-respect:
Fanon and Black Radicalism

Self-transformation and the transformation of others have constituted the radical interest in our century, whether in painting,
psychiatry or political action.

—Harold Rosenberg

It is precisely because the capacity for invention and self-
recreation is so universally held to be precious that the most
legitimately seductive arguments on behalf of war are arguments (in different guises) that war contributes to the re-
creation process.

—Elaine Scarry

The increasing attention the federal government gave to the civil
rights issue after 1954 was driven by an awareness that the way the
United States government responded to the demands of its black
citizens was closely monitored by the newly independent nations of
Asia and Africa. At the Bandung Conference in 1955, many of these
new nations formed a neutralist bloc, a *tiers monde*, jealous of its
autonomy vis-à-vis the Western or Eastern bloc alliances. To com-
pete with the Soviet Union for the support of these newly independent nations, the United States felt pressure to live up to its own
moral and constitutional values as they bore on the status of Afro-
Americans, a group which, as we have seen, seemed to be a kind of
internal colony within the United States.

Likewise, the post-1945 struggles against colonialism and efforts at
nation building had a significant effect upon the morale and vision of
the post-1954 civil rights movement. In the early days of the Mont-

gomery bus boycott, Martin Luther King noted that the "oppressed people of the world are rising up," while King's attendance at the independence ceremony in Ghana in 1957 and his visit to India late in the decade both made powerful impressions on him. Generally the importance of Gandhian *satyagraha* in the development of King's own philosophy of non-violent direct action has been amply documented.[1]

Yet the ways civil rights activists perceived the national liberation struggles in the Third World were many and various, if for no other reason than that the Third World was defined by its negative relationship to a condition that had recently been destroyed. In some parts of the Third World, such as China and Latin America, the struggle was not directed against political domination by the colonial powers so much as against powerfully entrenched indigenous economic and political interests backed by European colonial powers, the United States, and Japan.

On the other hand, much of Asia, Africa, and the Middle East had been under the direct political control of England, France, Holland, and Portugal. In these ex-colonial areas, the struggle was first political and cultural, then economic. Put another way: in many Third World countries the task was to reclaim national autonomy or to create a sense of peoplehood or nationhood more inclusive than traditional tribal or religious identities. It was in these countries in particular that what I have referred to as the "psychological" and "cultural" question was most acute.

Following from this, theorists of national liberation such as Frantz Fanon felt that true psychological liberation from colonial domination was impossible if independence was granted (as it was in some of the British and French colonies) rather than seized by armed struggle. By the 1960s national liberation struggles in Indo-China and Algeria and the successful Castro-led Cuban revolution provided the most dramatic examples of Third World self-determination and liberation. The logic of the situation seemed compelling: armed rather than non-violent struggle was necessary. And by the late 1960s, with anti-war sentiment growing rapidly in America, the position of some radicals, both white and black, was that if armed struggle were necessary in the peripheries, then the war should also be brought home to the "mother country" itself, there to re-create "one, two, . . . many Vietnams."

In what follows I want to examine SNCC's original commitment to non-violence, analyze the theory of liberation advanced by Fanon which was so at odds with non-violence, and then try to explain Fanon's appeal to black radicals in America after the mid-1960s. My claim will be that there were serious theoretical, psychological, and moral problems with Fanon's therapeutics of violence and that the Fanonist vision was particularly inappropriate in a non-colonial setting. Moreover, the reason—or at least a main reason—for Fanon's appeal to black radicals was that his vision resonated with and radicalized the search for freedom as a new sort of individual and group character, one of the crucial leitmotifs of the movement from the beginning. Such a transformational vision seemed a way out of the impasse the movement had reached by the mid-1960s.

The Turn to Violence: From Camus to Fanon

SNCC's original "statement of purpose" expressed a clear commitment to "the philosophical or religious ideal of nonviolence as the foundation of our purpose, the presupposition of our faith, and the manner of our action." It went on to contend that "love is the central motif of nonviolence" and that by "appealing to conscience and standing on the moral nature of human existence . . . reconciliation and justice become actual possibilities." Though probably more influenced by Nashville's James Lawson than Martin Luther King, SNCC's spare commitment was compatible, though not exactly identical, with King's political theology of non-violence.[2]

From the start, however, SNCC was less than unanimously committed to a specifically Christian foundation for non-violent direct action. When asked about King's position, Robert Moses suggested that "the majority of the students are not sympathetic to the idea that they have to love the white people they are struggling against . . . And there's the constant dialogue at meetings about non-violence and the meaning of nonviolence."[3] Drawing its support from many who were religiously tone-deaf, SNCC's commitment to nonviolence was as likely to reflect the secular ethics of Henry David Thoreau or Albert Camus as it was the Christian ethics of King or Gandhian *satyagraha*.

Moses for example was strongly influenced by the writings of Camus. He was particularly (and prophetically) struck by Camus's claim that those who revolted against oppression might in the process become "executioners"—in fact or in attitude—after having rebelled

successfully against their "victim" status. Somehow the back-and-
forth movement between master and slave, oppressor and oppressed, and the self-perpetuating nature of racism had to be overcome.
As Moses put it: ". . . the problem is whether . . . you can move
Negro people from the place where they are now the victims of this
kind of hatred, to a place where they don't in turn perpetuate this
hatred." Moses also subtly detached the commitment to non-violence and the refusal to hate from King's positive injunction to love
the oppressor. Camus's circumscribed ideal—"not a world in which
murder no longer exists (we are not so crazy as that!) but rather one in
which murder is not legitimate"—provided the basis, or at least one
of them, for a secular ethic of non-violence. It was not to prove as
durable as King's vision grounded in a faith and justified theologically. [4]

There were other, tactical justifications for non-violence within
SNCC and the movement generally. Beside the obvious facts that
black Americans lacked the numbers or equipment to defeat whites
and that selective violence, even in self-defense and under provocation, would likely alienate potential white support, Moses also
suggested that violence should not be encouraged due to the fact that
once the struggle was over black people had to live with white people
in the South and violence might create ineradicable barriers between
them. James Forman later reflected that non-violence had been
instrumentally important as a means to "heighten consciousness and
disrupt society," while Stokely Carmichael told Robert Penn Warren
that "I never took the approach we've got to teach [white people] to
love us. . . . But I was impressed by the way [the students engaged
in the sit-ins] conducted themselves, the way they sat there and took
the punishment." [5] Thus non-violent direct action was seen as but one
form of self-discipline and creative action; it was a valuable form of
political self-education and reflected a new attitude toward the self.
But, for many in SNCC, it was never, not at least for long, an end in
itself.

But the answer to the crucial questions at the heart of the
movement—How are the possibilities of self-respect and dignity
created?, and, What does it mean to be a free man or woman?—was
increasingly that a self-respecting person had the right and duty to
defend him/herself and his/her family. The outbreak of urban "riots"
in the summers of 1964 and 1965 suggested that the mood, at least
among Northern blacks, was no longer amenable to the ideas of non-

violence disseminated by King. For several years the influential
voice of Malcolm X had refused to eschew violence against whites, at
least in self-defense. For Malcolm and his followers, the non-violent
leadership of the black Southern ministers was part of the problem .
not the solution. It emasculated rather than empowered black men
and served only to confirm them in their impotence.

Such attitudes inevitably found welcome ears in SNCC ranks as
frustration, impatience, and anger grew apace. The psychology of the
dream deferred, of the heart too often broken, spread among SNCC
workers. In such a situation, Max Weber's coldly realistic words seem
apposite:

> Those, for example, who have just preached "love against violence"
> now call for the use of force for the *last* violent deed, which would then
> lead to a state of affairs in which *all* violence is annihilated.

To provide the theoretical justification for such a radical turn-around,
some in SNCC looked to the Martinique-born, French-educated,
Algerian revolutionary Frantz Fanon.[6]

The Fanonist Vision

Fanon's work was important in the development of black radicalism
in the 1960s not just because his work directly influenced figures such
as Carmichael and Forman (as well as the leadership nucleus of the
Black Panther Party in the San Francisco Bay area); it also revealed
the logic of the politics of self-respect, of freedom as self-transformation, pushed to its limits and gave an eloquent voice to the
psychological and cultural legacy of racial and colonial domination.
Couched in the inherently dramatic (though also difficult) idiom of
French Left-Existentialism, it drew heavily, if loosely, upon psychi-
atric and psychoanalytic theory. Indeed of all the radical theorists of
the 1960s, Fanon was far and away the most intriguing character.
Where most black American radicals lacked the training to "theorize"
domination or liberation, as opposed to articulating its effects, Fanon
demonstrated that such theoretical work could retain something of
the immediacy of both experiences and remain relevant to concrete,
popular struggles.[7]

Before focusing directly on Fanon, it is necessary to set forth
briefly what Fanon drew from Left-Existentialism. Perhaps the
single most formative influence behind this position were the lec-

tures on Hegel given in Paris between 1936 and 1939 by the Russian émigré Alexandre Kojève which many luminaries-to-be of French thought attended. Though Jean-Paul Sartre did not actually attend the lectures, the existentialist phase of his thought drew extensively on Kojève's interpretation of Hegel. Kojève's reading of Hegel took the master-slave relationship in *The Phenomenology of Spirit* as central not only to an understanding of Hegel but also to the development of a philosophical anthropology and a philosophy of history. For Kojève, the prototypical human situation involved the desire and struggle for recognition between two potentially self-conscious beings. This struggle involved a risk of life, ending with either the death of one or both combatants, in which case the struggle had been in vain, or with the capitulation of one to the other. With the latter came the origin of the categories of master and slave and hence human society. All history, contended Kojève, was therefore the "history of the working slave." But with the French Revolution and advent of Napoleon, history had come to completion, since on principle (though not yet in fact) all were recognized as equal and free in an Hegelian state.[8] After the final struggle, the slave becomes a Citizen and the "Master is simply killed, and he dies as a Master." Generally, " '[f]ellow citizens' would therefore be at the beginning identical to 'brother-in-arms.' " Thus the state, the locus of human freedom, originates in violent struggle.[9]

Presupposed in and implied by Kojève's foundational "scene" of struggle for recognition of worth, dignity, equality, and freedom—all roughly equivalent in Kojève's account—were several crucial ideas that reappear in Fanon's theory of domination and liberation. First, the basic human drive is desire for recognition from another desiring consciousness rather than the drive to make or produce (Marx), the realization of reason (orthodox Hegel), or the enjoyment of pleasure and avoidance of pain (Freud).[10] Second, risk and struggle are not biological drives or compulsions. Kojève's Hegel is not a Darwinian before the fact, for animals and humans differ to the degree that humans will risk their lives for prestige and honor, for designation by self and others as possessing a certain status and character as free beings. Thus human violence is not the result of straightforward frustration. It results from the desire for recognition and is embraced in order then to be free. This leads to a third major point—that human beings and human societies create themselves independently rather than according to some pre-ordained plan: they emerge through struggle. Mankind reaches the stage of full humanity when each recognizes the other as equal. From a retrospective point of view, history is a process of self-creation, the emergence of newness; but from a philosophical-anthropological view, history is the progressive realization of what is truly human, of what was always potentially there within and between self-conscious beings—freedom and mutual recognition.

The other theoretical tradition Fanon drew most heavily upon was modern depth psychology. As a psychiatrist (though not a trained psychoanalyst), Fanon conceptualized the relationship between individual and social self-consciousness, particularly between black French colonials and the colonial domination which played such a large part in determining their self-conception.[11] Thus in his first book, *Black Skin, White Masks* (1952), Fanon explored the social aetiology of individual psychic disturbance. Though Fanon occasionally cited Freud and Jung, he objected to what he considered Freud's too exclusively intrapsychic focus and Jung's essentialist concept of a collective unconscious. Rather he was drawn toward something closer to Alfred Adler's (psychoanalytically) heretical belief in the primacy of the ego-instincts and the centrality of the inferiority complex. Indeed Kojeve's Left-Hegelianism, its rearticulation by Sartre and incorporation by psychoanalyst Jacques Lacan in his now famous theory of the "mirror stage" comported quite well, as Fanon recognized, with an Adlerian orientation. Both the Hegelian tradition and the Adlerian position stressed the centrality of power and prestige in understanding conscious and unconscious motivations behind actions. In both traditions, the problem of self-identity—whose origins Lacan located in the "imaginary" register and grounded in a primordial mutual misrecognition—was central.

Indeed, Lacan served as an important theoretical bridge between psychoanalytic theory and a role psychology Fanon needed to analyze the complex interrelationships between colonizer and colonized, white and black, in the colonial setting. Fanon noted in *Black Skin* that Lacan's mirror stage made it clear that for whites "the real Other" is the black man "and conversely." But the Hegelian dialectic of recognition and misrecognition becomes rigidified into a dualism of opposites, since whites perceive blacks as purely "body image" rather than as a form of self-consciousness and for "the black man . . . historical and economic realities come into the picture." That is, black people are not even misrecognized by whites but are seen as natural resources or impulse centers. From the white point of view, blacks hardly enter into the dialectic of self-consciousness with whites at all: "what [the white man] wants from the slave is not recognition but work." And for blacks, domination is not only physical and economic; it is psychological and linguistic. How whites talk about and represent blacks decisively shapes how blacks represent themselves to themselves. What Fanon wanted to show in *Black Skin* was the way black people in the colonial setting could come to recognize themselves as having been (mis)-recognized historically by whites.[12]

But Fanon was also bent on undermining the structures and psychology of colonial/racial domination. In other words his original and fundamental "project" was to "cure" social, political, and cultural domination. Fanon set forth his political-cultural diagnosis most succinctly near the end of *Black Skin* when he wrote:

> Historically the Negro steeped in the inessentiality of servitude was set free by his master. He did not fight for his freedom . . . He went from one way of life to another, but not from one life to another.[13]

Though Fanon was adverting specifically to the experience of the Afro-Caribbeans, his more general claim was that freedom is won only through the (Hegelian) risk of life. The only thing the master can give the slave is negative political and legal freedom, freedom as equal status in relationship to the law. He cannot give the slave a new sense of self, for that must be chosen or created rather than accepted from those holding power.

More generally, Fanon's position in the early 1950s was that a change in the sense of self had to precede action. Specifically as a psychiatrist, he wrote that:

> my objective, once [the patient's] motivations have been brought into consciousness, will be to put him in a position to *choose* action (or passivity) with respect to the real source of the conflict—that is, toward the social structures.[14]

In moral and philosophical terms this would mean:

> To educate man to be *actional*, preserving in all his relations his respect for the basic values that constitute a human world, is the prime task of him who, having taken thought, prepares to act.[15]

To be human for Fanon, then, was to live in a world in which one was recognized as a subject and in which that recognition had been won through struggle with the other and within oneself. Such was the basis of his radical humanism, which however we judge its possibility, deserves better than the description afforded it by Homi Bhabha: a "simple, sentimental promise of a humanistic 'world of the You.'"[16]

But how could a colonial revolution succeed? In terms of political strategy, Fanon agreed with other contemporary theorists of armed struggle such as Che Guevara in rejecting both nationalist and/or Communist parties as captives of the status quo. Too timid to initiate colonial uprisings, nationalist parties were captured by and/or tended to speak for a new national bourgeoisie after the revolution had been successful. They merely replaced colonial domination with their own indigenous form of domination. Fanon distanced himself from orthodox Marxists by rejecting the colonial industrial and urban working class as the carriers of the revolution. Not only few in number, this proletariat was privileged and "pampered" rather than radically oppressed. Instead Fanon, like Mikhail Bakunin almost a century before in Russia, then Europe's Third World, looked both to the peasantry and to the uprooted peasantry come to the cities as the twin pillars of the revolution. The former would supply the discipline; the latter, the energy and anger. In this projected alliance, the traditional hostility between the city and the countryside would be overcome.[17]

A second, essential element in the creation of a successful revolution was, according to Fanon, the creation of a revolutionary culture. Not only did Fanon reject the Marxist theory of the vanguard role of the party or of the proletariat, he also rejected racial or tribal conceptions of culture grounded in the glories of a unified African past. Though strongly influenced by the theory and poetics of Negritude in the late 1940s, Fanon came to see that Negritude was valuable only insofar as it called into question the primacy of the metropolitan European culture. But, as what Patrick Taylor has called an "abstract populism," Negritude offered no viable basis for a cultural politics.[18] African culture was no more a "real" thing because African people asserted it than it was a badge of inferiority because Europeans so considered it.

Similarly, in his writings on Algeria, Fanon stressed the way individual and social relations—doctor/patient, parent/child, brother/sister, husband/wife—were transformed in and by the struggle for liberation. Because the older culture had become "closed, fixed in the colonial status" and had undergone "cultural mummification," it was of little use as the basis for a revolutionary culture. Nor was any form of theocratic-religious state the answer.[19] What was needed was a "national culture . . . a fighting literature, a revolutionary literature, and a national literature":

> the whole body of efforts made by a people in the sphere of thought to describe, justify and praise the action through which the people has created itself and keeps itself in existence.[20]

Authentic culture, along with the new revolutionary self, was created in and by the struggle not inherited and preserved inviolate against outside forces.

But finally even national consciousness/culture was not enough for Fanon: "Nationalism is not a political doctrine, nor a programme . . . a rapid step must be taken from national to political and social consciousness . . . in other words into humanism."[21] Unlike the corrupt European form of humanism which justified racism even as it advocated universal values, a contradiction embodied in the teaching of Enlightenment values in colonial schools, the new revolutionary humanism would speak without incoherence or self-contradiction.

Though his theory of revolutionary politics and culture was part of an emerging post-Marxist revolutionary consensus during the 1960s, Fanon added a more controversial—and by now notorious—element to his theory: the centrality of violence in the recasting of the psyche of the colonized. "Concerning Violence," the first chapter of *The Wretched of the Earth*, set forth the issue without equivocation. The "settler . . . brought the native into existence." The result is a "Manichean" stand-off between the two worlds of the colonizer and the colonized. If "decolonization is quite simply the replacing of a certain 'species' of men by another 'species' of men," then colonial domination can only be "called into question by absolute violence." The "nationalist reformist" position which advocates non-violence and "bring[s] pressure to bear on the forces of colonialism and . . . allow[s] the people to work off their energy" must be abandoned as a kind of "therapy by hibernation."[22]

Fanon then proceeded to analyze the functions of violence in the colonial setting. When directed against the indigenous population, as it had been at Sharpeville in 1960, it illuminated the situation in South Africa for the outside world and may even have put pressure on the superpowers to respond for the sake of their own prestige and image. Moreover, the use of violence against the colonizers represented an "ironic turning of the tables," since now the colonizer appears as the one who only understands the language of violence. And of course violence was of use in achieving specific objectives.[23]

There was nothing unusual in such considerations concerning violence. What was unusual was the way Fanon assigned violence a value beyond these concerns. For Fanon went on to assert that violence was

> a royal pardon. The colonised man finds his freedom in and through violence. This rule of conduct enlightens the agent because it indicates to him the means and the end.

More pointedly, violence creates solidarity among its perpetrators; it "invests their characters [those under colonial rule] with positive and creative qualities . . . bands them together as a whole . . . mobilises the people."[24] Finally:

> At the level of individuals, violence is a cleansing force. It frees the native from his inferiority complex and from his despair and inaction; it makes him fearless and restores his self-respect.[25]

Thus in *Wretched* Fanon reversed the sequential and causal relationship between therapy and action. In *Black Skin* therapy was a preparation for action; in *Wretched* action became therapeutic in and of itself. In sum, then, Fanon was claiming that violence had an "internal," positive, and therapeutic effect on those who wielded it. It purged the colonized of their old self-conceptions and indicated a willingness to act with others. The "new man" is the man of violence against the oppressor.

American Reception and Influence

It is difficult to gauge the precise influence of Fanon on SNCC and black radical groups such as the Black Panther Party with whom some SNCC leaders struck up a short-lived alliance in early 1968. After *Wretched* appeared in English in 1965, it circulated among SNCC workers. James Forman struck a defiantly Fanonist note in his autobiography when he wrote that "only violence can totally free a colonized people." Panther defense minister Huey P. Newton grouped Fanon with Mao and Che Guevara as major influences on his thinking. Newton himself was introduced to Fanon's work by Bobby Seale who had allegedly read *Wretched* six times. Eldridge Cleaver also testified to the popularity of Fanon among black prison inmates and referred to *Wretched* as "the Bible" of black militancy. Indeed, one black journalist reported of young black rioters that "No one of them hasn't read the Bible . . . Fanon . . . you'd better get this book. Every brother on a rooftop can quote Fanon."[26]

There were several ironies at work in Fanon's influence on black radicals. First, both Martin Luther King and Fanon had incorporated considerable amounts of Hegel in their visions of politics, yet King had of course separated the struggle for recognition from the use of violence. Second, whereas Camus, the Algerian *pied noir* who had attempted to remain neutral during the Algerian War, provided much of the ethical grounding for SNCC's early position on non-violence, Fanon, who had forged his theory of therapeutic violence while working with Algerians against the French, influenced SNCC's later shift toward militancy. Fanon explicitly rejected Camusian efforts at neutrality, a prime example, he felt, of the failure of the French and European Left to shake off the colonialist legacy.

Moreover, in both *Black Skin* and in *Wretched*, Fanon suggested that the situation of blacks in the United States was not comparable to the situation of the colonized in a genuine colony. In the former, civil rights were legally established (even if not enforced) and whites recognized blacks to the point of being obsessed with them. Indeed whites sometimes aided blacks in their struggle. By contrast what Fanon found so debilitating about the colonial situation was the invisibility of blacks. It was not so much that they were misrecognized as that they were not recognized at all. At best they were seen as French men and women with black skins and at worst, as already mentioned, as natural resource-beings. Beside that, as Fanon emphasized in his last work, "every culture is first and foremost national" and thus the methods appropriate in North Africa or the West Indies might not be apposite in the United States.[27] Thus ironically Fanon provided the materials, albeit in fragmentary form, to undermine rather than to support the colonial analogy and use of violent struggle by black Americans.

Yet Fanon's writings did find strong echoes in the experience of SNCC in the South and with militants in the Northern and Western ghettoes. By 1967 SNCC workers were traveling throughout the Third World and making contacts with radicals and liberation movements there. Cleveland Sellers went to Japan; Julius Lester and Charles Cobb to Vietnam; Courtland Cox to the War Crimes Tribunal; Carmichael to Cuba and elsewhere; and Howard Moore and Forman to Zambia. Representatives were sent to the UN and SNCC took a position in support of the Palestine Liberation Organization in 1967, a move which exacerbated the growing estrangement of liberal and Jewish support from the movement. In a SNCC pamphlet, Forman asserted that the struggle for black liberation in America was "indivisible" from the rest of the world because "We are a colonized people in the United States . . . suffering from a white Western racism which can never be eliminated under capitalism."[28]

Similarly Carmichael sounded more radical when he addressed a conference in Havana in 1967 than he had in *Black Power:* "Our world can only be the Third World; our only struggle, for the Third World; our only vision, of the Third World." Such a pronouncement did not presuppose or point to Marxian class conflict between bourgeoisie and proletariat but a conflict between the proletarian societies of the Third World and the affluent white societies of the First and Second Worlds. Though Carmichael contended that black people were "a colony within the U.S.," he granted that it was not "possible to take over the entire country militarily and hold large areas of land." Black radicals could only constitute a "disruptive force" within the country, a point of view ratified by the Black Panthers whose basic premise was that the conflict within the United States was between the "black colony" and the "white mother country."[29]

SNCC radicals found Fanon's attacks on established radical parties and reformist groups very much to their liking. Fanon's caustic claim that non-violence was a diversionary release of energy, along with his secular vision, undoubtedly reenforced their deep scepticism regarding Martin Luther King. Indeed as SNCC looked north and west to the ghettos, melding into a loose alliance with the Black Panthers, they increasingly depended upon (some) students, unemployed youths, and the lumpenproletariat in general rather than the black working class or the black farmers and middle class in the South. Ex-prisoners turned writers, including Malcolm X and Cleaver (and later Huey Newton, Bobby Seale, and George Jackson), and the leadership of the Black Panther Party itself seemed to confirm the radical potential of a black urban underclass.

But it should be noted that the black radical analysis ignored the importance Fanon placed upon the "peasantry," while enthusi-astically embracing his championing of the lumpenproletariat. An-other area where SNCC and the Panthers tended to ignore Fanon was in their emphasis upon an explicitly black radicalism as opposed to the revolutionary populism Fanon advocated and the "blind alley" he felt "Negro-ism" and the "racialis[ing]" of culture to be.[30] The Panthers did eschew romanticizing things like "soul food" and had major confrontations with "pork chop nationalists." But though they did not forego white alliances, the Party's ethos was inevitably strongly black and hostile to whites.

If Fanon's analysis of the colonial world influenced black radicalism in America, the impact of his theory of violence was as pervasive but harder to pinpoint. It takes no complex theory of dialectics to see that a people whose very existence under and after slavery was permeated by violence might adopt it as a kind of antidote or countersolution to the violence inflicted upon them. As Elaine Scarry has suggested (in another context):

> If self-hatred, self-alienation, and self-betrayal . . . were translated out of the psychological realm where it has content and is accessible to language into the unspeakable and contentless realm of physical sensa-tion it would be intense pain.[31]

To be free of psychological and physical pain, an individual or group may choose to reciprocate against those who have caused it.

Historically considered, the apotheosis of violence is by no means foreign in the annals of revolutionary struggle, even in America. As we have seen, Frederick Douglass was eager that black men demon-strate their manhood and patriotism by fighting for their freedom in the Civil War. Such reasoning was expressed with heavy sarcasm by a character—a Native American as it happens—in Martin Delany's *Blake: or The Huts of America:* "If you want white men to love you, you must fight im!" Such a political justification of violence, echoed in the republican notion of *virtu* as the necessary virtue of all (male) citizens, has also been accompanied by a religious hallowing of violence in the cause of freedom. Many Abolitionists accepted what Lawrence Friedman refers to as John Brown's "righteous violence" as expressed in his "Without the shedding of blood there can be no remission of sins."[32] For them violence was not just an instrument for achieving certain concrete and limited goals but it took on a religious, even redemptive function. Indeed President Lincoln was known to connect the shedding of blood with the hallowing of the Union's cause, though he, like Martin Luther King over a century later, was willing to offer his own life as well as someone else's for the larger cause of freedom. Finally in modern writing, the role that violence plays in imparting meaning to the life of Richard Wright's Bigger Thomas or its evocation in the early plays of Amiri Baraka (Leroi Jones) or Norman Mailer's flirtation with the meaning-giving capacity of violence indicates the creative power and almost religious charge that some types of violence are sometimes taken to possess.

Yet Fanon's therapeutics of violence seemed different somehow. Though its resonance undoubtedly owed something to the human desire for revenge, to the [male] tradition of risking one's life to show one's honor and worth, and to the quasi-religious tradition of redemption of some larger cause by dying for it, this was not the whole story. Nor could it be said only to appeal to the insulted and injured, the social outcasts and the rejected. William Grier and Price Cobb's *Black Rage* (1968) suggested that the black bourgeoisie was just as devastated by the corrosive effects of suppressed anger as their less fortunate counterparts in the ghettos. Thus Fanon's appeal was not simply a function of class and status; indeed his ideas appealed to black people with intellectual interests or pretensions, whatever their class origins. [33]

Finally, it is not correct to say that Fanon made violence an end in itself, since he still conceived of it in instrumental terms. But it was his emphasis upon the internal, transformational effects of violence, violence as a way of changing one's self-image, that made Fanon's thoughts on violence so distinctive. When positively valorized, using violence is normally considered a sign of an existing desire or motive (such as revenge) or of a quality (such as courage). But for Fanon the use of violence was a way of bringing a new state of mind into existence; it was not a way of demonstrating the existence of a quality or virtue, but the very means of engendering it. Finally, Fanon advanced a political/psychological thesis on the way to becoming a religious vision, a form of therapy metamorphizing into a redemptive politics, what Marie Perinbam has referred to as "holy violence." [34]

Assessment

How then can we evaluate Fanon's therapeutics of violence? Several related matters should be established as a way of both framing and leading into the discussion. First, in certain contexts violence is neither irrational, inhuman, or ineffective. When applied in self-defense or in certain sorts of revolutionary situations or in a "just" war, violence can and does accomplish its purposes, notwithstanding the cliche to the contrary that "violence never solves anything." Collective violence can on certain occasions be defended as a way of rectifying injustice, since, as Barrington Moore has written, "the costs of moderation have been at least as atrocious as those of revolution, perhaps a great deal more." And Scarry has also identified violence as one way of demonstrating the "capacity of a people to substantiate . . . its own beliefs, its own territorial and ideological self-definition." Indeed, it has even been used as a measure of a people's "capacity for self-renewal or self-recreation." Only when the application of violence is incommensurable with or inappropriate to the ends pursued, assuming those ends are justifiable, does violence become irrational (as opposed to moral/immoral). These are hard and difficult truths which analysts of violence and war have forced us to confront, for unless we do so, we will never figure out different, less costly ways to "substantiate" our values and positions or to engage in "self-renewal." Thus violence is not somehow more or less "human" than non-violence.[35]

Nor is there much to be gained from explaining human violence by positing natural propensities.[36] Human violence is by definition mediated by processes of thought and imagination, embodied in symbol and instrument, and multitudinous in form. Human beings give themselves reasons for their actions, as well as being subject to causal forces, and these reasons (values, beliefs, ideologies, etc.) play an important motivating role themselves. Indeed Fanon's therapeutics of violence implicitly acknowledges this, since what is at issue for the colonized is not literal survival, but dignity, prestige, and self-respect. Thus violence is not somehow more "natural" than non-violence.

Similarly, the attractions of violence and emotions associated with it should not be dismissed as simply pathological. As J. Glenn Gray has testified, in combat situations there may be a (welcome) loss of individuality, a sense of merging into one unit of solidarity and comradeship (as opposed to friendship), and, even more ominously, a delight in destruction. This solidarity in which "I" is replaced with "we" can also mean, claims Gray, that "dying has lost its terrors."[37] On this point Fanon and some of his defenders can be criticized, for, as Eugene Genovese has emphasized, violence must be "collective and disciplined—that is, political—but then it is precisely the collective effort, not the violence, that does the healing." Indeed Marie Perinbam's defense of Fanon's advocacy of "holy violence," which she sees as a powerfully sublime spirit of "release and creation," is really a defense of the effects of collective action upon individual and social spirit, behavior and self-image, rather than the effect of violence per se. In other words, Perinbam can defend this encompassing form of violence precisely because she includes in its definition and effects those beneficial qualities which collective action, whether violent or not, may produce.[38] Fanon was certainly aware of the importance of collective action in the creation of new forms of cultural and political life, but there is no doubt that violence was the critical ingredient in their production.

Granting all this, are there any moral objections to violence—as opposed to judgments of efficacy—to be raised against Fanon's position? Indeed the effect of Fanon's transvaluation of values, of his refusal not just to condemn violence—unless we are absolute pacifists, there are circumstances in which we all, even if grudgingly, accept violence as an option in certain situations—but to identify the use of violence with the creation of a free self, a "new man," makes conventional judgments about violence seem flatfooted. Though Jean-Paul Sartre's prefatory comments to *The Wretched of the Earth* bring to mind George Orwell's charge from the 1930s that W. H. Auden was always somewhere else when the trigger was pulled, Sartre does foreground with blood-chilling acuity the reversal of values implied in Fanon's writing:

> The rebel's weapon is the proof of his humanity. For in the days of the revolt you must kill: to shoot down a European is to kill two birds with one stone, to destroy an oppressor and the man he oppresses at the same time: there remains a dead man, and a free man.[39]

Or at least such a reversal of values is advocated in *Wretched*. In *A Dying Colonialism*, compiled from his journalism of the late 1950s, Fanon discussed voilence with less *sang-froid:*

> The Algerian leaders who, in view of the intensity of the repression and the frenzied character of the oppression, thought they could answer the blows received without any serious problems of conscience, discovered that the most horrible crimes do not constitute a sufficient excuse for certain decisions.[40]

Why *did* the Algerian leaders feel pangs of conscience and why are the cold-bloodedness of the later Fanon and the verbal enthusiasm for violence expressed by SNCC leaders and various Panther spokesmen so disturbing? Does the fact that violence is generally interdicted mean that it is always accompanied by guilt and ambivalence, even when it can perhaps be justified? One might posit, as did Rousseau, an innate sentiment of pity toward creatures in pain and by extension an innate reluctance to inflict pain. Something like it, now given a Darwinian gloss, might provide the basis for a natural repugnance toward murder and torture. Yet, appeals to nature are dubious and our attitude toward violence seems most powerfully determined by what our culture tells us it should be; indeed Rousseau granted that his postulated sentiment of pity was all but absent in civilized life. Moreover, the cancerous proliferation of ideological torture and its justification in this century suggests the relative ease with which we can overcome our repugnance toward violence. Perhaps the only "advance" now is that torture is carried on away from the public view. It is incidentally no answer to attribute the resurgence of violence to the decline of religion: torture was morally and legally justified throughout the "Christian" world well into the nineteenth century.[41]

One secular answer to the question of why violence is wrong and/or why we are made queasy by its justifications is a Kantian one. In this view, violence represents the paradigmatic case of objectifying another consciousness, of turning a subject into an object. But to use the language of subject and object suggests another quite different sort of violence (as well as constituting a reminder that violence is not a unitary thing at all)—violence whose aim is to inflict pain upon a person just because she or he *is* a subject, that is, torture. For torture depends on the assumption that physical pain and the fear accompanying it are only effective if the "object" of the violence not only registers but also recognizes what the agent is doing to him or her. Rocks cannot be tortured; and there seems little point to torturing a tree or even an animal (though there are pathologies whose symptoms include inflicting pain on animals). But it is precisely the point of torture that it has a point—to be recognized as having absolute control, a kind of micro-totalitarianism. The torturer wants the person being tortured to recognize him or her and also, as Scarry has suggested, to render the person being tortured mute and dispossess him or her of a world. The torturer tries to produce not an object but an objectified subject, the modern equivalent of the idea of the slave.[42]

The reason for raising the matter of torture is that though Fanon did not discuss torture inflicted by Algerian freedom fighters, his justification of violence presents no obstacle to justifying torture or any other form of violence. Moreover, inflicting violence becomes "legitimate," not because of what it does to the enemy and his or her capacities, but because of what it does to the colonized who embraces it. What is therapeutic or cathartic—"cleansing" in his words—are its effects on those who engage in it. Though apparently not under the influence of Fanon at the time, Eldridge Cleaver's decision to rape white women as an "insurrectionary" act, after first practicing on black women, illustrates the solipsistic nature—whether taken individually or collectively—of this sort of violence. But such violence solidifies rather than undermines what Fanon referred to as the morally narcissistic worlds of colonizer and colonized, white and black, so convincingly delineated in *Black Skin*.[43]

This in turn suggests that the world which Fanon's theory proposes is profoundly dualistic rather than dialectical; it reflects the Manichean reality, rather than attempting to point out the falsity of such a split vision. As David Caute has noted, Fanon's analysis tends, despite its theoretical provenance, to essentialize the categories of colonizer and colonized and thus assume that they are without self-division. At issue here is not some putative failure on Fanon's part to assert that because colonizer and colonized are both human their conflict can be easily resolved—or resolved at all. Rather Fanon sets up the relationship between settler and native (colonizer and colonized, white and black) in a way that makes it conceptually impossible to recognize the ways in which native influenced settler and vice-versa and to understand that in some respects they have internalized aspects of each other. Thus he finds it hard to explain how the pair remain interrelated even after the end of colonial rule. "The colonized," wrote Albert Memmi in reference to Fanon's work, "lives on in the decolonized man."[44] The reverse, it should be added, is also true.

Indeed Kojeve had already raised the question of what happens after the Master is killed but "dies as a Master." If this happens, the Slave never receives recognition as an equal from the Master and "Hegel does not explain how a Master can be recognized by another Master . . . One could, however, allow that the state is born from the mutual recognition of the victors of a collective fight for recognition."[45] But it might also be argued that the vision of final mutual recognition is utopian, since there is no reason that, lacking the full recognition from dead Masters, the new Masters should not perpetuate instead of transcend the master/slave relationship in their endless quest for recognition. Such, it might be suggested, may be the theoretical logic underlying post-revolutionary authoritarian regimes that stifle internal dissolution by creating an "other" as a threat. Thus the assumptions underlying Fanon's theory of violence suggest a perpetuation rather than supersession of the system of domination.

Put another way, there is no theoretically or existentially convincing way to say when enough is enough. This lack of a check on the momentum of violence is revealed in Patrick Taylor's sympathetic gloss on Fanon:

> The act of killing the colonizer is not in itself liberating . . . the consciousness of freedom that comes with the killing of the tyrant within, rather than violent action, is what constitutes revolutionary activity.[46]

The problem with such a sympathetic reading is that it makes Fanon's advocacy of violence seem either morally dubious, since there may be other ways to "kill the tyrant within" than killing the tyrant "without"; or, by locating the crucial killing as an internal psychological act, it offers no way of developing shared criteria for determining when enough (quantitatively) is enough (qualitatively). In reading Fanon in this more nuanced way, Taylor augments rather than diminishes the potential murderousness of Fanon's vision of psychic self-healing, in whose name anything is permitted.

These moral and conceptual issues aside, is Fanon's description/ prediction of the psychological effects of exercising revolutionary violence plausible? Though not addressing the issue of the therapeutic effects of violence as such, there is some evidence that there are decreases in certain indicators of social pathology during times of collective protest. (There also may have been a decline in gang organizations in the 1960s in American cities.) In *A Dying Colonialism* Fanon described some of the crucial changes in the family and in the relationship between the sexes during the Algerian War. But there is little evidence that the "new" men and women of the revolution endured for any length of time after the French had departed. Perinbam suggests that Fanon never claimed that the changes wrought by "holy violence" would be permanent; but this seems a damaging concession given the redemptive significance Fanon attributes to violence in *Wretched*.[47] Finally, though it constitutes little more than anecdotal evidence, the last chapter of *Wretched*, entitled "Colonial War and Mental Disorders," includes cases of "reactionary" (i.e., reactive) psychoses in Algerians who had engaged in violence against the French colonizers. This suggests provisionally that Fanon's own evidence fails to support the claims for the therapeutic effects of violence.

Part of the problem is that, though talk of the "new" man (and woman) was common in (cultural) rhetoric of the 1960s, it was never really clear what this idea meant (as opposed to specific, relatively modest transformations such as the acquisition of self-respect). Leaving aside relationships with former colonizers—or in America with white people—relatively little attention was devoted to what a "new" culture might imply about social structures, including family relationships and relations between the sexes; economic systems, including attitudes toward work and money; and politics, including the mechanisms for and extent of participation. In all these spheres, the radical alternative tended to be the inverse of existing arrangements, with a vague commitment to socialism often thrown in for good measure. The culture and society of liberation tended to be the mirror image of the old one and thus still conceptually linked to it. The notion of a total transformation of human nature was and remains essentially religious, one whose fulfillment was to come through perpetual political and military mobilization. One can only agree with Eugene and Elizabeth Fox-Genovese that the "new" man and woman were "an impossibility and therefore an unworthy aim."[48]

Specifically, the vision of the family and the relationship between men and women articulated by American black male radicals such as Malcolm X or Cleaver was literally and psychologically reactionary, anything but new in substantive terms. They projected a revision/ reversion of things toward some imaginary past period of patriarchal control, while the male, phallocentric cast of black self-respect itself became increasingly explicit. Self-respect and pride were increasingly synonymous with the achievement of "manhood" and the ability to intimidate. Eldridge Cleaver's embarrassingly cloying and kitschy "To All Black Women, From All Black Men" was the least obviously chauvinistic of the black radical versions of what the new relationship between black men and women was to be. Indeed nothing better illustrated Fanon's warning about the reactionary dangers of getting stuck at the level of "blackness" and infatuation with some imaginary notion of past cultural wholeness. White patriarchal domination was to be destroyed, only to be replaced by the "fraternal" contract among (generally male) revolutionaries who then would reestablish black male patriarchy of sorts.[49]

Thus a cultural conservative such as Philip Rieff had a strong point when he heaped scorn on "rapists grown didactic," an obvious reference to Cleaver. Indeed Rieff refused to take black power seriously as long as its ideal typical figure was "Caliban" or "Supernigger" rather than, say, W. E. B. DuBois or even Fanon himself. What Rieff foresaw was neither a traditional nor radical but a barbaric anticultural vision in which the "personification of freedom, for the race therapists as for the racists, remains the black transgressive."[50] The "best" of the new black culture looked distressingly like the worst of the old white one.

Indeed the extreme black radical scenarios in America lent credence to the charge that certain forms of 1960s radicalism were closer to fascism than socialism. The apotheosis of violence and redemption through the gun, the emphasis upon a return to an earlier form of cultural simplicity, the anti-intellectualism and fear of criticism, the excessive appeals to masculinity and heterosexuality, the propensity toward racial explanations and the cult of personality all were disturbing, even if not fascist in the technical sense of the term. Again, the parallels with the fringes of nineteenth-century Russian radical anarchism or with left-wing Peronism seem unmistakable.[51]

One way to suggest the complexity of the situation to which Fanon's powerful simplicities were taken to be an answer is to ask if the culture of the colonized or of American black people was as uniform and unvariegated as American devotees of Fanon suggested? Since the 1960s, studies of Afro-American culture during and after slavery have emphasized the degree to which that culture was not just a deviation from or inferior version of the dominant white society. The culture and institutions of slaves were not totally permeated by the power and values of the slave-owning class. Indeed the slave population, and by extension black American society, was and is divided along class, status, and regional lines. But if this was even roughly the case for a slave population and for a black minority culture after slavery, it would seem to follow that neither post-World

War II Afro-Americans nor colonized populations in the Third World could be understood solely in terms of their condition as oppressed people living in a "mummified" culture. Ralph Ellison's question, "can a people . . . live and develop for over three hundred years simply by *reacting?*" answers itself in the negative.[52]

Fanon's great theoretical mistake was to follow too closely Sartre's essential thesis in *Anti-Semite and Jew* that "the Jew is one whom other men consider a Jew." As Fanon wrote at the beginning of *Wretched*, "it is the settler who has brought the native into existence and who perpetuates his existence."[53] And his starting point in *Black Skin* had been, as Chester Fontenot suggests, to assume that to accept and use the colonizer's language was to become part of his/her world, denuded of any other resources. Or so it seemed. On one level, Fanon was making a point about power and self-image in a particularly dramatic way. But he did neglect the positive aspects of the fact that there was a way of life, a culture as it were, in place when the colonizer first arrived. This is not to imply that pre-colonial cultures, south or north of the Sahara, are somehow "original" or unitary, for they too have a history. It is to suggest that Fanon almost totally ignored the creative importance of Islam in Algeria, a culture older than the European one which came to dominate it. Put another way, the settler may bring the native into existence, but neither figure's identity is exhausted by the category "settler" or "native," "colonizer" or "colonized." The point about the Hegelian or DuBoisian notion of "double consciousness" is that it is "double" not unitary.[54]

Indeed, Fanon's version of the dominated consciousness of the colonized bore more than passing resemblance to Stanley Elkins' "Sambo" and certainly Fanon's *oeuvre* constituted a major contribution to what Elkins has referred to as the "literature of damage" concerning the way of life of dominated peoples. Fanon would certainly have taken exception to the spirit of Orlando Patterson's claim that "there is absolutely no evidence from the long and dismal annals of slavery to suggest that any group of slaves ever internalized the conception of degradation held by their master."[55] Where Fanon differed from Elkins was in reasoning that if domination were the all-pervading fact of black life and culture, then the only answer was *the* ultimate one: a fight to the death, since compromise and reform would only further confirm the domination.

More generally, Fanon's example suggests that the type of analysis

Elkins advanced of the black American experience need not have conservative implications or be seen as a counsel of despair. The mistake of Elkins and Fanon lay not in assuming some degree of internalization and psychological-cultural deformation in the oppressed but in attributing too much undiluted power to the oppressor and placing him/her too much at the center of the focus. It is not just that the oppressor is not essentially superior; it is also that the oppressor is not responsible for everything in and about the world of the oppressed. Put more generally: the total domination thesis of Elkins and Fanon makes it imperative to think about radical change, yet also makes it much more difficult to imagine from where the impetus for such change might come.

On the other hand, emphasizing diversity within a colonized population or emphasizing the pluralist nature of black American culture is not without its problems. Though the structures of domination may be more loosely jointed than Fanon's analysis allows, for that reason the lives of those living under domination may also be harder to change in one uniform direction. As we have seen, many black women in the South engaged in political action for the first time during the movement days. Yet their traditional role in the family was maintained. Similarly, black men made no automatic connection between their new sense of empowerment and the need to consider the changing role of black women in the family, the community, or the civil rights movement itself. As already pointed out in connection with black radicals, emphasis upon self-respect and assertion can easily become identified as a peculiarly *male* need or prerogative, since one indication of the alleged impotence of black men is the amount of independence and "voice" black women allegedly have.

A final way of critiquing Fanon's therapeutics of violence is to explore the contradictions between the models of the psyche implicit in his analysis. Despite his experience in psychiatry and perhaps because of the overwhelming emphasis he placed on social and cultural forces in the shaping of individual personality, Fanon offered no explicit theory or model of psychic functioning. His central claim that "violence is a cleansing force . . . [which] makes [the individual] fearless and restores his self-respect" indicated that Fanon was working with two incompatible models of the psyche. The "cleansing" metaphor sees the essential effect of action as quantitative, similar to the view of repression as a damming-up whose negative effects can be eradicated by removing that which hinders action or by applying a "cleansing force" to expunge something. But his other model is that of the psyche as a producer and repository of meanings and images rather than the site of the clash of forces. From the point of view of the "meaning" model, the problem is not just or primarily that the energies or actions of the colonized are repressed but that their self-image is a deformed and negative one. The goal becomes one of replacing one meaning with another, of destroying an old identity and creating a new one through action.

This is far from an irrelevant quibble. The quantitative model having to do with unblocking and cleansing suggests that cure for psychological domination can be achieved through a cathartic action alone, while the qualitatively tinged trope of self-respect suggests that a new self-understanding is necessary as well. If we take the psychoanalytic cure as a kind of simulacrum (not instrument) for the creation of this new self-understanding, we see that it is not concerned with releasing frustrations per se, but with reclaiming and reexperiencing, understanding and then working through, the reasons for and causes of existing repressions and resistances. Patrick Taylor is correct—an individual or group self-image is not changed simply by action, since to claim so begs the question of what image informs that action and more importantly because simply acting to lift a repression tends to assume that it is possible to restore the original object of desire. Seen from this perspective, the self-image or *imago* of the colonized is grounded in unconscious processes and structures internalized from the colonizer's world. So far Fanon would have agreed. But this self-image must be raised to awareness and worked through experientially and verbally rather than just "acted out." By itself acting out tends to repeat by reversal (from passive to active slave) rather than through a transcending act of learning (passive slave to active subject.)

This is not to say, moving back to the political realm, that literally defeating the oppressor makes no psychological difference to the oppressed. But it probably doesn't make all the difference and, as suggested above, may not be central to therapeutic action at all. In a strange way, Fanon was too optimistic and underestimated the powerful hold that unconscious images had on individual and collective self-conception. He might have emphasized much more strongly that the "cleansing" was only barely started by the revolutionary action itself and had to be pursued in a long process of rethinking the relationship of the individual and the community after the oppressor was out of the picture. The proper model was neither therapeutic nor transformational but pedagogic. Unfortunately, Fanon only touched on it at the end of *Wretched*.

Two Theories of Action: Fanon and Arendt

It remains finally to evaluate Fanon's theory of political action in relation to Arendt's vision of politics and relate both to the situation within which SNCC operated after the mid-1960s. Violence as a form of public action is very close to Arendt's vision of politics—since it involves action in concert for a common political goal. But it is also quite distant, since it abandons persuasive speech for coercive force. It represents the failure of politics and the loss of the common world so necessary for politics. Indeed Glenn Gray has speculated that "The appeal of violence . . . results from the increasing difficulty of acting effectively as distinguished from mere behavior or reacting."[56] Thus political violence is a kind of political heresy, something that closely resembles free action but arises from the compelling force of the passion for rectification and revenge induced precisely by the frustration of free action and lack of recognition.

Indeed, another crucial difference between Fanon and Arendt is that Arendt rarely, if ever, discussed the psychological need for political action and she certainly never dreamt of discussing its effects in therapeutic terms.[57] At best "public happiness" was not a goal so much as a by-product or side-benefit of political action. Indeed as one of the essential human capacities, political action needs no explanation for its presence, only for its absence. By contrast, for Fanon and for the entire civil rights movement, including Martin Luther King at times, the psychological need to act together in concert and the effects of that action on individual and group self-conception were of crucial importance. At best, Arendt might have said, as she did in "Civil Disobedience," that the motives for political action are various and what counts is the action in concert not the motivation of the individuals involved.

Though Arendt has been criticized for insisting on the conceptual distinction between violence and politics, consideration of Fanon's thought, in which the two are all but synonymous, makes Arendt's deep suspicion of such an identification more comprehensible.[58] As a student (and defender) of political foundings and revolutions, Arendt clearly had to acknowledge the importance of violence in those phenomena. Indeed her early writings spoke eloquently of the imperative of Jewish self-defense and the need for Jews to fight for their own freedom. Still, she could never integrate violence into her theory of politics or freedom, for the obvious reason that persuasive speech—as opposed to violence—was so central to what she understood both politics and freedom to mean.

On the other hand, because Fanon never developed any way of talking about the distinction between politics and violence, he offered no vision of a post-revolutionary political order or why it should be any different than the old colonial order. His is the clearest expression of the modern tendency of "realists" and "radicals" to assume that politics-legitimacy-interest-power-domination-force-violence exist in a continuum and/or that all of these concepts can be reduced to variations on violence and force. For Fanon, who assumed the continuity of violence and political action, the courage to engage in collective violence was the "virtue" term in his proto-political theory, that which members of the body politic had to manifest and act on to be truly political and hence free beings. To risk one's life for the people was both to create and to demonstrate one's status as a free person. Where Arendt emphasized political action and the subsequent need to create "lasting institutions" so as to preserve political freedom, Fanon's concern was with political self-creation through action and prior to the institutionalization of freedom.

But Arendt, like Memmi, was less than sanguine about the possibility that the "brotherhood of the battlefield" would survive the cessation of hostilities.[59] Similarly to the pariah community, the band of embattled brothers and sisters—which SNCC saw itself as—was a poor model for the ideal political community of participation and debate, of argument and dissent. For, independence of judgment and imagination must be kept under tight control in combat conditions. One reason most revolutions have difficulties with institutionalizing or preserving democratic forms is that the habit of self-government is not a habit nurtured by or even often very possible in revolutionary conditions.[60] Arriving at decisions in a democratic fashion, i.e., through argument and compromise, often strikes professional soldiers and veteran revolutionaries as temporizing and even decadent. Arendt's analysis of the relationship between violence (specifically war) and politics suggests that a new political order must be wary of perpetuating the psychology of violence with its emphasis upon resolute, decisive, and unitary action.

Though courage was certainly one of the central political virtues for Arendt, she did warn of the anti-political nature of the presence of death so palpable in the brotherhood of the battlefield.[61] Obsession with death, coupled with the goal of liberation, runs like a leitmotif through James Forman's writings: "Only when we overcome the fear of death—only then—can we really live for the liberation of man." Later in *The Making of Black Revolutionaries* he writes that "we must deny death. It is the greatest act of defiance, an act of defiance necessary to make a revolutionary."[62] The great danger in such a view is that the struggle to overcome the fear of death will become itself the point of action. If that happens, death is not just confronted but courted as that which defines one's existence, while the political goal of creating a new political community with "lasting institutions" is all but forgotten. Indeed, as suggested in the previous chapter, something like this happened in SNCC. The fascination with death, also manifested in the escalating rhetoric of violence after 1966, may help explain the self-defeating nature of the later efforts of SNCC and the Black Panthers and their obsession with provoking "whitey."

We are back again to the "unreality" of SNCC politics after the mid-1960s and its loss of "common sense." Such a criticism refers not to SNCC's rejection of existing political and social structures, but to its refusal to take those structures into account and, more damagingly, its failure to gauge accurately the level of consciousness or capability of its own constituency. Part of the problem was that the movement (and not just SNCC) was never really required to formulate its goals beyond ending Jim Crow and disfranchisement. When it did set its sights elsewhere, it lacked the time or energy or patience (or outside support from indigenous radical forces) to think hard about the institutions which might best preserve something of the participatory impulse and the newly acquired self-respect so central to the movement's experience. That is, in failing to make political sense of its own experience of politics, SNCC failed to figure out how to institutionalize freedom. Having run out of creative tactics and effective strategies and scorning institutional coherence or theory, it had nothing really to fall back on except either the rhetorical vision of violence combined with an irrelevant Third World–ism or a retreat into cynicism.

*

Finally the tragedy of SNCC was exemplified in its trajectory from non-violence to violence, from indigenous community organization to affirmations of solidarity with the Third World. It was stranded in the no-man's land of the revolutionary consciousness without a revolutionary situation, a decolonized psyche outside a colonial setting. Put another way, where Rev. Martin Luther King began by wanting to save souls and ended by hoping to cure them and where Dr. Frantz Fanon began wanting to cure souls and ended by trying to save them, SNCC was caught in the cross-fire between these two conceptions of what revolutionary politics is about—salvation or cure. No wonder it was torn apart.

Conclusion

Politics is a strong and slow boring of hard boards.

Max Weber

Change is initiated by the principled few, not the compromising many; by the "crazies" in the streets, not by politicians on the hustings.

Garry Wills

Between the civil rights movement and the central European "revolutions" of 1989, there are enough similarities to suggest that the fate of the civil rights movement in America might illuminate the events in central Europe as the genuine sublimities of 1989 gave way to the intractable realities in the early 1990s. In fact, what happened in Europe in the late 1980s and early 1990s can sharpen our perspective on what the civil rights movement was "about." In reference to such parallels, I would like briefly to take up three questions: What was the civil rights movement? What were its effects on participants? and, What role did the media specifically play in the rise and fall of the movement as well as in any changes in our general conception of politics?

What Was the Movement?

We have yet to find an appropriate vocabulary to describe the civil rights movement. Many, then and now, labeled (and thereby condemned) the movement as "reformist," thus emphasizing the conventional nature of movement goals. There is no doubt that the first, obvious goal of the movement was the dismantling of the Jim Crow system in the South. In that respect it *was* a reform movement. But the desire for freedom expressed in the biblical idiom of collective liberation, in the psycho-political quest for transformed sense of self, and in the political emphasis upon participatory freedom, that is, genuine self-determination encompassing both individual and collective dimensions, suggested that the movement had more in mind than the goals entailed by liberal reform. Moreover, the willingness to employ various forms of direct action meant that pressure was exerted on the "state system" from outside the conventional political institutions. Not only did the movement not work through regular channels as defined by the political parties or representative bodies; it also went beyond the normal scope of civil disobedience, at least as it had been seen in America, and restored the idea of the "people in the streets" to political respectability.

And yet the movement was not revolutionary in the sense understood by most people in the mid-1960s. It scarcely fit the Marxist formula of a proletarian revolution guided by a vanguard party. Violent overthrow of the government or of the established order was scarcely contemplated by the movement's mainstream. Nor, as already pointed out, did the Fanonist idea of a revolutionary alliance between peasantry and lumpenproletariat have much resonance in America. Religious institutions and values, as well as traditional cultural values deriving from Southern Afro-American culture and general American political culture, were integral to the movement. In sum, the civil rights movement neither wanted totally to "transform" America nor merely to "reform" it.[1]

The best way to describe the civil rights movement is, I think, as a movement of political rejuvenation or revitalization. Though institutional reforms were certainly high on its agenda, its uniqueness lay in its effort to alter the existing political ethos as well. Rather than adopting what Albert Hirschman has called the "exit" option, the movement sought to find an appropriate political "voice" within which to enunciate a political vision and with which to revitalize the "public forum" where politics could flourish. But it was not a familiar voice in the general din of conventional political voices.[2]

The civil rights movement, along with the anti-Vietnam War movement and the emerging women's movement, forced the nation to confront more than the gap between its professed ideals and the realities of the Jim Crow South. It also triggered a rethinking on the academic and popular level of what those ideals meant in themselves. It is no coincidence that since the 1960s there has been a revival of political and social theory in America. The point of this study has been to look at the ways experiences of movement participants and attempts to understand what the movement represented have enriched our general conception not only of the meaning of rights, equality, and democracy, but especially of politics, citizenship, and freedom, pressing us to ask whether they have a unitary meaning at all. Thus the movement in effect revived the effort to rediscover or re-create the "spirit of the laws" rather than simply tinkering with the mechanisms and structures of government.

Seen as a whole, the movement suggests the limited purchase "domination" theories in social and political thought have on political realities. Here I refer to work advanced or inspired by Frankfurt School theorists such as Theodor Adorno, Max Horkheimer, and Herbert Marcuse, by post-structuralists such as Michel Foucault, and by theories of hegemony suggested by Antonio Gramsci. In unnuanced form, such work posits, then analyzes, an all but unbreachable totality, within and against which resistance in thought or action seems impossible.[3] The problems with such theories are threefold: empirically, they are not very convincing; theoretically, they are incoherent and self-contradictory; and politically, they are counter-productive. The history of the civil rights movement suggests that, despite the fact that people are "objectively" oppressed, even victimized, it can happen that at some point they cease to act like victims. Through political action and the stories they tell of it, they begin to create, as Fanon suggested, a new culture of resistance and often, as Fanon failed to stress, rediscover a lost tradition of alternatives to ponder and models to emulate. In emphasizing "freedom," however various its meanings, the civil rights movement refused to follow the scripts suggested by radical social and political theorists. This is not to say that there were no determining structures or institutional forces that profoundly shaped, even limited, the goals and strategies of the civil rights movement. But the example of the civil rights movement should force radical theorists and historians to be as assiduous in ferreting out the ways oppressed people find to resist domination and take collective action as they are in explaining the impossibility of resistance and action—up to the moment when resistance and action suddenly break loose. What the civil rights movement showed was that the American/Afro-American political tradition contained elements that could be turned against the very established institutions that claimed to be acting in the name of that tradition.

Put another way, movements like the civil rights movement should bring historians and political theorists to recognize, as I have repeatedly emphasized, that neither the theory nor the practice of politics is identical with the pursuit of interests or power or control of the instruments of violence alone. Rather, a healthy polity, even—and particularly—a post-revolutionary polity, should periodically generate revitalization movements to serve as politically imaginative counterweights to the existing system and the "normal" political psychology by which it operates. Such movements are not aberrations or signs of political pathology. Though I don't fully accept his Weberian dichotomy, Garry Wills draws an interesting contrast between the politician concerned with stability and the prophet who speaks out for change: "The politicians maintain our country . . . 'save' it in a sense. The prophets make it worth saving."[4] The great challenge facing revitalization and revolutionary movements alike is, as Arendt stressed, to establish lasting institutions for the preservation of freedoms. The tragic failure of the civil rights movement was that it failed to think long and hard about ways to preserve the varieties of freedom it championed—which is precisely the great challenge presently facing the revolutions of central Europe.

Political Morality and Psychology

The Aristotelian question—what is the relationship between the good "man" [person] and the good citizen—is also a question implicitly raised by the civil rights movement. In the case of the movement, the question is: Do the political characteristics of a free people—self-respect, the capacity for courage and solidarity, an eagerness to act politically—imply a commitment to other goods such as liberal tolerance or aesthetic creativity?

For the sake of consistency, if nothing else, one hopes for unity of vision across the political, ethical, and aesthetic spheres, that somehow the creative person makes a good citizen who acts in a moral fashion. But that such a unity does or can exist under the conditions of modernity is another matter. For instance philosopher Laurence Thomas asserts that "I do not take self-respect to be tied to having an acceptable moral character."[5] Wills observes that contemplation of those who have made a career out of politics—such as Richard Nixon—offers little consolation to those who hope that participation in public life has a salutory effect on personal character. He writes:

Participatory politics is not the way to make men happy, whole, humane. We should have learned that long ago, simply by observing the effect of politics on its most intimate participants—the pros, the politicians themselves.[6]

Finally, coming closer to home, the fate of ex-SNCC chairman and one-time mayor of Washington, D.C., Marion Barry as well as of several of his associates who were veterans of the movement suggests that the virtues required of and the experience acquired by young radicals were poor protection against the temptations of "public service" as conventionally defined.

Still, Wills's position is far from impregnable. First, service as an elected official does not exhaust the meaning of a political life. Politics inevitably corrupts and, Wills adds, requires a kind of middling, compromising mentality, only if we equate electoral politics with what politics "really" is. Moreover, as Wills knows, politics is a practice that has its own attendant virtues, valuable in themselves: it has its own "internal goods."[7] A self-respecting political actor, whether aiming for order through compromise or change through conflict, must be judged on how well she or he achieves those political ends, aside from whether she or he is a loving parent or faithful spouse or creative writer. We don't question the value of physical fitness because an extremely fit thief outruns a police officer; nor do we question the importance of intense personal relationships just because they seem to exclude public involvement. The specifically political point about Nixon or Barry is not that they were crooks and/or hooked on drugs; it is that they violated a public trust as elected officials and displayed poor political judgment. In short they were poor politicians.

Such a defense of politics is convincing as far as it goes, but some would say it does not go quite far enough. It is a kindergarten truth that because the practice of politics affects vast numbers of people, the "internal goods" and political virtues belonging to politics must be balanced against its "external" effects, no matter how much political virtuosity, courage, etc., characterizes the good politician or courageous political participant. One problem with seeing politics as a discrete practice demanding specific virtues is that it renders politics immune to any independent standard of value or judgment. One modern corrective for "virtue" politics, or politics judged on its own standards and engaged in by those allegedly possessing certain qualities, is the institution of rights and liberties beyond the control of the politically virtuous, whether an elite or the citizen-body generally. What the politically virtuous want and what is good by no means automatically coincide.[8]

Indeed, the *polis,* as well as a movement of free and virtuous citizens who claim to possess certain qualities of character or common characteristics, will tend to divide the world between themselves, those who belong together by virtue of their virtue, and those who don't. Such a movement aims for homogeneity of characteristics and experience and is drawn to a worldview in which uniformity is a positive good. In *The Origins of Totalitarianism* Arendt underscores this proclivity for political *Gemeinschaften* to repress or extrude difference.

> The reason why highly developed political communities, such as the ancient city-states or the modern nation-states, so often insist on ethnic homogeneity is that they hope to eliminate as far as possible those natural and always present differences and differentiations which by themselves arouse dumb hatred, mistrust, and discrimination. . . .
> The 'alien' is a frightening symbol of the fact of difference as such, of individuality . . .[9]

This passage is particularly interesting since it refers not to Nazi Germany or some modern racist or ethnically homogeneous order but to the Greek city-state that she so celebrated in her subsequent writing. What Arendt suggests is that exclusion of those who seem different can not be attributed solely to conscious or unconscious projections or to the desire for revenge against former oppressors. Generally, the possession of political self-respect and the capacity for self-determination entails nothing that forbids invidious distinctions between "us" and "them." Thus we should be less than shocked by the fact that one sector of the civil rights movement embraced black ethnic and racial exclusivity. A sense of civic consciousness and virtue can easily become transformed into religious, ethnic, or racial exclusivity. Of this the history of Eastern Europe is a melancholy example.

Martin Luther King did of course envisage a form of political action that tried to promote solidarity across racial lines and at the same time respect difference and individuality. Radicals had serious problems with King's politics of *agape,* since it seemed to imply that white people as the oppressors were necessary for blacks to achieve self-respect. They rejected King's reading of the oppressor-oppressed relationship and instead turned to the truncated version suggested by

Fanon. Thus the civil rights movement failed to discover a way to incorporate a tolerance of difference and otherness into the notion of a free self; a failure, it should be noted, no greater than the historical failure of the (white) American republic to do the same.

What are the lasting effects of political participation and of the creation of a new and freer political self? In its more extreme forms the politics of self-transformation become a secular version of religious conversion or a political form of psychotherapy. But these are dangerous and wrong-headed models for conceptualizing the psychological changes to which participants in the civil rights movement attest. It is better to understand political self-transformation as a form of education, as a slow process that builds a self-critical component into the process itself. Gandhi and King, as well as the early Fanon, emphasized the need to prepare for action. If this is done, then the transformational capacities of action are put into perspective. Direct confrontation, including risk of life, has an indubitable effect on one's sense of self. But changes in the self linked with action should be seen as a by-product rather than the main point of political action. It is also no accident that Gandhi and King built on the existing cultures of their people rather than urging them to discard their old way of life completely. Elements of continuity, as well as of transformation, are essential.

Still, there is evidence that involvement in the movement permanently altered the psychological and emotional lives of some of its participants. After conducting extensive interviews with a number of people involved in the movement and then reinterviewing them several years later, William Beardslee wrote:

> The fundamental concerns they voiced before—the overwhelming importance of closeness to others . . . the handling of anger, the new sense of self, the taking of action rather than being passive, the development of faith in the work over time, the reconciliation of Movement experience with the rest of their own life experiences, and the acceptance of self with limitations—all remain true. What is different, and in some ways even more unusual than in the original observations, is the length of the commitment of these men and women, now extending over twenty years in most cases.[10]

Clearly for those Beardslee consulted, self-transformation was no superficial or temporary thing. Nor had it diminished these participants' sense of interiority and psychological complexity, as Wills's

pronouncements on the baleful consequences of leading a political
life would suggest. Of course the original "high" of political action
could not last. But the civil rights movement certainly had lasting
(and beneficial) effects on many of its participants.

Politics and Representation

There is still no essay dealing with the impact of the media, particularly television, on changes in the nature of politics which can match
what Walter Benjamin's "The Work of Art in the Age of Mechanical
Reproduction" did for the relationship between aesthetics and tech-
nological reproduction. Indeed, it is easy to forget that the civil rights
movement was, according to veteran Southern journalist and political analyst Harry Ashmore, the "first great national story" covered by
American television, a technology which had only emerged as a
national force in the early 1950s.[11] If the civil rights movement (and
the various public movements of dissidence and resistance in the
1960s) helped make television, network television and the national
(and regional) press were certainly crucial to the success and, I think,
the failure of the movement. The media is one of those institutional/
structural determinants without which neither the failures nor the
successes of the civil rights movement can be understood.

But such a claim is not based on any straightforward, intentional
hostility of the media toward the civil rights movement. Most of the
national and larger regional papers that covered the movement were
broadly sympathetic to its aims; indeed, the role played by white
Southern journalists in thoroughly and sympathetically reporting the
unfolding of events, their tracking of the thrust and counter-thrust
between the white Southern political establishments and the movement, was considerable and invaluable. As John Lewis later said,
many in the movement saw journalists as something like "sympathetic referees." They tried to use the press to "dramatize the issues"
that were then disseminated across the nation.[12] Indeed, the movement garnered world-wide attention and sympathy from the images
beamed around the world of police dogs attacking demonstrators in
Birmingham in 1963. Later the media coverage of the Selma campaign, particularly the attack on marchers on the Edmund Pettus
Bridge by Sheriff Jim Clark and his men, would arouse national
indignation and push President Johnson and the Congress toward
swifter action on the Voting Rights Act of 1965. In the decade when

Marshall McLuhan first talked of the existence of a "global village" brought into existence by communication satellites, the civil rights movement, together of course with the Vietnam War, became a truly international phenomenon.[13]

More thoughtful newspaper and television journalists have come to realize the limitations of their coverage of the movement, mainly in terms of what they didn't or couldn't cover. Under the pressure of events and daily deadlines, it was difficult, says Ashmore, to convey the "underlying story" about, say, the historical context, or to draw back and assess the "longer range" issues, or to be very analytical about the whole phenomenon. More interestingly, according to Eugene Roberts, the journalists never told the story of the "fear and despair" that built up within the movement over time. The journalistic ethic of "get it right" competed with the similarly strong imperative to "get it first."[14] As several journalists commented at a conference on the Media and the Civil Rights Movement at the University of Mississippi in 1987, commercial network television will still not finance nor show a series such as *Eyes on the Prize* which took 14 years to complete. Commercial sponsorship would not be forthcoming.

But aside from what it must omit, media coverage also distorts what is shown. Though he concentrates primarily on the coverage of the New Left, the thrust of Todd Gitlin's *The Whole World is Watching* (1980) pertains to the civil rights movement and to the larger issue of the effect on politics itself of "live" coverage. Gitlin suggests that since the "archetypal news story is a crime story," protest movements tend to be treated that way. More important, he notes, journalists need a "peg," a "significant" event or action to hang the story on. It particularly needs to identify and ratify spokespersons from the group, to create "movement star-celebrities," but it also can decide whether and when to break them. Gitlin also found that media coverage encouraged the inflation of rhetoric and general militancy since it produced a lively story yet not surprisingly tended to cover the "moderate alternative," whatever or whoever it might be at any given time, more favorably.[15]

All of this certainly happened in and to the civil rights movement. But there are several factors in particular which suggest the way the internal nature, aims, and strategy of the movement were affected by media coverage. First Gitlin's analysis suggests that if the news is to be "new," then rapid acceleration of events, changes in leadership, and transformation of aims are built into the relationship between the media and the movement. After a point the internal momentum driven by the media no longer is synchronized with the needs or wishes or consciousness generally of the movement's constituency. "Sealed off from the possibility of experienced social observation," Gitlin observes, "the celebrities become inferior strategists. . . . The media represented a surer constituency for revolution . . ." To put it another way: as media coverage increased, "face to face organizing dried up."[16]

The latter point is particularly important for the civil rights movement and may help explain the failure of SNCC in particular to continue its efforts in community organizing and setting up new organizations. By disseminating images of protest and then militancy, the media was an instrument for increasing publicity and even political awareness of a sort. But the ease with which political consciousness can be raised suggests the rapidity with which it can fade. The danger of television particularly (as opposed to print journalism) is not so much the content (sex, violence, radical challenges to existing order, racist language); it is the rapidity of presentation and the difficulty of staying with an issue long enough to explore its strategic or theoretical implications. Even a talented speaker such as Jesse Jackson has by now in his career been reduced to speaking in jingles and ingenious but highly perishable doggerel. One wonders if Dr. King's slow and sometimes ponderous speaking style would have needed changing had he lived past 1968. And the chief weakness of *Eyes on the Prize*, especially part II, was that it rarely if ever stopped to analyze issues. In retrospect, is John Lewis correct that black power was nonsense? Why did Muhammed Ali, shown in one segment of the documentary with Malcolm X, remain a supporter of Elijah Muhammed when Malcolm broke with the Nation of Islam?

In terms of political thought, particularly the idea of participatory freedom and citizen participation, the media's need for the striking image and sensational event (a fiery speech, police brutality) encouraged what is perhaps already a tendency in radical political movements composed largely of young people: a preference for mass meetings and demonstrations or for action of any sort over both grassroots organizing and small-group discussion of issues and aims. If, as already suggested by James Miller, there are two strands to participatory politics—the "action" approach and the "speech" approach—television surely encourages the former rather than the latter. Debating and arguing require that people pay attention, while marches and demonstrations can be attended to, or not, as an image and an experience rather than as an occasion for thought. [17]

Finally, the most general theoretical and historical perspective suggests that the nature of public space in the age of instantaneous dissemination of images has to be rethought and redefined. For this, the idea of the "simulacrum," one of the central tropes of the "postmodern," becomes genuinely relevant. [18] The notion of the simulacrum suggests a world where, because of the instant reproducibility and transmission of images, it has become difficult to distinguish the original from the copy, the real from the imitation. In Arendtian terms, there are now two kinds of public space of appearance where thought and action go on: an "actual" one and the one "broadcast" and "disseminated" by a third party (the media). As a result it becomes nearly impossible to distinguish between what "really happened" at Tiananmen Square or Wenceslas Square in 1989 or at the Lincoln Memorial in August 1963 and the way they have been preserved on television and film, purveyed by and consumed by those of us who were not directly involved. No doubt such images of a public space turned to genuinely political purposes are powerfully instructive and provide important models for emulation. But it is much more difficult to make "the strong and slow boring of hard boards" of community organizing and political argumentation in public of as much interest. Moreover, it is not that mediation by images lessens the power or intentionally distorts what actually happened as such. In fact, images may at times trigger off a stronger immediate reaction than actual presence at an event might. But the final paradox is that images of political action and/or speech in the public forum are increasingly consumed while alone or in private. Insofar as they are consumed in this way, the danger is that they further weaken rather than augment our sense of an actual political space where oppositional forces can speak and act against those who seek to stifle either or both.

Notes

Introduction

1. Taylor Branch, *Parting the Waters: America in the King Years, 1954–63* (New York: Simon and Schuster, 1988), 145; 172.

Recent studies of black political culture include Vincent Harding, *There Is a River* (New York: Vintage, 1983), V. P. Franklin, *Black Self-determination* (Westport: Lawrence Hill, 1984), and Sterling Stuckey, *Slave Culture* (New York: Oxford Univ. Press, 1987). Eric Foner, *Reconstruction: America's Unfulfilled Revolution, 1863–77* (New York: Perennial, 1988) has a very useful chapter on the meaning of freedom for ex-slaves during Reconstruction. Valuable sociological studies of the movement include Doug MacAdam, *Political Process and the Development of Black Insurgency, 1930–1970* (Chicago: Univ. of Chicago Press, 1982) and Aldon Morris, *The Origins of the Civil Rights Movement* (New York: Free Press, 1984).

2. Robert Korstad and Nelson Lichtenstein, "Opportunities Found and Lost: Labor, Radicals and the Early Civil Rights Movement," *Journal of American History* 75, #3 (Dec. 1988): 786–811.

3. J. Mills Thornton, Comment on William Chafe's "The End of One Struggle, The Beginning of Another," in *The Civil Rights Movement in America*, ed. Charles Eagles (Jackson: Univ. Press of Mississippi, 1986), 149.

4. Pat Watters and Reese Cleghorn, *Climbing Jacob's Ladder* (New York: Harcourt, Brace and World, 1967) is practically the only book dealing with the movement that so much as cites a political theorist: John Stuart Mill, on political participation, while Watters's thesis in *Down to Now* (New York: Pantheon, 1971) posits that the movement was engaged in much more than politics as usual. David Garrow's *Protest at Selma* (New Haven: Yale Univ. Press, 1978) and Charles Hamilton and Stokely Carmichael's *Black Power* (New York: Vintage, 1967) offer at least a beginning exploration of the point of political participation as something more than instrumental for protection of interests.

The story is much the same with legal and constitutional histories of the movement or with studies of constitutional issues arising in and from movement activities. Rarely, if ever, do we have any discussion of what a "right" is as opposed to what our rights are, what the definition(s) of freedom might be rather than just what our freedoms are. Besides Richard Kluger,

Simple Justice (New York: Knopf, 1976), see also J. Harvey Wilkinson, III, *From Brown to Bakke* (New York: Oxford Univ. Press, 1979), and more recent studies on particular legal and constitutional issues, Michael Belknap, *Federal Law and Southern Order: Racial Violence and Constitutional Conflict in the Post-Brown South* (Athens: Univ. of Georgia Press, 1987), Jack Bass, *Unlikely Heroes* (New York: Simon and Schuster, 1981), and Abigail Thernstrom, *Whose Votes Count? Affirmative Action and Minority Voting Rights* (Cambridge: Harvard Univ. Press, 1987).

Though not directly related to legal thought dealing with the civil rights movement, Mark Tushnet's "Rights: An Essay in Informal Political Theory," *Politics and Society* 17, #4 (Dec. 1989): 403–52, does provide an accessible account of some of the definitional issues associated with the political/legal concept of rights.

5. Ricks is quoted in James Forman, *The Making of Black Revolutionaries* (New York: Macmillan, 1972), 457. A conceptual weakness, for instance, of Kate Millett's *Sexual Politics* (London: Sphere Books, 1971), one of the founding texts of radical feminism, lies in its assumption that "the essence of politics is power" (p. 25). For an alternative position, see chapter 2 of Hannah Arendt's *On Violence* (New York: Harcourt, Brace and World, 1970), in which she distinguishes between politics as force and domination and politics as persuasion based on popular consent, the true source of political power.

6. A. J. Polan's *Lenin and the End of Politics* (London: Methuen, 1984) is both historically and theoretically convincing on this issue as it is examined in the history of the Soviet Union.

7. See Tushnet, "Rights: An Essay in Informal Political Theory," as well as Sheldon Wolin, "Revolutionary Action Today," *Democracy* 2, 4 (Fall 1982): 17–28. One of the chief weaknesses of much rights-based liberalism is its lack of a strong commitment to political participation as a good in its own right.

8. See Wini Breines, *The Great Refusal: Community and Organization in the New Left, 1962–1968* (New York: Praeger, 1982), who also emphasizes the importance of SNCC on the development of the (white) New Left idea of "projective" politics. Jane Mansbridge's *Adversary Democracy* (New York: Basic Books, 1980) has the great merit of actually being based on empirical investigations of various forms of political decision making.

9. The classic analysis of the liberal tradition is Louis Hartz's *The Liberal Tradition in America* (New York: Harcourt, Brace and World, 1955). For a theoretical statement of the various political traditions at work in contemporary Anglo-American political culture, see Charles Taylor, "Philosophy and Its History," in *Philosophy in History*, ed. R. Rorty, Q. Skinner, and J. B. Schneewind (Cambridge, U.K.: Cambridge Univ. Press, 1984), 17–31, especially 26. Historical works establishing the pertinence of the civic

humanist/republican tradition in America are Bernard Bailyn, *Ideological Origins of the American Republic* (Cambridge: Harvard Univ. Press, 1967); Gordon Wood, *The Creation of the American Republic, 1776–1787* (Chapel Hill: Univ. of North Carolina Press, 1969); and J. G. Pocock, *The Machiavellian Moment* (Princeton: Princeton Univ. Press, 1975). John Diggins, *The Lost Soul of American Politics* (New York: Basic Books, 1984) challenges claims for the historical or theoretical importance of republican political thought in American history and represents a return to the original thesis of liberal consensus, though with an added Calvinist element.

10. Don Herzog, *Happy Slaves: A Critique of Consent Theory* (Chicago: Univ. of Chicago Press, 1989), xiii.

11. Here I refer primarily to works such as John Rawls, *A Theory of Justice* (Cambridge: Harvard Univ. Press, 1971) and Robert Nozick, *Anarchy, State and Utopia* (New York: Basic Books, 1974). Ronald Dworkin, *Taking Rights Seriously* (Cambridge: Harvard Univ. Press, 1977) is also central in recent liberal theory. Because Dworkin's work is in jurisprudence and legal theory, he has more reason to neglect the experience of politics. A good defense of the liberal theoretical tradition, though not without a critical thrust, is Amy Gutman, *Liberal Equality* (Cambridge, U.K.: Cambridge Univ. Press, 1980), while Michael Sandel, *Liberalism and the Limits of Justice* (Cambridge, U.K.: Cambridge Univ. Press, 1982) and Ian Shapiro, *The Evolution of Rights in Liberal Theory* (Cambridge, U.K.: Cambridge Univ. Press, 1986) take a more uniformly critical position with respect to liberal political thought.

There are a few works in social and political thought that attempt to deal with the political legacy of the movement. Michael Walzer, *Obligations: Essays on Disobedience, War and Citizenship* (New York: Simon and Schuster, 1971) includes several essays arising out of issues raised by the movement, while more recently Leonard Harris (ed.), *Philosophy Born of Struggle: Anthology of Afro-American Philosophy from 1917* (Dubuque: Kendall/Hunt, 1983) is a valuable compilation of essays by black scholars and thinkers. Adolph Reed, "The 'Black Revolution' and the Reconstitution of Domination," in *Race, Politics, and Culture* (Westport: Greenwood Press, 1986), 61–95, analyzes the movement from a position influenced by the Frankfurt School; and Cornel West, *Prophesy Deliverance! An Afro-American Revolutionary Christianity* (Philadelphia: Westminister Press, 1982) mixes Christianity, Marxism, and recent Continental thought.

12. Nancy L. Rosenblum, *Another Liberalism: Romanticism and Reconstruction in Liberal Thought* (Cambridge: Harvard Univ. Press, 1987), 3.

13. Here the work of communitarian and neo-republican theorists such as Arendt, Wolin, Hannah Pitkin, Bernard Crick, Benjamin Barber, and Ronald Beiner with their emphasis upon political action and judgment, and that of neo-Hegelians such as Jean-Paul Sartre, Albert Memmi, and Frantz

Fanon, who emphasize the dialectics of domination and liberation, can help in constructing a phenomenology of political action, a semantics of political discourse, and a moral psychology of political participation.

Arendt's concepts of politics and the political are set forth in *The Human Condition* (Garden City, N.Y.: Anchor Books, 1959), "What Is Freedom?" in *Between Past and Future* (Cleveland; Meridian Books, 1961), 143–71, and *On Revolution* (New York: Viking Compass, 1963). See also Sheldon Wolin, *Politics and Vision* (London: Allen and Unwin, 1961); Hannah F. Pitkin, *Wittgenstein and Justice* (Berkeley: Univ. of California Press, 1972) and "Justice: On Relating Private and Public," *Political Theory* 9, #3 (Aug. 1981): 327–52; Bernard Crick, *In Defense of Politics* (Harmondsworth, U.K.: Penguin, 1983); Ronald Beiner, *Political Judgment* (London: Methuen, 1983); and Benjamin Barber, *Strong Democracy* (Berkeley: Univ. of California Press, 1984).

Hegel's canonical "Lordship and Bondage" is found in *The Phenomenology of Spirit* trans. J. B. Baillie (New York: Macmillan, 1931). Its modern social and political influence was transmitted to French thought by Alexandre Kojève's Paris lectures in the 1930s, some of which have been collected in Kojève, *Introduction to the Reading of Hegel*, ed. Allan Bloom (New York: Basic Books, 1969). See also Albert Memmi, *Colonizer and Colonized* (New York: Orion Press, 1965) and *Dominated Man* (Boston: Beacon, 1968) as well as, of course, Frantz Fanon, *The Wretched of the Earth* (New York: Grove Press, 1963). I will discuss Fanon's position more fully in Chapter 7. Though the master/slave dialectic would seem to be all and only about power as domination, it is in fact most centrally concerned with the struggle for recognition and the (im)possibility of mutuality.

14. Major published works of movement oral history are Robert Penn Warren, *Who Speaks for the Negro?* (New York: Random House, 1965); Robert Coles, *Children of Crisis* (Boston: Atlantic-Little Brown Books, 1967); Robert Hamburger, *Our Portion of Hell: Fayette County, Tennessee: An Oral History of the Struggle for Civil Rights* (New York: Links Books, 1973); Howell Raines, *My Soul Is Rested* (New York: Bantam Books, 1978); William Beardslee, *The Way Out Must Lead In*, 2nd ed. (Westport: Lawrence Hill, 1983); and Joan Turner Beifuss, *At the River I Stand: Memphis, the 1968 Strike, and Martin Luther King* (Memphis: B and W Books, 1985).

Chapter 1: The Repertory of Freedom

1. For general discussions of freedom, see Leonard Krieger, "Stages in the History of Political Freedom," in *Nomos* IV [Liberty], ed. Carl J. Friedrich (New York: Atherton Press, 1962), 1–28; Orlando Patterson, *Slavery and Social Death* (Cambridge: Harvard Univ. Press, 1982) and "The Unholy Trinity: Freedom, Slavery and the American Constitution," *Social*

Research 54, #3 (Autumn 1987):543–78; Richard Flathman, *The Philosophy and Politics of Freedom* (Chicago: Univ. of Chicago Press, 1987); and Albrecht Wellner, "Models of Freedom in the Modern World," *The Philosophical Forum* XXI, 1–2 (Fall-Winter 1989–90):227–52. I should emphasize that I am making no claim that leaders or participants had any or all of these conceptions of freedom explicitly in mind when they used the term "freedom."

2. See William Connolly, *The Terms of Political Discourse,* 2nd ed. (Oxford, U.K.: Martin Robertson, 1983) for a discussion of "essentially contested" political concepts.

3. William Beardslee, *The Way Out Must Lead In,* 2nd ed. (Westport: Lawrence Hill, 1983), 123. Beardslee conducted his original interviews in 1972 and then reinterviewed most of his subjects in 1980.

4. For this notion of rights as specifications on freedom, see Daniel T. Rodgers, *Contested Truths: Keywords in American Politics Since Independence* (New York: Basic Books, 1987), 219; and Agnes Heller, "Freedom as a Value Idea and the Interpretation of Human Rights," in *Eastern Left, Western Left* (Atlantic Highlands, N.J.: Humanities Press, 1986), 146–60.

5. Michel Foucault, "Truth and Power," in *Power/Knowledge,* ed. Colin Gordon (New York: Pantheon, 1980), 109–33; and also *The History of Sexuality,* vol. 1 (New York: Vintage Books, 1980).

6. Besides Patterson, see Edmund Morgan, *American Slavery, American Freedom* (New York: Norton, 1975); David Brion Davis, *The Problem of Slavery in Western Culture* (Ithaca: Cornell Univ. Press, 1966) and *The Problem of Slavery in the Age of Revolution: 1770–1823* (Ithaca: Cornell Univ. Press, 1975) as well as *Slavery and Human Progress* (New York: Oxford Univ. Press, 1984). Michael Kammen, *Spheres of Liberty: Changing Perceptions of Liberty in American Culture* (Madison: Univ. of Wisconsin Press, 1986) offers a quick overview of the idea of freedom in the United States.

7. Quoted in Kammen, *Spheres of Liberty,* 20.

8. *Ibid.,* 33–34; see also Wood, *The Creation of the American Republic.*

9. Benjamin Constant, "The Liberty of the Ancients Compared with That of the Moderns" (1819), in *Political Writings,* ed. and trans. Biancamaria Fontana (Cambridge, U.K.: Cambridge Univ. Press, 1988), 307–28, cited on pp. 310–11, 315–17; and Stephen Holmes, *Benjamin Constant and the Making of Modern Liberalism* (New Haven: Yale Univ. Press, 1984).

10. Constant, "The Liberty of the Ancients . . . ," 327.

11. Eric Foner, *Reconstruction, 1863–77* (New York: Perennial Library, 1989), chap. 6; Robert J. Kaczorowski, "To Begin the Nation Anew: Congress, Citizenship and Civil Rights after the Civil War," *American Historical Review* 92, #1 (Feb. 1987):45–68; and Rodgers, *Contested Truths,* 109, 139–43. For the development of the idea of citizenship in the ante-bellum years, see also James Kettner, *The Development of American Citizenship, 1608–*

1870 (Chapel Hill: Univ. of North Carolina Press, 1978); and Harold Hyman and William M. Wiecek, *Equal Justice Under Law: Constitutional Development, 1835–1875* (New York: Harper and Row, 1982). The upshot of all of these works is that the Civil War and early Reconstruction saw a significant revision in the idea of what citizenship entailed, at least for a time. Even moderate Republicans came to believe by the late 1860s that black male citizenship should include political rights.

12. Constant, "The Liberty of the Ancients . . . ," 327. See also Larry Siedentop, "Two Liberal Traditions," in *The Idea of Freedom*, ed. Alan Ryan (Oxford, U.K.: Oxford Univ. Press, 1979), 153–74, for a discussion of the French political liberals and Richard Krouse, "'Classical' Images of Democracy in America: Madison and Tocqueville," in *Democratic Theory and Practice*, ed. Graeme Duncan (Cambridge, U.K.: Cambridge Univ. Press, 1983), 58–78.

13. W. E. B. DuBois in August Meier, Elliott Rudwick, and Francis L. Broderick (eds.), *Black Protest Thought in the Twentieth Century*, 2nd ed. (Indianapolis: Bobbs-Merrill, 1971), 68–69.

14. Randolph Bourne, "Trans-National America," in *War and the Intellectuals*, ed. Carl Resak (New York: Harper Torchbooks, 1964), 111–12.

15. Isaiah Berlin, "Two Concepts of Liberty," in *Four Essays on Liberty* (London: Oxford Univ. Press, 1969), 125. The original version appeared in 1958. The introduction to the 1969 edition contains a long discussion in response to criticisms of Berlin's original essay.

16. Constant, "The Liberty of the Ancients . . . ," 323.

17. Berlin, "Two Concepts . . . ," 127.

18. *Ibid.*, 132, 148. Rousseau's "force them to be free" is a politically ominous way of talking about the less outrageous Kantian notion of autonomy as obedience to the laws one has set for oneself. In a political context this can be seen as one way of talking about the obligation of a citizen in a democracy to obey the laws of the polity. There should be no argument that citizens can be forced to obey the law; it is another matter to identify such action, or the law mandating it, with freedom.

19. Berlin, "Two Concepts . . . ," 165, lviii (written in 1969).

20. Berlin, "Two Concepts . . . ," 128, 131; and C. B. MacPherson, "Berlin's Division of Liberty," in *Democratic Theory: Essays in Retrieval* (Oxford, U.K.: Clarendon Press), 96–97.

21. Rosenblum, *Another Liberalism*, 70–71; Gerald Dworkin, *The Theory and Practice of Autonomy* (Cambridge, U.K.: Cambridge Univ. Press, 1988), 14–15; Harry G. Frankfurt, *The Importance of What We Care About* (Cambridge, U.K.: Cambridge Univ. Press, 1988), 20. Frankfurt does see what he calls first-order freedom as insufficient to define personhood, where most thinkers would see it as sufficient; J. R. Schneewind, "The Use of Autonomy in Ethical Theory," in *Reconstructing Individualism*, ed.

T. Heller, M. Sosna, and D. Wellberry (Stanford: Stanford Univ. Press, 1986), 64–75; and Flathman, *The Philosophy and Politics of Freedom*, 176, 217.

22. See Flathman, *The Philosophy and Politics of Freedom*, 177–178; and Dworkin, *The Theory and Practice of Autonomy*, 14–15; for points regarding the confusion of autonomy with negative freedom; Henry David Thoreau, *Walden* (New York: Signet, 1960), 10.

23. For a discussion of the way freedom should be seen in terms of the capacity for "intelligent choice," see John Dewey, "Philosophies of Freedom" (1928), in *John Dewey: On Experience, Nature, and Freedom*, ed. Richard Bernstein (New York: Liberal Arts Press, 1960), 262–87.

24. On Arendt's direct influence, see Breines, *The Great Refusal;* James Miller, "Modern Democracy: From France to America," *Salmagundi* 84 (Fall 1989): 175–202; and Jean Bethke Elshtain, "Hannah Arendt's French Revolution," *ibid.*, 203–13, for testimonies to Arendt's influence on the student left in the early 1960s and on movements such as Solidarity in Poland. I have not seen any evidence of her influence on the political thinking coming out of the civil rights movement itself.

25. Hannah Arendt, "What Is Freedom?," *Between Past and Future*, enlarged ed. (New York: Viking Press, 1968), 146; *On Revolution* (New York: Viking Compass, 1963), 24–25; "What Is Freedom?," 148.

26. Arendt, "What Is Freedom?," 148.

27. *Ibid.*, 153–69.

28. Arendt, *The Human Condition* (Garden City, N.Y.: Anchor Books, 1959), 177.

29. Ferenc Feher, "Redemptive and Democratic Paradigms in Radical Politics," in *Eastern Left, Western Left* (Atlantic Highlands, N.J.: Humanities Press, 1986), 61–76.

30. Michael Walzer, *Exodus and Revolution* (New York: Basic Books, 1985) makes the point about the Exodus "event" as a story rather than an idea and discusses its importance in the history of Western political thought for radical (though not messianic or other-worldly) visions of social and political liberation.

31. See Erich Auerbach, *Mimesis* (Garden City, N.Y.: Anchor Books, 1957), chaps. 1–8, for examples of figural interpretation, and see Sacvan Bercovitch, *The Puritan Origins of the American Self* (New Haven: Yale Univ. Press, 1975) for its relevance to the origins of American self-conception.

Simon Schama, *The Embarrassment of Riches* (London: Fontana Press, 1988), 35, 112–13, discusses the importance of the Exodus model and national Christianity in the setting of the Dutch republic and alludes to its importance in South African, American, and Israeli history as well.

32. Elaine Pagels, *Adam, Eve and the Serpent* (New York: Vintage Books,

1988), 98–126. Pagels claims that pre-Augustinian Christianity had a radical notion of "negative" freedom at its core. That is, the individual was free to choose a life in Christ and this was theologically a genuine form of freedom. Thus by her account not all forms of Christian freedom are necessarily forms of obedience.

33. Rodgers, *Contested Truths*, 78. See also Vincent Harding, *There Is a River* (New York: Vintage Books, 1983), 45, 55.

34. Foner, *Reconstruction*, 54, and chap. 3; Ronald Walters, "The Boundaries of Abolitionism," in *Anti-Slavery Reconsidered*, ed. Lewis Perry and Michael Fellman (Baton Rouge: Louisiana State Univ. Press, 1972), 3–32.

35. Quoted in Foner, *Reconstruction*, 72, 76.

36. *Ibid.*, 78; Harding, *There Is a River*, 264.

37. See Foner, *Reconstruction*, chaps. 3 and 7; Leon Litwak, *Been in the Storm So Long* (New York: Knopf, 1980), chap. 10; and Harding, *There Is a River*, 263–327.

38. Foner, *Reconstruction*, 282, 291.

39. Harding, *There Is a River*, 293, 296.

40. David Walker, *Appeal to the Colored Citizens of the World, but in particular and very expressly, to those of the United States of America*, ed. Charles M. Wiltse (New York: Hill and Wang, 1965), 2.

41. *Ibid.*, 29, 65.

42. Harding, *There Is a River*, 87; Douglass quoted in John Bracey, August Meier, and Elliott Rudwick (eds.), *Black Nationalism in America* (Indianapolis: Bobbs-Merrill, 1970), 60; soldier quoted in Litwak, *Been in the Storm*, 64; Arnett quoted in Carol V. R. George, "Widening the Circle: The Black Church and the Abolitionist Circle, 1830–60," in *Anti-Slavery Reconsidered*, eds. Perry and Fellman, 89, 93.

43. Quoted in Bracey *et al.*, *Black Nationalism*, 56.

44. Henry Highland Garnet, "An Address to the Slaves of the United States of America" (1843), reprinted *ibid.*, 70–71.

45. Martin Delany, "The Political Destiny of the Colored Race, on the American Continent" (1854), reprinted *ibid.*, 88–89.

46. *Ibid.*, 89–92, 95, 101.

47. Walters, in *Anti-Slavery Reconsidered*, 8; Harding, *There Is a River*, xviii–xix.

48. Harold Cruse, *Plural But Equal* (New York: Morrow, 1987), 75; Genna Rae McNeil, *Groundwork: Charles Hamilton Houston and the Struggle for Civil Rights* (Philadelphia: Univ. of Pennsylvania Press, 1983), 133. Also see Mark V. Tushnet, *The NAACP's Legal Strategy vs. Segregated Education, 1925–1950* (Chapel Hill: Univ. of North Carolina Press, 1987).

49. Raymond Wolters, *Negroes and the Great Depression: The Problems of Economic Recovery* (Westport: Greenwood, 1970), 220; Ralph Bunche in Meier *et al.*, *Black Protest Thought*, 196.

50. W. E. B. DuBois, *Dusk of Dawn: An Essay Toward an Autobiography of a Race Concept* (New York: Schocken Books, 1968), 205; Wolters, *Negroes and the Great Depression*, 230–65.

51. August Meier and Elliott Rudwick, *Black History and the Historical Profession, 1915–1980* (Urbana: Univ. of Illinois Press, 1986), 176.

52. Clayborne Carson, *In Struggle: SNCC and the Black Awakening of the 1960s* (Cambridge: Harvard Univ. Press, 1981), 14–15.

53. V. P. Franklin, *Black Self-Determination* (Westport: Lawrence Hill, 1984), 29–67, makes this point in reference to black sacred music and the failure of the black radicals and academics of the 1930s to understand its (only barely) encoded political message.

Chapter 2: The Experience of Politics

1. The history of SNCC can be found in Howard Zinn, *SNCC: The New Abolitionists* (Boston: Beacon Press, 1965) and Clayborne Carson, *In Struggle: SNCC and the Black Awakening of the 1960s* (Cambridge: Harvard Univ. Press, 1981).

The funding of the VEP was arranged by the Kennedy administration through private foundations and initially threatened to divide SNCC, since some SNCC members felt that it was an effort to blunt the organization's militancy, as indeed it was. But, ironically, the VEP didn't have that effect at all. In *Parting the Waters* (New York: Simon and Schuster, 1988), Taylor Branch notes on the matter of Justice Department protection of voter registration activity that "two years in office had made Justice officials more rather than less timid about criminal prosecutions in their showcase area of voting rights" (p. 640).

2. William Chafe, *Civilities and Civil Rights: Greensboro, N.C. and the Black Struggle for Freedom* (New York: Oxford Univ. Press, 1980), 99. Chafe's book is a fascinating study of the political mobilization of Greensboro and of the frustrating effects of the white establishment's commitment to "civility" which stymied as often as it aided integration. John Ehle's *The Free Men* (New York: Harper and Row, 1965) makes much the same point about the ambiguous virtue of white civility in the desegregation of restaurants in Chapel Hill, North Carolina, in 1963–64.

3. See Robert Bellah, *et al.*, *Habits of the Heart* (New York: Harper Torchbooks, 1984) for the point about the origins of American protest movements.

4. Pat Watters, *Down to Now* (New York: Pantheon, 1971) contains extensive transcriptions of mass meetings, while William Beardslee, *The Way Out Must Lead In*, 2nd ed. (Westport: Lawrence Hill, 1983), 60; Pat Waters and Reese Cleghorn, *Climbing Jacob's Ladder* (New York: Harcourt, Brace and World, 1967), 156; and Branch, *Parting the Waters*, 524–61, illuminate the workings of the mass meetings and the role of the freedom

songs in them. Particularly valuable on this topic is the interview with
Bernice Reagon in Dick Cluster (ed.), *They Should Have Served That Cup of
Coffee* (Boston: South End Press, 1979), 11–30, and her *Voices of the Civil
Rights Movement: Black American Freedom Songs, 1960–1966* (Washington,
D.C.: Smithsonian Institution, 1980).

5. See Reagon, *Voices*, 8, as well as Frank Adams with Myles Horton,
Unearthing Seeds of Fire: The Idea of Highlander (Winston-Salem: John
F. Blair, 1974), 74, for changes in the titles and lyrics.

In *Black Self-Determination* (Westport: Lawrence Hill, 1984), 29–67,
V. P. Franklin argues against the standard view that black religion (and hence
spirituals) were traditionally "otherworldly and compensatory" and that they
depicted God freeing the slaves rather than the slaves freeing themselves.
His point is that slave religion was always religious and political, sacred and
secular.

6. Reagon in Cluster (ed.), *Cup of Coffee*, 20.

7. Cited in Robert Hamburger, *Our Portion of Hell* (New York: Links
Books, 1973), 71. Fayette County in West Tennessee was an exception to the
general pattern of outside intervention by civil rights organizations to help
start grass-roots organizations, at least after the attention paid to Tent City in
1960–61. The leadership of the movement there was largely indigenous.
Hamburger's interviews were taped in 1971–72.

Adolph Reed, *The Jesse Jackson Phenomenon* (New Haven: Yale Univ.
Press, 1986) criticizes Aldon Morris for overemphasizing the religious
provenance of the movement.

8. Adams with Horton, *Unearthing*, 206; Aldon Morris, *The Origins of
the Civil Rights Movement: Black Communities Organize for Change* (New
York: Free Press, 1984), 146, 148.

9. Branch, *Parting the Waters*, 263; Septima Clark, *Ready from Within:
Septima Clark and the Civil Rights Movement,* ed. Cynthia Stokes Brown
(Navarro: Calif.: Wild Trees Press, 1986).

10. See Watters, *Down to Now*, 113, for this point about the new
perception of what it meant to go to jail, especially for middle-class black
Southerners.

11. For this definition of experience, see Fred Dallmayr, *Polis and Praxis:
Exercises in Contemporary Political Theory* (Cambridge: MIT Press, 1984),
49.

There has been considerable debate in recent theory about the status of
the "self" or "subject." As I use the concept of "self," I am not assuming any
fixed, pre-given, and entirely coherent entity called the self; but I do assume
that any meaningful discussion of ethical or political matters implies that
individuals generally possess enough self-coherence to reflect upon what
they are doing and to make judgments for themselves. That is, they are

potential agents. By extension, though the self is shaped and mediated by all sorts of forces, it is not thereby consigned to an epistemological-experiential "iron cage" without chance of modification. That is, experience can—and sometimes does—lead to new self-understanding: though the self has no metaphysical essence, it does have a history and is part of an on-going self-constructed story. For a sophisticated analysis of the "situated" self, see Richard Flathman, *The Philosophy and Politics of Freedom* (Chicago: Univ. of Chicago Press, 1987), and for a discussion of the "judging" self, see Richard H. King, "Self-Realization and Solidarity: Rorty and the Judging Self," in *Pragmatism's Freud,* ed. Joseph H. Smith and William Kerrigan (Baltimore: Johns Hopkins Univ. Press, 1986), 27–51.

    12. John Lewis in Beardslee, *The Way Out,* 34.

    13. Elizabeth Sutherland (ed.), *Letters from Mississippi* (New York: McGraw-Hill, 1965), 60; Powdermaker quoted in Jacqueline Jones, *Labor of Love, Labor of Sorrow* (New York: Basic Books, 1985), 222; Annie Devine quoted in Anne Romaine, "The Mississippi Freedom Democratic Party through August, 1964," M.A. Thesis, University of Virginia, 1970, p. 54; Marion Page, Interview, Civil Rights Documentation Project, Morland-Spingarn Collection, Howard University (1969), p. 4. (Hereinafter cited as CRDP; the pages in each interview are numbered separately; the year of the interview is given in parentheses.)

    14. See Jones, *Labor of Love,* 99–104, chap. 8.

    15. Bertram Wyatt-Brown, *Southern Honor* (New York: Oxford Univ. Press, 1982). Though Wyatt-Brown's study is confined to the white antebellum South, I assume that the culture of honor did not disappear in April 1865, nor do I assume that it was confined to the white population.

    16. Quoted in Jones, *Labor of Love,* 280–87, 299.

    17. Robert Coles, *Children of Crisis* (Boston: Atlantic Monthly Press, 1967), 67. Coles was of course the pioneer in gathering oral histories of participants in the civil rights movement; Anne Moody, *Coming of Age in Mississippi* (New York: Laurel Books, 1968), 125; Louis Lomax, *The Negro Revolt* (New York: Signet Books, 1963), 65.

Much of the testimony I cite in this chapter comes from Mississippi and other areas across the South where conditions were particularly oppressive. In this sense it is not entirely typical. At the same time it was the purpose of the civil rights movement to go into areas that needed organizing and changing and thus individuals most directly affected by the movement would be in these "hard-core" areas.

    18. Watters and Cleghorn, *Climbing,* 154, 127.

    19. Square Mormon in Hamburger (ed.), *Our Portion,* 244.

    20. The poem is reprinted in Watters, *Down to Now,* 117–23. Watters does not identify the black minister who composed it. In a speech in 1959,

Martin Luther King repeated the phrase "we just want to be free" several times. See John Ansboro, *Martin Luther King: The Making of a Mind* (Maryknoll, N.Y.: Orbis Books, 1982), 197.

21. See Martin Luther King, *Stride Toward Freedom* (New York: Harper and Row, 1958), 128, for an account of a similar experience.

22. Lawson's views are summarized by Branch, *Parting the Waters*, 260.

The dialectic of seeing and being-seen, the power of the "look" or "gaze" (*le regard*), is central to Jean-Paul Sartre's analysis of the ontology of interpersonal relationships in *Being and Nothingness* (New York: Philosophical Library, 1956). A literary exemplification of this dialectic can be found near the end of Faulkner's *Light in August* (New York: Modern Library, 1950) as the dying Joe Christmas looks back at his killers: "They are not going to lose it [the look] in whatever peaceful valleys, beside whatever placid and reassuring streams of old age, in the mirroring faces of whatever children they will contemplate old disasters and newer hopes" (p. 407).

23. Ernest Gaines, *The Autobiography of Miss Jane Pittman* (New York: Bantam Books, 1972), 228, 236.

24. Watters and Cleghorn, *Climbing*, 54; Beardslee, *The Way Out*, 8.

25. Both the Jacob and the Angel and Jericho poems are untitled and anonymous. I found them in SNCC Series XV, State Project Files (Mississippi), Box 101, File 2, Martin Luther King, Jr. Center for Nonviolent Social Change, Atlanta, Georgia.

26. Harding, *There Is a River*, 112.

27. Norman Yetman, *Life Under the Peculiar Institution* (Huntington: Robert E. Krieger, 1976), 11–20, 130–33.

28. George Armstrong Kelley, "Notes on Hegel's 'Lordship and Bondage,' in *Hegel*, ed. Alasdair MacIntyre (Garden City: Anchor Books, 1972), 195. Kelley suggests that the sources for Hegel's master-slave conflict may have included the Cain and Abel, Polyneices and Eteocles, and Jacob and the Angel stories. Again, Faulkner offers a literary exemplification in "Fire in the Hearth," in *Go Down, Moses* (New York: Modern Library, 1942), when Lucas Beauchamp and Roth Edmonds confront each other across a bed in the latter's house.

29. The biblical account of the confrontation of Jacob with the Angel is found in Genesis 32:25–30. Commentaries suggest that the Angel may be the biblical version of the "spirit" of the river bank which must be defeated to ensure safe passage, an evil demon, the spirit of Jacob's wronged brother Esau, an Angel, or God himself. It is interesting to note several similarities and differences with the Oedipus story in which the young Oedipus quarrels with a stranger at a crossroads and kills him, that stranger of course being his father. Both stories involve an ambiguous triumph at a place of transition or "crisis," that triumph being a marker in a progression toward political leadership. Oedipus kills his father, but Jacob is spared and wrests a blessing

from his adversary. Jacob is lamed in the fight, while Oedipus has already been lamed by the shackles placed on his ankles as an infant.

30. In the four-fold schema of medieval textual interpretation, there was a literal, a figural or symbolic, an ethical or psychological, and an anagogic or universal level of meaning. Figural readings linked the Old and New Testaments; ethical readings were concerned with the Bible as the source of exemplary figures and action for personal emulation; and anagogic readings read the scriptures as a key to universal history. See Erich Auerbach, *Mimesis* (Garden City: Anchor Books, 1957), chaps. 1–8, for the explanation and exemplification of figural interpretation; Northrop Frye, *Anatomy of Criticism* (Princeton: Princeton Univ. Press, 1957); and Fredric Jameson, *The Political Unconscious* (Ithaca: Cornell Univ. Press, 1981), 69–75.

31. Watters and Cleghorn, *Climbing*, 134, 126.

32. See Kimberley Benson, "I yam what I yam: The Topos of (Un)naming in Afro-American Literature," in *Black Literature and Literary Theory*, ed. Henry Louis Gates, Jr. (London: Methuen, 1984), 151–72.

33. Hamburger, *Our Portion*, 67; Perry Hamer in Tracy Sugarman, *Stranger at the Gates* (New York: Hill and Wang, 1966), 115–16; Wilola Mormon in Hamburger, *Our Portion*, 47; Mary Lane, CRDP (1969), p. 4.

34. Annie Devine, CRDP (1968), p. 9; John Hulett, CRDP (1968), p. 30.

35. McLaurin in Sugarman, *Stranger*, 132; Sherrod in Watters and Cleghorn, *Climbing*, 7; Searles in Watters, *Down to Now*, 158.

36. Watters and Cleghorn, *Climbing*, 8; Reagon in Cluster (ed.), *Cup of Coffee*, 23–24; Sally Belfrage, *Freedom Summer* (New York: Fawcett Crest, 1966), 97.

37. Bevel in Watters and Cleghorn, *Climbing*, 127. In *Parting the Waters* Branch paraphrases a frenzied sermon of Bevel's during the Birmingham campaign in 1963: "To heal themselves with freedom, he cried, all they had to do was walk—walk to the mass meeting, walk to the courthouse, walk to jail" (p. 735); Lewis in Beardslee, *The Way Out*, 8.

38. Moody, *Coming of Age*, 289, 371; Horton in Hamburger, *Our Portion*, 228–331; Hamer in Sugarman, *Stranger*, 121; Fannie Lou Hamer, CRDP (1968), p. 40.

39. Charles McDew, CRDP (1967), p. 78.

40. Alice Walker, *Meridian* (New York: Washington Square Press, 1976), 205. The phrase "political death" is a variation on Orlando Patterson's claim in *Slavery and Social Death* (Cambridge: Harvard Univ. Press, 1982) that slaves suffer from "social death" or an obliteration of essential kinship or family ties.

41. Quoted in Robert J. Norrell, *Reaping the Whirlwind: The Civil Rights Movement in Tuskegee* (New York: Knopf, 1985), 41; Lillian McGill, CRDP (1969), p. 27; Isaac Richmond, CRDP (1968), p. 47.

42. Quoted in Hamburger, *Our Portion*, 62; Watters, *Down to Now*, 336–37.

43. "Mode of experience" comes from Sheldon Wolin, "Hannah Arendt: Democracy and the Political," *Salmagundi* 60 (Spring–Summer 1983):18. In *On Revolution* (New York: Viking Compass, 1963), Arendt emphasizes the experience of public happiness in connection particularly with the founding generation of the American republic.

44. The term "saints of endurance" is Craig Werner's in "Tell Old Pharoah," *Southern Review* 19 (Oct. 1983):711–35.

45. Rosa Parks, CRDP (1967), p. 67; Sheyann Webb and Rachel West Nelson, *Selma, Lord, Selma* as told to Frank Sikora (University: Univ. of Alabama Press, 1980), 124; Unita Blackwell, CRDP (1968), p. 10; Watters, *Down to Now*, 7.

46. Quoted in Seth Cogin and Philip Dray, *We Are Not Afraid* (New York: Bantam Books, 1988), 470.

Chapter 3: Self-interest and Self-respect

1. For self-interest in the American context, see Gordon Wood, *The Creation of the American Republic, 1776–1787* (Chapel Hill: Univ. of North Carolina Press, 1969); John Diggins, *The Lost Soul of American Politics* (New York: Basic Books, 1984); and Daniel T. Rodgers, *Contested Truths: Keywords in American Politics since Independence* (New York: Basic Books, 1987), 176–211.

2. For the wider historical and conceptual context for understanding self-interest, see Albert O. Hirschman, *The Passions and the Interests* (Princeton: Princeton Univ. Press, 1977); Richard Flathman, *The Philosophy and Politics of Freedom* (Chicago: Univ. of Chicago Press, 1987), 238–44; Robert Frank, *Passions Within Reason: The Strategic Role of the Emotions* (New York: Norton, 1989); and William Griffith and Robert S. Goldfarb, "Amending the 'Rational Egoist' Model to Include Norms" (unpublished).

3. Historical-theoretical attacks on "ideological" politics (of left- and right-wing varieties) can be found in Karl Popper, *The Open Society and Its Enemies*, 2 vols. (London: Routledge and Kegan Paul, 1945); J. R. Talmon, *The Rise of Totalitarian Democracy* (London: Secker and Warburg, 1952); Hannah Arendt, *The Origins of Totalitarianism* (New York: Harcourt, Brace & Co., 1951); and Isaiah Berlin, "Two Concepts of Liberty," in *Four Essays on Liberty* (London: Oxford Univ. Press, 1969). Students of American political culture such as Daniel Boorstin, *The Genius of American Politics* (Chicago: Univ. of Chicago Press, 1953) and Louis Hartz, *The Liberal Tradition in America* (New York: Harcourt, Brace and World, 1955) assumed the existence of an atheoretical liberal consensus, though Hartz in particu-

lar had his doubts about its contemporary viability and explained rather than celebrated the lack of radical ideologies to challenge the liberal one. For one of the classical expressions of the interest-group position, see Joseph Schumpeter, *Capitalism, Socialism, and Democracy,* 3rd ed. (New York: Harper Torchbooks, 1962), 232–302. The *locus classicus* of the liberal pluralist attack on right-wing ideological politics can be found in Daniel Bell (ed.), *The Radical Right* (Garden City, N.Y.: Doubleday Anchor, 1964); while John Murray Cuddihy, *No Offence: Civil Religion and Protestant Taste* (New York: Seabury Press, 1978) offers a stimulating analysis of the link between religious and political pluralism. An early attack on liberal pluralism from the Left can be found in C. Wright Mills, *The Power Elite* (New York: Oxford Univ. Press, 1955). Michael Rogin, *The Intellectuals and McCarthy: The Radical Specter* (Cambridge: MIT Press, 1967) challenges the historical and social analyses underlying the liberal pluralist position; and Theodore Lowi, *The End of Liberalism* (New York: Norton, 1969) wades in with a critique of the policy implications of pluralist politics.

4. Richard Hofstadter, "Pseudo-Conservative Revolt" (1955), 84, and Daniel Bell, "Interpretations of American Politics" (1955), 71, in *The Radical Right,* ed. Daniel Bell.

5. For recent accounts of the Old Left/New Left split, see Maurice Isserman, *If I Had a Hammer . . . The Death of the Old Left and the Birth of the New Left* (New York: Basic Books, 1987) and James Miller, *"Democracy Is in the Streets": From Port Huron to the Siege of Chicago* (New York: Simon and Schuster, 1987).

6. My discussion of self-interest leans heavily on William Connolly, *The Terms of Political Discourse,* 2nd ed. (Oxford, U.K.: Martin Robertson, 1983), 45–83; Alasdair MacIntyre, "Egoism and Altruism," *Encyclopedia of Philosophy,* vol. 2 (New York: Collier-Macmillan, 1967): 462–66; and Rodgers, *Contested Truths.*

7. See Bayard Rustin, "From Protest to Politics (1965)," in *Black Protest Thought in the Twentieth Century,* ed. A. Meier *et al.* (Indianapolis and New York: Bobbs-Merrill, 1971), 444–60.

8. V. O. Key, *Southern Politics* (New York: Random House, 1949), 15–16; see also Richard H. King, *A Southern Renaissance* (New York: Oxford Univ. Press, 1980), 249–56. For the most recent study of Southern politics in the Key tradition, see Merle and Earl Black, *Politics and Society in the South* (Cambridge: Harvard Univ. Press, 1987). In his "The Populist Heritage and the Intellectuals," *The Burden of Southern History* (New York: Vintage, 1961), 153, C. Vann Woodward chides the liberal pluralists who tended to see the Populists and "populism" as the chief threats to the politics of civility and as precursors of the McCarthyite spirit. Woodward claims that the Populists pursued "interest" not "status" or "class" politics; that is, they

were neither proto-Marxists nor Fascists before the fact, but militants in the mainstream of American politics.

9. Frank, *Passions Within Reason*, xi.

10. Jane Mansbridge, "Self-Interest in Political Life," *Political Theory* 18, 1 (February 1990): 132–53. 140.

11. Diggins, *The Lost Soul of American Politics*, 105.

12. Connolly, *Terms of Political Discourse*, 45–83.

13. Griffith and Goldfarb, "Amending the 'Rational Egoist' . . . ," 8.

14. Frank, *Passions Within Reason*, ix.

15. This, I take it, is similar to the basic point of rule utilitarians who do not insist that each practice or institution maximize pleasure or activity, only that it should contribute to overall or long-term maximization of utility. Criminals, for instance, are punished in the name of overall greatest good of the greatest number, even though presumably punishment does not maximize their pleasure per se. See John Rawls, "Two Concepts of Rules," *The Philosophical Review* 64 (1955):3–32.

Though both are consequentialist positions, interest theory differs from utilitarianism in not aiming at the greatest good of the greatest number but at the minimal condition that can support an on-going pursuit of individual or group interest. Nor does utilitarianism claim to describe what the motivations for action are, as does explanatory interest theory; rather it is concerned with what they should be, as is the normative notion of interest theory.

16. Alasdair MacIntyre, "Egoism and Altruism," 462–66. MacIntyre has suggested that Aristotle's notion of "well-being" is the proper yardstick for understanding and evaluating political institutions as it potentially encompasses action based on self-interest and group welfare. See his *A Short History of Ethics* (New York: Macmillan, 1966), 57–83, for a discussion of Aristotle and well-being.

17. Bernard Williams, "The Idea of Equality," in *Philosophy, Politics and Society*, 2nd series, ed. P. Laslett and W. G. Runciman (Oxford, U.K.: Basil Blackwell, 1969), 114; Carol Gilligan, "In a Different Voice: Women's Conceptions of Self and Morality," in *The Future of Difference*, ed. Hester Eisenstein and Alice Jardine (New Brunswick: Rutgers Univ. Press, 1987), 306; Thomas Hill, "Servility and Self-respect," in *Rights*, ed. David Lyons (Belmont: Wadsworth, 1979), 116; Laurence Thomas, "Self-respect: Theory and Practice," in *Philosophy Born of Struggle*, ed. Leonard Harris (Dubuque: Kendall/Hunt, 1983), 174, 176; Bernard Boxill, "Self-respect and Protest," in *Philosophy Born of Struggle*, ed. Leonard Harris (Dubuque: Kendall/Hunt, 1983), 190–98.

18. Bernard Williams, "A Critique of Utilitarianism," in *Utilitarianism*, ed. J. J. C. Smart and B. Williams (Cambridge, U.K.: Cambridge Univ. Press, 1973), 104. The thrust of Williams's objections to utilitarianism—that it fails to understand or credit personal integrity or commitment—applies to an extent to the ethics and politics of self-interest. But the real problem with

the politics of self-interest is not that it doesn't acknowledge the separateness of selves but that its notion of what constitutes a self is inadequate.

19. Michael Walzer, *Spheres of Justice* (New York: Basic Books, 1983), 279. Walzer says that self-respect derives from keeping abstract standards or principles, while self-esteem has to do with the opinion of others.

20. See of course Stanley Elkins, *Slavery* (Chicago: Univ. of Chicago Press, 1959); Salmon Rushdie, *Shame* (London: Jonathan Cape, 1983); and Elaine Scarry, *The Body in Pain* (New York: Oxford Univ. Press, 1985).

21. Orlando Patterson, *Slavery and Social Death* (Cambridge: Harvard Univ. Press, 1982).

22. Williams, "The Idea of Equality," 110.

23. Stanley Cavell, "Being Odd, Getting Even: Threats to Individuality," *Salmagundi* 67 (Summer 1985), 104, 108.

24. "Other" in this context refers to any form of self-consciousness which (mis-)recognizes my existence and thus implicitly or explicitly acknowledges my difference.

25. See, for instance, Neil McMillen, *Dark Journey* (Urbana: Univ. of Illinois Press, 1989), an exhausting account of black life, including the lack of a public life, in Mississippi up to 1940.

26. Bernard Boxill, "Self-respect and Protest," 193, 197.

27. Nor does Arendt develop a consistent or clear account of self-formation. Suzanne Jacobitti, "Hannah Arendt and the Will," and B. Honig, "Arendt, Identity and Difference," *Political Theory* 16, #1 (Feb. 1988): 53–76 and 77–98, come to quite different conclusions about the adequacy of the conception of the self in Arendt's work. Jacobitti claims that Arendt needs a notion of agency to complete her theory of action and freedom, while Honig claims that Arendt is precisely concerned not to unify the self and thereby detach freedom from action. For Arendt, she claims, identity is not identical with autonomy but emerges in and is revealed by action and speech.

28. G. W. F. Hegel, *The Phenomenology of Mind*, trans. J. B. Baillie (London: George Allen and Unwin, 1955), 228–40. This section of Hegel's text is actually translated "Lordship and Bondage." I use "Hegelian" here to refer not just to Hegel's analysis but also to those analyses deriving from it: particularly Jean-Paul Sartre, *Being and Nothingness* (1958), Albert Memmi, *The Colonizer and Colonized* (1965), Frantz Fanon, *Black Faces, White Masks* (1967) and *The Wretched of the Earth* (1963), which I mentioned in Chapter 1 and which I will take up in depth in Chapter 7.

The applicability of the master-slave paradigm to American slavery in the work of Eugene Genovese and David Brion Davis has been questioned by John Diggins, "Comrades and Citizens: New Mythologies in American Historiography," *American Historical Review* 90, #3 (June 1985): 616–19 and Richard H. King, "Marxism and the Slave South," *American Quarterly* 29, #1 (Spring 1977): 117–31. Diggins wonders whether the claim that the actual laboring slave comes to "know" more than the master is historically sustainable and doubts that the Southern master wanted the slave to emulate his way of life, while I think the added element of racism dilutes the master's need for recognition from the slave, since racial inferiority implies permanent not circumstantial inequality. In addition Fredric Jameson notes that conceptualizing domination in purely personalistic (Hegelian) terms neglects the importance of impersonal and structural modes of domination, a point that a Foucaultian also might make. See Jameson, "Periodizing the 60s," in *The 60s Without Apology*, ed. Sohnya Sayres, *et al.* (Minneapolis: Univ. of Minnesota Press, 1984), 190.

However all that may be, Hegel's analysis is still the necessary starting point for understanding the psychology of domination and self-formation, whether at an individual or group level, not to mention the internal structures of the self. G. A. Kelly, "Notes on Hegel's 'Lordship and Bondage,'" in *Hegel*, ed. Alasdair MacIntyre (Garden City, N.Y.: Anchor Books, 1972), 189–217, and M. H. Abrams *Natural Supernaturalism* (New York: Norton, 1971), 356–72, contain valuable accounts of the intellectual origins and effects of the master-slave paradigm. Abrams in particular stresses the way external relations of opposition (self/other; mind/nature) were internalized (as oppositions between body and soul, intuition and perception) in Romantic thought and literature after the onset of disillusionment with the French Revolution. Abrams refers to this as the "politics of vision" whose goal was re-union of contending opposites at a higher level. Thus it is impossible to restrict Hegel's analysis either to the intra- or the interpersonal level, since it bears on both.

29. Frederick Douglass, *Narrative of the Life of Frederick Douglass* (Garden City: Doubleday Dolphin, 1963). W. E. B. DuBois, *The Souls of Black Folk*, in *Three Negro Classics*, intro. John Hope Franklin (New York: Avon Books, 1965).

30. Douglass, *Narrative*, 82. For the general point about the secular nature of *Narrative*, see Ann Kibbey, "Language in Slavery: Frederick Douglass's *Narrative*," in *Prospects 8*, ed. Jack Salzman (Cambridge, U.K.: Cambridge Univ. Press, 1983), 163–82. Also Robert Stepto, *From Behind the Veil* (Urbana: Univ. of Illinois Press, 1979) is highly illuminating on the place of Douglass's *Narrative* in Afro-American writing. See also Richard Wright, *Black Boy* (New York, Signet, 1951), and Anne Moody, *Coming of Age in Mississippi* (New York: Dell, 1968).

31. Stanley Elkins, "The Slavery Debate," *Commentary* 60 (Dec. 1975): 40–54.

32. Moody, *Coming of Age*, 88–89; Richard Wright, *American Hunger* (New York: Perennial, 1979).

33. Moody, *Coming of Age*, 263, 129.

34. Kibbey, "Language in Slavery," 163–82.

35. Douglass, *Narrative*, 35. There is nothing particularly novel about the thesis that power corrupts—the master's power particularly. It was a staple of abolitionist discourse and indeed one of the main arguments used by Southern white opponents of slavery from Jefferson through Helper.

36. *Ibid.*, 14, 42–43.

37. *Ibid.*, 43.

38. Douglass, *My Bondage and My Freedom*, intro. Philip S. Foner (New York: Dover, 1969), 247. This, his second autobiography, was originally published in 1855.

39. Douglass, *Narrative*, 73; Douglass, *My Bondage and My Freedom*, 244.

40. Douglass, *My Bondage*, 247. This passage is an example of what Patterson refers to as the dishonored status of the slave.

41. Douglass, *Narrative*, 74.

42. Scarry, *The Body in Pain*, esp. chap. 1.

43. Henry Louis Gates, introduction, *Our Nig or Sketches from the Life of a Free Black* by Harriet E. Wilson (London: Allison and Busby, 1983), xlvii.

44. Wilson, *Our Nig*, 105, 108.

45. Hazel V. Carby, *Reconstructing Womanhood: The Emergence of the Afro-American Woman Novelist* (New York: Oxford Univ. Press, 1987). See also bell hooks, *Ain't I a Woman: Black Women and Feminism* (London: Pluto Press, 1982), 159; Quandra Prettyman, "Visibility and Difference: Black Women in History and Literature—Pieces of a Paper and Some Ruminations," in *The Future of Difference*, ed. Eisenstein and Jardine (New Brunswick: Rutgers Univ. Press, 1985), 246.

46. Zora Neale Hurston, *Their Eyes Were Watching God* (New York: Negro Univ. Press, 1969), 74.

47. Douglass, "The Heroic Slave," reprinted in *Violence in the Black Imagination: Essay and Documents*, ed. Ronald Takaki (New York: G. P. Putman, 1972), 75, 77; see also Robert Stepto, "Storytelling in Early Afro-American Fiction: Frederick Douglass's 'The Heroic Slave,'" in *Black Literature and Literary Theory* ed. Henry Louis Gates (London: Methuen, 1984), 175–86. It should be added that whatever the power and literary merit of Douglass's *Narrative*—which I think are considerable—Douglass was certainly no writer of fiction.

48. Waldo Martin, Jr., *The Mind of Frederick Douglass* (Chapel Hill: Univ. of North Carolina Press, 1984), 62. There is no avoiding the explicit gender reference in this passage.

49. Douglass, *Narrative*, 83–84.

50. *Ibid.*, 76–77.

51. G. W. F. Hegel, *Phenomenology of Mind*, 238, 237. Douglass, *Narrative*, 85.

52. Joel Williamson, *The Crucible of Race: Black-White Relations in the*

American South Since Emancipation (New York: Oxford Univ. Press, 1984), 399–413.

53. W. E. B. DuBois, *The Souls of Black Folk,* 214.

54. Hurston, *Their Eyes,* 21.

55. DuBois, *Souls,* 214–15.

56. For this emphasis upon cultural pluralism, see Manning Marable, W. E. B. *DuBois: Black Radical Democrat* (Boston: Twayne, 1986).

57. DuBois, *Souls,* 216, 219.

58. *Ibid.,* 220, 219.

59. See Addison Gayle (ed.), *The Black Aesthetic* (Garden City: Double-day Anchor, 1971) for essays and manifestoes on this topic.

60. Barbara Johnson, "Metaphor, Metonymy and Voice in *Their Eyes Were Watching God,*" in *Black Literature and Literary Theory,* 212; hooks, *Ain't I a Woman.*

Chapter 4: Martin Luther King and the Meanings of Freedom

1. Stanley Cavell, *The Senses of Walden* (San Francisco: North Point Press, 1981), 33. Cavell's point about overpraising but undervaluing was made in reference to Thoreau's reputation; Alice Walker, *In Search of Our Mothers' Gardens* (London: Women's Press, 1984), 156.

2. Recent major studies of King and SCLC, institutional biographies as it were, are Adam Fairclough, *To Redeem the Soul of America* (Athens: Univ. Georgia Press, 1987); David Garrow, *Bearing the Cross* (New York: Morrow, 1986); Thomas R. Peake, *Keeping the Dream Alive* (New York: Peter Lang, 1987); and Taylor Branch, *Parting the Waters: America in the King Years, 1954–63* (New York: Simon and Schuster, 1988). Major studies of King's thought include Haynes Walton, *The Political Philosophy of Martin Luther King, Jr.* (Westport: Greenwood, 1971); Kenneth Smith and Ira Zepp, Jr., *Search for the Beloved Community* (Valley Forge, Pa.: Judson Press, 1974); and John Ansboro, *Martin Luther King, Jr.: The Making of a Mind* (Maryknoll, N.Y.: Orbis Books, 1982).

3. The first three books cited in note 2 are at pains to de-emphasize the importance of King for the movement generally or for SCLC particularly. Whatever their other merits, they remain unconvincing on that theme.

4. William Beardslee, *The Way Out Must Lead In,* 2nd ed. (Westport: Lawrence Hill: 1983), 98; Walker, *Mothers' Gardens,* 122, 124, 145, 159; Clayborne Carson, "Reconstructing the King Legacy: Scholars and National Myths," in *We Shall Overcome: Martin Luther King, Jr. and the Black Freedom Struggle,* ed. Peter J. Albert and Ronald Hoffman (New York: Pantheon, 1990), 246.

5. Walker, *Mothers' Gardens,* 121.

6. Harold Cruse, *Resistance and Rebellion* (New York: Morrow, 1968),

127; Ralph Ellison in Robert Penn Warren, *Who Speaks for the Negro?* (New York: Random House, 1965), 346–47.

7. John Edgar Wideman, *Brothers and Keepers* (New York: Penguin, 1985), 113, 114.

8. Cruse, *Resistance*, 66.

9. *Ibid.*, 61. See Sara Evans, *Personal Politics* (New York: Vintage, 1980) for an account of the emergence of feminism in the civil rights movement.

10. Cruse, *Resistance*, 114. See Ralph Ellison, *Shadow and Act* (New York: Signet, 1966) and Albert Murray, *The Omni-Americans* (New York: Avon, 1970) for analyses of black American culture which emphasize its Southern roots.

11. Hannah Arendt, *The Human Condition* (Garden City, N.Y.: Doubleday Anchor, 1959), 11–13, is a basic statement of her objection to the idea of a fixed human nature in general or individual identity in particular. Her idea is that only "god" could have the vantage point to detect what is essentially human.

12. See Smith and Zepp, *Search for the Beloved Community*, and John Ansboro, *Martin Luther King, Jr.: The Making of a Mind* for King's theological and philosophical training. Ansboro notes that King claimed Hegel as his favorite philosopher (p. 122) and was strongly influenced by Hegel's analysis of the master-slave relationship (p. 298).

13. Quoted in David Lewis, *King: A Critical Biography* (Baltimore: Penguin, 1971), 109.

14. See Emerson, "Fate," *Selected Writings of Ralph Waldo Emerson* (New York: Modern Library College Edition, 1981), 686. Both David Garrow and Taylor Branch identify the Birmingham campaign in 1963 as the point after which King finally fully accepted his destiny as a leader.

15. Martin Luther King, *Chaos or Community* (Harmondsworth, U.K.: Pelican, 1969), 98–99. This is the title of the British edition of *Where Do We Go From Here?* (1967).

16. Garrow, *Bearing*, 58; and "Martin Luther King, Jr. and the Spirit of Leadership," in *We Shall Overcome*, ed. Albert and Hoffman, 11–34; Lerone Bennett, *What Manner of Man?* (London: George Allen and Unwin, 1966), 75–76; and also Elie Landau, *King: A Filmed Record, Montgomery to Memphis* (1970), reel 3.

17. Quoted in Lewis, *King*, 236. Garrow makes surprisingly little of King's two attempts at suicide. He includes the first in a list of "scrapes" ("jumping or falling from the second floor . . .") and hurries past the second attempt (pp. 34–35). It should be said that there is a strange reluctance generally on the part of King's biographers to do anything at all approaching a psychoanalytic profile of King.

18. Reinhold Niebuhr, *Moral Man and Immoral Society* (New York: Scribner's, 1932), chap. 9. See also Richard W. Fox, *Reinhold Niebuhr* (New

York: Pantheon, 1985). Taylor Branch, *Parting the Waters*, 81–87, claims Niebuhr's influence on King was stronger than that of Walter Rauschenbusch or Gandhi. He also notes King's reversal of Niebuhr's claim that social injustice is more difficult to correct than are individual shortcomings (p. 802).

19. These are Erik Erikson's words about Gandhi in *Gandhi's Truth* (New York: Norton, 1969), 144.

20. Garry Wills, "Dr. King on the Case," *Lead Time* (Garden City, N.Y.: Doubleday, 1983), 29–50.

21. Quoted in Lewis, *King*, 236.

22. *Ibid.*, 254.

23. Quoted in Garrow, *The FBI and Martin Luther King, Jr.* (New York: Penguin, 1983), 217–18.

24. Stephen B. Oates, *Let the Trumpet Sound* (New York: New American Library, 1982), 232.

25. Robert Stepto, *From Behind the Veil* (Urbana: Univ. of Illinois Press, 1979).

26. Of the early biographers Bennett makes this point particularly well, while Garrow convincingly documents the mounting physical exhaustion and emotional depression in the last three years of King's life.

27. This positive assessment of King's response to the difficult public tasks of his last two years is emphasized by Manning Marable, "Toward an Understanding of Martin Luther King, Jr.," in *From the Grassroots* (Boston: South End Press, 1980), 51–58; and Taylor Branch, "Uneasy Holiday," *New Republic* (Feb. 3, 1986), 22–27.

28. King, *Chaos or Community*, 66.

29. *Ibid.*, 98; see also Lillian Smith, *The Winner Names the Age* (New York: Norton, 1978).

30. King, *Strength to Love*, 50. The classic work on this subject is Anders Nygren, *Agape and Eros* (London: SPCK, 1954); while Gene Outka, *Agape: An Ethical Analysis* (New Haven: Yale Univ. Press, 1972) offers a comprehensive overview of the various theological understandings of *agape* in contemporary theology.

31. Smith and Zepp, *Search for the Beloved Community*, claim that King rejected Nygren's astringent view that *agape* commands us to love our enemies only because God loves them and not because they are created in God's image (pp. 63–66). Ansboro, *The Making of a Mind*, affirms this claim about King (p. 27) but recognizes that the passage cited in the text seems to indicate King's acceptance of Nygren's position.

32. King, *Stride Toward Freedom* (New York: Harper and Row, 1958), 107; the second part of the quotation is found in Smith and Zepp, *Search for the Beloved Community*, 113.

33. Quoted in J. Robert Cox, "The Fulfillment of Time: King's 'I Have a Dream' Speech (August 28, 1963)" in *Texts in Context: Critical Dialogues on*

Significant Episodes in American Political Rhetoric, eds. Michael C. Leff and Fred J. Kauffeld (Davis, Cal.: Hermagoras Press, 1989), 181–204; Smith and Zepp, *Search for the Beloved Community*, 25–26; King, *Why We Can't Wait* (New York: Signet, 1964), 61.
More generally, see Sacvan Bercovitch, *The Puritan Origins of the American Self* (New Haven: Yale Univ. Press, 1975), and *The American Jeremiad* (Madison: Univ. of Wisconsin Press, 1978) for the white origins of the sense of chosenness and the centrality of the jeremiad. For the black origins of similar themes, see Vincent Harding, *There Is a River* (New York: Vintage, 1983); V. P. Franklin, *Black Self-Determination* (Westport: Lawrence Hill, 1984); and Cornell West, *Prophesy Deliverance!* (Philadelphia: Westminister, 1981).

34. King, *Why We Can't Wait*, 93.

35. King, *Chaos or Community*, 129.

36. King, *Stride*, 37, 215. In her memoir of the boycott, Jo Ann Robinson writes: "Many of the elderly boycotters felt that the black masses had really grown up in dignity, self-composure, and reserve. Dignity seemed to prevail with almost everyone" (*The Montgomery Bus Boycott and the Women Who Started It*, ed. David J. Garrow [Knoxville: Univ. of Tennessee, 1987], 167).

37. King, "Love, Law and Civil Disobedience," in *A Testament of Hope*, ed. James M. Washington (New York: Harper and Row, 1986), 45; King, *Why We Can't Wait*, 30.

38. King, *Chaos or Community*, 44–46, 57.

39. King, *Why We Can't Wait*, 80; *Stride*, 101.

40. King, *Strength to Love*, 55; see Martin Buber, *I and Thou* (New York: Charles Scribner's Sons, 1958).

41. King, *Why We Can't Wait*, 39, 100.

42. King, *Chaos or Community*, 28.

43. *Ibid.*, 71, 84. It is ironic that psychologist Kenneth Clark, who was extremely critical of King's non-violent approach, was one of the main purveyors of the "ghetto-as-pathology" rhetoric as illustrated by his *Dark Ghetto* (New York: Harper Torchbook, 1967). The label "hermeneutics of suspicion" can be found in Paul Ricoeur, *Freud and Philosophy* (New Haven: Yale, 1970), 32–36.

44. *Ibid.*, 102–3, 106, 112.

45. *Ibid.*, 92, 91.

46. King, *Why We Can't Wait*, 81, 94.

47. King makes the point about the First Amendment basis of direct action in his *Playboy* interview of 1965 collected in James M. Washington (ed.), *A Testament of Hope*, 357. See also Richard H. King, "Justice Black and Dr. King," *European Contributions to American Studies XII* (Amsterdam: Free University Press, 1988), 100–118.

48. King's indictment of white Southern moderates and acceptance of the extremist label owed much to Lillian Smith, particularly her "The Right Way

Is Not a Moderate Way" (1956), in *The Winner Names the Age*, 67–75. A copy of this essay can be found in the King Papers at Boston University along with early letters from Smith to King.

49. In *Stride* King writes that "one of the great glories of democracy is the right to protest for right" (p. 62), while Stephen Oates records that at Montgomery King said, "One of the great glories of American democracy is that we have the right to protest for rights" (pp. 78–79). The voice recording in the Landau film indicates that King said, "The great glory of American democracy is the right to protest for right" at Montgomery, while at Memphis he modified it to "The greatness of America is the right to protest for right." There is of course a difference between what is "right" and "a right." Right is a moral term, while rights are legal/constitutional entities, the exercise of which may be morally wrong.

In *Origins of Totalitarianism*, 2nd ed. (Cleveland: Meridian Books, 1958), Arendt refers to the "right to have rights." Although eschewing any reference to natural rights as such, Arendt explained the phrase as the right "to live in a framework where one is judged by one's action and opinions" and "to belong to some kind of organized community" (p. 53). See Stephen J. Whitfield, *Into the Dark* (Philadelphia: Temple Univ. Press, 1980), 110–12, for the influence of Arendt's idea of a "right to have rights" on Supreme Court decisions of the 1950s and 1960s.

50. King, *Why We Can't Wait*, 82–83. The conceptual core of "Letter" can be found in "Love, Law and Civil Disobedience" (1961). It is there that King explicitly acknowledges that natural law thinking is foreign to most people.

51. King, *Why We Can't Wait*, 83. See Hugo Bedeau, "On Civil Disobedience," *Journal of Philosophy* 58 (1961): 653–66; and John Rawls, *A Theory of Justice* (Cambridge: Harvard Univ. Press, 1971), chap. 6, for the "rectification" view. April Carter, *Direct Action and Liberal Democracy* (London: Routledge and Kegan Paul, 1973) is a less theoretically and more historically oriented discussion of the various ways of analyzing civil disobedience.

Rawls cites King's "Letter" at the beginning of his discussion of civil disobedience in *A Theory of Justice* (p. 364). However, Rawls notes that his notion of civil disobedience is based on political rather than religious or metaphysical criteria. In the terms I use in the next chapter, Rawls accepts King's procedural but not his substantive criteria. Ultimately, however, the distinction between substantive and procedural criteria breaks down since the procedure based on mutual acknowledgment and keeping promises, i.e., justice as fairness, is part of the substantive notion of justice. In his "Disobeying the Law," *Journal of Philosophy* 58 (1961), Richard Wasserstrom suggests that there may be an "obligation to break the laws" (p. 653). See also Morton White, *The Philosophy of the American Revolution* (New York: Oxford Univ. Press, 1970) for a discussion of the relationship between duty and rights in the Lockean tradition where a duty implies a right.

52. King, *Chaos or Community*, 58; Wilson Carey McWilliams, "Civil Disobedience and Contemporary Constitutionalism," *Comparative Politics* 1 (Jan. 1969): 222. I do not claim that King had such a participatory or revelatory notion of freedom in mind.

53. Hannah Arendt, "Civil Disobedience," *Crises of the Republic* (New York: Harcourt, Brace and Jovanovich, 1972), 56. In *A Theory of Justice* Rawls makes a similar distinction between "civil disobedience" and "conscientious refusal" (pp. 368–89). See also Marshall Cohen, "Civil Disobedience in a Constitutional Democracy," *Massachusetts Review* 10 (Spring 1969): 211–26. This criticism of Arendt has been voiced by George Kateb, *Hannah Arendt: Politics, Conscience, Evil* (Oxford, U.K.: Martin Robertson, 1981), chaps. 1 and 3.

54. King, *Why We Can't Wait*, 38.

55. McWilliams, "Civil Disobedience . . . ," 222; King, *Why We Can't Wait*, 39.

Chapter 5: Martin Luther King: Authorship and Ideas

1. See Taylor Branch, *Parting the Waters* (New York: Simon and Schuster, 1988), 363, 747.

2. Hannah Arendt, *On Revolution* (New York: Viking Press, 1965), 127.

3. A recent article on this topic is Keith Miller, "Composing Martin Luther King, Jr.," *PMLA* 105, #1 (Jan. 1990): 70–82.

4. In his *The Kennedy Imprisonment* (New York: Pocket Books, 1983), Garry Wills notes that John Kennedy was the author of *Profiles in Courage* primarily in the sense that he "authorized" it (pp. 139–43). I was told about Nader's having a ghostwriter in the mid-1970s.

5. Quoted in David Garrow, *Bearing the Cross: Martin Luther King, Jr., and the SCLC* (New York: Morrow, 1983), 649. For discussions of the multiple meanings of authorship, see Roland Barthes, "The Death of the Author," *Image-Music-Text* (London: Fontana Collins, 1977), 142–48; and Michel Foucault, "What Is an Author?," *Language, Counter-Memory, Practice*, ed. Donald F. Bouchard (Ithaca: Cornell Univ. Press, 1977), 113–38. Though Barthes's is the more striking piece, Foucault's is actually more useful in this context. I have taken the term "author-function" from him, referring to the function of the name which authorizes the circulation of certain texts all bearing that name.

6. Garrow, *Bearing the Cross*, 112.

7. Miller, "Composing Martin Luther King, Jr.," 76. About the influence of Hegel, Miller writes "[The Rev. A. D.] Williams had taught that lesson [growth through struggle] to King's father. If the elder King failed to

pass it on, his son still did not need to consult Hegel to learn about struggle" (p. 77).

8. *Ibid.*, 77–78.

9. *Ibid.*, 79.

10. See Michael Harrington, *Fragments of the Century* (New York: Saturday Review Press, 1973). Other thinkers such as Paul Goodman and the early C. Wright Mills were more forthright in their rejection of Marxism, while Herbert Marcuse wrote *Eros and Civilization* (Boston: Beacon, 1955) without once mentioning Marx's name and substituted the term "Critical Theory" for Marxism.

11. Adam Fairclough, "Was Martin Luther King a Marxist?" *History Workshop Journal* 15 (Spring 1983): 183; see also his *To Redeem the Soul of America* (Athens: Univ. of Georgia Press, 1987), 29–32.

12. Vincent Harding, *The Other American Revolution* (Los Angeles: Center for Afro-American Studies, 1980).

13. *Ibid.*, 150.

14. Interview with Ella Baker, CRDP (1968), p. 16.

15. Cornel West, "The Religious Foundations of the Thought of Martin Luther King, Jr.," in *We Shall Overcome: Martin Luther King, Jr. and the Black Freedom Struggle*, ed. Peter J. Albert and Ronald Hoffman (New York: Pantheon, 1990), 116–17. Though West cites liberal Christianity as a major influence on King, he neglects to mention Niebuhr's influence.

16. Clayborne Carson, "Reconstructing the King Legacy: Scholars and National Myths," *ibid.*, 243.

17. James M. Washington (ed.), "Playboy Interview," *A Testament of Hope: The Essential Writings of Martin Luther King, Jr.* (New York: Harper and Row, 1986), 364, 365.

18. In *Black Self-Determination* (Westport: Lawrence Hill, 1984), V. P. Franklin points to this dichotomy when he contrasts "political" and "cultural" self-determination (p. 8).

19. Max Weber, "Politics as a Vocation," *From Max Weber*, ed. H. H. Gerth and C. Wright Mills (New York: Oxford Univ. Press, 1958), 126.

20. Philip Rieff's *The Triumph of the Therapeutic* (New York: Harper Torchbook, 1968) is one of the earliest and the best analyses of the shift in cultural discourse from moral and religious to psychological and therapeutic descriptions of the self. See also Robert Boyers (ed.), *Psychological Man* (New York: Harper Colophon, 1975), for a general critique and discussion of Rieff's thesis.

21. Jennifer Radden, *Madness and Reason* (London: George Allen and Unwin, 1985), 15.

22. Michel Foucault, *The Order of Things* (New York: Pantheon, 1970), 318–22.

23. Radden, *Madness and Reason*, 8.

24. At least since Wilhelm Reich there has been a suspicion that cancer has psychological causes instead of or—as well as—environmental or other undiscovered causes. If this was shown to be the case, it would serve to support rather than to undermine my case, since it would move what seems to be a biological disturbance into the realm of psychology. But one (frightening) consequence of the psychologization of the illness is the covert re-moralization of the disease and the attribution of responsibility to the sufferer. For a recent attack on the alcoholism-as-a-disease thesis, see Herbert Fingarette, "Alcoholism: The Mythical Disease," *Public Interest* 91 (Spring 1988): 3–22.

25. Amelie O. Rorty, "*Akrasia* and Conflict," *Inquiry* 23 (1980): 193–212. See also Richard Flathman, *The Philosophy and Politics of Freedom* (Chicago: Univ. of Chicago Press, 1987), 98–107. The classic definition of *akrasia* is weakness of the will; in other words, acting against one's better judgment.

26. In her essay cited above, Rorty claims that this is the classical (Socratic) view of *akrasia* (p. 195), though I am obviously using it in a different context.

27. Pat Watters, *The South and the Nation* (New York: Pantheon, 1969), 351. See also Hannah Arendt, *Eichmann in Jerusalem* (New York: Viking Compass, 1965), and "Thinking and Moral Considerations," *Social Research* 38, #3 (1972): 417–46.

28. A. Rorty, "*Akrasia* and Conflict," 197. For Harding's use of the term "wounded healer" see Vincent Harding in Albert and Hoffman (eds.), *We Shall Overcome*, 165; and King in Washington, "Playboy Interview," *Testament*, 349.

29. King, *Why We Can't Wait*, 83.

30. Ronald Dworkin, *Taking Rights Seriously* (Cambridge: Harvard Univ. Press, 1977), 99. See also Richard Wasserstrom, "Disobeying the Law," *Journal of Philosophy* 58 (1961): 641–53; and "The Obligation to Obey the Law," in Hugo Bedau (ed.), *Civil Disobedience* (New York: Pegasus Books, 1969), 256–68, for discussions of the "what if everyone did it" objection to civil disobedience.

Related to Dworkin's position is the objection to the belief that willingness to suffer the consequences of breaking a law justifies civil disobedience by itself. But as Marshall Cohen has pointed out, it was Justice Oliver Wendell Holmes rather than Gandhi or Thoreau (or King) who offered this justification for civil disobedience. As many have noted, this position is nonsense, since murderers or bank robbers could justify their crimes in this way. See Marshall Cohen, "Civil Disobedience in a Constitutional Democracy," *Massachusetts Review* 10 (Spring 1969): 214.

31. John Rawls, *Theory of Justice*, 366.

32. See Cohen, "Civil Disobedience," 219.

33. Wasserstrom, "Disobeying the Law," 473; William L. Taylor, "Civil

Disobedience: Observations on the Strategies of Protest," in Bedau (ed.), *Civil Disobedience,* 90–105; and Arendt, "Civil Disobedience," *Crises of the Republic* (New York: Harcourt Brace Jovanovich, 1972), 53 (citing remarks by Charles Black).

34. Hugo Bedau, "On Civil Disobedience," *Journal of Philosophy* 58 (1961): 655.

35. Fred Berger, "Symbolic Conduct and Freedom on Speech," *Freedom of Expression,* ed. Fred Berger (Belmont, Cal.: Wadsworth, 1980), 148.

36. Arendt, "Civil Disobedience," 49–102.

37. These three rationales for free expression are suggested in David Cole's "Agon at Agora: Creative Misreadings in the First Amendment Tradition," *Yale Law Journal* 95, #5 (April 1986): 857–907. Cole's article is a stimulating application of Harold Bloom's theory of the "anxiety of influence" to great dissenting opinions by Justices Holmes, Brandeis, and Brennan.

38. The meaning I give to "public forum" is suggested by but not identical with Harry Kalven's use of the term in his "The Concept of the Public Forum: *Cox v. Louisiana,*" *Supreme Court Review* (Chicago: Univ. of Chicago Press, 1965), 1–32.

39. Hugo Black, *A Constitutional Faith* (New York: Knopf, 1968), 45.

40. "Justice Black and the Bill of Rights," CBS News Special, Dec. 3, 1968 (Justice Black interviewed by Eric Severeid and Martin Agronsky).

41. Berger, "Symbolic Conduct . . . ," *Freedom of Expression,* 151–56.

42. Reinhold Niebuhr, *Moral Man and Immoral Society* (New York: Scribner's, 1932), 172, 240.

43. King, *The Trumpet of Conscience* (New York: Harper and Row, 1968), 15.

44. King, *Chaos or Community,* 126.

45. See Vinit Haksar, *Civil Disobedience, Threats and Offers: Gandhi and Rawls* (Delhi: Oxford Univ. Press, 1986) for a discussion of the role of civil disobedience in a fundamentally just society, where Rawls basically assumed civil disobedience to be justified or potentially effective.

46. David Garrow, *Protest at Selma* (New Haven: Yale Univ. Press, 1978), chap. 7; see also Watters and Cleghorn, *Climbing Jacob's Ladder* (Harcourt, Brace and World, 1967) for an earlier version of Garrow's charge.

47. April Carter, *Direct Action and Liberal Democracy* (London: Routledge and Kegan Paul, 1973), 89.

48. Erik Erikson, *Childhood and Society,* 2nd ed. (New York: Norton, 1963), 285.

49. In both the theological and naturalistic arguments much hinges on the force of the term "natural." One view would see the natural as synonymous with "necessary" and "inevitable": thus if violence is natural, it is inevitable. But another, more plausible view would be that to describe something as natural is not to say much more than that it is a possibility or, at most, a

propensity. Moreover, a Darwinian emphasis upon the survival of adaptive traits suggests that there is a multitude of natural traits which may work against one another. Indeed instincts might best be considered to be transcendental concepts which are needed to ground an explanation of behavior. We obviously have evidence that violence exists, but any statement about the origins, force, desirability, or inevitability of a violent instinct is an interpretation, a function of a theory. Indeed Roy Schafer has urged in his *A New Language for Psychoanalysis* (New Haven: Yale Univ. Press, 1976) that we should de-reify concepts such as "aggression" or "violence" and talk rather of "aggressive" or "violent" behavior, i.e., we should replace nouns with adjectives when we describe thought or action.

50. Kenneth Clark, *The Dark Ghetto* (New York: Harper Torchbooks, 1965), 213–22. See also Robert Penn Warren, *Who Speaks for the Negro?* (New York: Random House, 1965), 313–25, for an interview with Clark.

51. Clark, *Dark Ghetto*, 218–19. In an interview with King in 1963, Clark attributed the view that non-violent behavior fits white stereotypes of blacks to Malcolm X. See Washington (ed.), *Testament*, 365–66.

52. Ralph Ellison in Warren, *Who Speaks for the Negro?*, 340, 341, 342.

53. Erik Erikson, *Gandhi's Truth* (New York: Norton, 1969), 423–36. See Kenneth Clark, "Implications of Adlerian Theory for an Understanding of Civil Rights Problems and Action," *Journal of Individual Psychology* 23 (Nov. 1967): 181–90, for an account of Clark's Adlerian position.

54. Vincent Harding, CRDP (1968), pp. 32–34; James Farmer quoted in Carter, *Direct Action and Liberal Democracy*, 90.

55. Hannah Arendt, *The Human Condition* (Garden City, N.Y.: Anchor Books, 1959), 218.

56. Friedrich Nietzsche, *The Use and Abuse of History* (Indianapolis: Bobbs-Merrill, 1957). Keeping promises and mutual acknowledgment are particularly important in contractarian views of society and politics. See, for instance, John Rawls's conception of the "original position" in "Justice as Fairness," *Philosophy, Politics and Society*, 2nd series, ed. Peter Laslett and W. G. Runciman (Oxford: Basil Blackwell, 1962), 132–57.

57. King, *Strength to Love*, 49.

Chapter 6: SNCC, Participatory Politics, and the People

1. Halberstam told this story at the conference "Covering the South: A National Symposium on the Media and the Civil Rights Movement" held at the University of Mississippi, April 3–5, 1987. The conference generally is a gold mine of anecdotes and insights about the movement and its relationship with the print and visual media.

2. Howard Zinn, *SNCC, the New Abolitionists*, 2nd ed. (Boston: Beacon, 1965); Clayborne Carson, *In Struggle: SNCC and the Black Awakening in the*

1960s (Cambridge: Harvard Univ. Press, 1981); Stokely Carmichael and Charles Hamilton, *Black Power* (New York: Vintage, 1967); James Forman, *Sammy Younge, Jr.* (New York: Grove Press, 1968) and *The Making of Black Revolutionaries* (New York: Macmillan, 1972); Cleveland Sellers with Robert Terrell, *The River of No Return: The Autobiography of a Black Militant and the Life and Death of SNCC* (New York: Morrow, 1973) are essential texts about SNCC or by veteran SNCC workers.

   3. Franco Venturi, *Roots of Revolution: A History of Populist and Socialist Movements in Nineteenth-Century Russia* (London: Weidenfeld and Nicolson, 1960), 471–72; Isaiah Berlin, "Russian Populism," *Russian Thinkers*, ed. Henry Hardy and Aileen Kelly (New York: Pelican Books, 1979), 210–38. See also Lewis Feuer, *The Conflict of Generations* (New York: Basic Books, 1969) for a more politically motivated work that establishes the parallels between the radicals of the 1960s and the *narodniki* of the 1870s.

   4. Alice Walker, *Meridian* (New York: Washington Square Press, 1976); Rosellen Brown, *Civil Wars* (New York: Knopf, 1984). Both of these novels were written by women who had been involved in the movement to some degree and both are concerned with what it means to live a political life after the high point of politicization, in this case the civil rights movement, has passed.

   5. David Garrow, *Bearing the Cross* (New York: Morrow, 1986), 131–33; Julian Bond, CRDP (1968), p. 20; John Lewis, CRDP (1967), p. 50.

   6. Kirkpatrick Sale, *SDS* (New York: Random House, 1973); Todd Gitlin, *The Whole World Is Watching* (Berkeley: Univ. of California Press, 1980); Wini Breines, *The Great Refusal: Community and Organization in the New Left* (New York: Praeger, 1982); Adolph Reed, Jr. (ed.), *Race, Politics and Culture: Critical Essays on the Radicalism of 1960s* (New York: Greenwood, 1986); Sohnya Sayres *et al.*, *The 60s Without Apology* (Minneapolis: Univ. of Minnesota Press, 1984); James Miller, *"Democracy Is in the Streets": From Port Huron to the Siege of Chicago* (New York: Simon and Schuster, 1987); and Maurice Isserman, *If I Had a Hammer . . . : The Death of the Old Left and the Birth of the New Left* (New York: Basic Books, 1987).

   7. C. Wright Mills, "The New Left" (1960), *Power, Politics and People* (New York: Oxford Univ. Press, 1967), 267.

   8. See Forman, *The Making of Black Revolutionaries*.

   9. Miller, *"Democracy Is in the Streets,"* 103; Garrow, *Bearing the Cross*, 137, 141. Staughton Lynd later wrote that the emergence of participatory democracy and consensus in SNCC was an "historical mystery." See "Prospects for the New Left," *Liberation* 15, #10 (Winter 1971): 21–22. Certainly the theoretical and philosophical foundations of participatory democracy had been laid out in the late 1950s and early 1960s by thinkers such as C. Wright Mills, Paul Goodman, Sheldon Wolin, Hannah Arendt,

and Michigan philosopher Arnold Kaufmann. Kaufmann was active both in organizing the first teach-ins against the Vietnam War and also as a teacher at Tuskegee Institute in 1965.

10. Ella Baker, CRDP (1968), pp. 39, 37; Baker in Anne Romaine, "The Mississippi Freedom Democratic Party through August 1964," MA Thesis, University of Virginia, 1969, p. 369; Baker, CRDP, p. 80; and Baker in Ellen Cantarow, *Moving the Mountain: Women Working for Social Change*, with Susan G. O'Malley and Sharon H. Strom (Old Westbury, N.Y.: Feminist Press, 1980), 53, 70.

11. Miller, *"Democracy Is in the Streets,"* 140–54.

12. Charles Sherrod, "Albany," SNCC papers, mss in Box 2, Folder 1, Martin Luther King Center for Social Change, Atlanta, Georgia, p. 1, p. 13; "Non-Violence," mss in Box 2, Folder 2, King Center, n.p.; "What We Can Do on Campuses," *ibid.*, n.p. The last entry was written sometime around the summer of 1964.

13. Unita Blackwell, CRDP (1968), p. 10; Mary Booth, CRDP (1968), p. 12; Annie Devine in Romaine, "The Mississippi Freedom Democratic Party," p. 244; Mary Lane, CRDP (1969), p. 3; Julian Bond, CRDP (1968), p. 37.

14. Neil McMillen, *Dark Journey: Black Mississippians in the Age of Jim Crow* (Urbana: Univ. of Illinois Press, 1989), 9, 285, 293.

15. Robert Moses, untitled report, *Liberation* 14 (Jan. 1970): 15; Moses in Romaine, "The Mississippi Freedom Democratic Party," p. 54; Moses in Robert Penn Warren, *Who Speaks for the Negro?* (New York: Random House, 1965), 98; Moses in Romaine, p. 60; Lawrence Guyot in Romaine, pp. 87, 93.

16. Edward Brown, CRDP (1967), pp. 62, 64. Edward Brown is the brother of H. "Rap" Brown, Carmichael's successor as SNCC chairman.

17. Staughton Lynd, "The New Radicalism and 'Participatory Democracy,'" *Dissent* 12, #3 (Summer 1965): 328. Lynd emphasized that participatory democracy did not seem appropriate for economic planning, a point also raised in Richard Flacks, "On the Uses of Participatory Democracy," *Dissent*, 13, #4 (Nov.–Dec. 1966):701–8.

18. Doug McAdam, *Freedom Summer* (New York: Oxford Univ. Press, 1988), focuses more on the effects of Freedom Summer on the largely white group of volunteers than the effects of the volunteers on Mississippi. Often stimulating, McAdam devotes surprisingly few pages to the subject of the freedom schools.

Ideas such as these were definitely "in the air" in the 1960s. In his writings Paul Goodman had stressed the need for people to take initiative in forming their own institutions, schools in particular. Since education was one of Goodman's chief interests, his writings on the subject helped stimulate the development of alternative schools and "free" universities throughout the

1960s. See for instance *Compulsory Mis-Education and the Community of Scholars* (New York: Vintage, 1966).

19. "Mississippi Politics and COFO's Political Program in Mississippi," SNCC papers, unit VII, part 2, King Center, p. 3.

20. "Overview of the Freedom Schools," State Project Files—MFDP, Series XV, Box 101, King Center, n.p.

21. Liz Fusco, "Freedom Schools in Mississippi, 1964," MFDP, XVI, Box 106, King Center, pp. 1–3.

22. Thelma Eubanks, "Opinion: The Way to Freedom," *Freedom's Journal* (McComb) 1, #1 (July 24, 1964): 4; Marionette Travis, "Hope," *Freedom's Journal* 1, #3 (August 11, 1964): 3.

23. C. T., "Speaking of Freedom," *Freedom Courier* (Greenwood) 1, #1 (July 16, 1964); Retha Barnes, in *The Press of Freedom* (Gulfport) 2 (July 27, 1964); Judie F. in *Freedom News* (Palmer's Crossing), (July 23, 1964); *Freedom's Journal* 1, #3 (August 11, 1964): 3.

24. Fannie Lou Hamer in Romaine, "The Mississippi Freedom Democratic Party," 244.

25. "A Proposal for a Freedom Information Center," AXV, III, King Center, p. 300.

26. "Mississippi Politics . . . ," SNCC papers, p. 13.

27. C. Wright Mills, *The Power Elite* (New York: Oxford Univ. Press, 1956), chap. 13.

28. Carson, *In Struggle*, 133–52.

29. See Gitlin, *The Whole World Is Watching*, especially 156–86, for a discussion of this problem in the New Left in general. Gitlin also notes that "face-to-face organizing dried up" (p. 203) in the wake of media attention to leaders who were good copy and provided them with a startling "news-making" image.

For the "missed opportunity" see McAdam, *Freedom Summer*, 126; Carson on Carmichael, *In Struggle*, 199.

30. Forman, *Making of Black Revolutionaries*, 430.

31. Julius Lester, "The Angry Children of Malcolm X" (1966), in *Black Protest Thought in the Twentieth Century*, 2nd ed., ed. A. Meier, *et al.* (Indianapolis: Bobbs-Merrill, 1971), 473; quoted in Pat Watters, *Down to Now* (New York: Pantheon, 1971), 285.

32. Lester, "The Angry Children . . . ," 480–81.

33. Chicago Office of SNCC, "We Want Black Power" (1967), in *Black Protest Thought*, 487.

34. Rousseau's *The Social Contract* is the centerpiece of his political thought, particularly the notion of the general will. For analyses of it and related topics, see Andrew Levine, *The Politics of Autonomy: A Kantian Reading of Rousseau's Social Contract* (Amherst: Univ. of Massachusetts Press, 1976); James Miller, *Dreamer of Democracy* (New Haven: Yale Univ.

Press, 1984); and Judith N. Shklar, *Men and Citizens: A Study of Rousseau's Social Theory* (Cambridge, U.K.: Cambridge Univ. Press, 1985).

35. Garrow, *Bearing the Cross*, 458.

36. Carmichael and Hamilton, *Black Power,* chap. 1.

37. Christopher Lasch, "Black Power: Cultural Nationalism as Politics," *The Agony of the American Left* (New York: Vintage, 1968), 115–68. Lasch also notes that Carmichael and Hamilton's analysis stresses class alliances across racial lines at times which in turn undermine their ethnic and colonial analogies (p. 143).

38. Harold Cruse, "Revolutionary Nationalism and the Afro-American" (1962), in *For a New America*, ed. James Weinstein and David W. Eakins (New York: Vintage, 1970), 364, 347, 351, 349, 367.

39. Cruse, Reply to R. Greenleaf in *For a New America*, 382–83.

40. Lester, "The Angry Children . . . ," 471; Ricks quoted in Forman, *The Making of Black Revolutionaries*, 457.

41. Garrow, *Bearing the Cross*, 707.

42. Lewis Black, CRDP (1967), pp. 9–10; Paul Puryear, CRDP (1968), p. 18; John Wilson, CRDP (1968), p. 28.

43. Harold Cruse, *The Crisis of the Negro Intellectual* (New York: Morrow, 1967), 347–81. Cruse was particularly concerned to make this point in reference to black leader Robert Williams of Monroe, N.C., who advocated armed self-defense, though his program was, as Cruse notes, thoroughly integrationist.

44. Hannah Arendt, *On Violence* (New York: Harcourt, Brace and World, 1970), 35–56.

45. Cruse, *The Crisis of the Negro Intellectual*, 394. This is not to say that Cruse went much further with his point. He gave no indication as to what such constitutional changes might consist of or under what circumstances they might be approved.

46. *Ibid.,* 12–13. Despite his Virginia origins, Cruse betrayed little interest in Southern black culture and less knowledge of the civil rights movement. See Lasch as well as Eugene Genovese, "The Legacy of Slavery and the Roots of Black Nationalism" (1966), in *For a New America*, 394–420, for essential agreement with Cruse's analysis.

47. Carmichael and Hamilton, *Black Power*, 34–35.

48. Hannah Arendt, *On Revolution* (New York: Viking Press, 1965), 70.

49. Lester, "The Angry Children . . . ," 483.

50. *Ibid.*

51. Hannah Arendt, *Men in Dark Times* (New York: Harcourt, Brace and World, 1968), 12–13.

52. Carson, *In Struggle*, 240–43.

53. There is an enormous literature on the subject of racism from many different points of view. Here I have found helpful Albert Memmi, "Attempt

at a Definition," in *Dominated Man* (Boston: Beacon Press, 1969), 185–89; Erik Erikson, "Race and the Wider Identity" (1966), in *Identity: Youth and Crisis* (New York: Norton, 1968), 295–320; William Nye, "The Emergent Idea of Race: A Civilizational-Analytic Approach to Race and Racism in the U.S.," *Theory and Society* 5 (1978):345–72; George Fredrickson, *White Supremacy* (New York: Oxford Univ. Press, 1981), xi–xxv.

54. Carmichael and Hamilton, *Black Power*, 3.

55. *Ibid.*, 4.

56. Put another way, institutions may validly discriminate on the basis of shared principles or beliefs. A religious organization may discriminate against those who do not accept its articles of belief or confess its faith; but it must also be possible for anyone to join who does accept those principles. The case is similar with aliens and the right to vote.

57. Chicago Office of SNCC, "We Want . . . ," *Black Protest Thought*, 487–90; Albert Memmi, *The Colonizer and the Colonized* (New York: Orion Press, 1965), 130–31.

58. Arendt, *Men in Dark Times*, 16.

59. See Arendt, *On Revolution*, 68–75, for her differences with Rousseau. Contrary to James Miller's claim in *Dreamer of Democracy*, Arendt is by no means a Rousseauean.

60. Vincent Harding, "Black Radicalism: The Road from Montgomery," in *Dissent: Explorations in the History of American Radicalism* (Dekalb: Northern Illinois Univ. Press, 1968), 341.

61. Lewis in William Beardslee, *The Way Out Must Lead In*, 2nd ed. (Westport: Lawrence Hill, 1983), 8.

62. Forman, *The Making of Black Revolutionaries*, 307; Zinn, *SNCC*, 168; Moses, *The Making of Black Revolutionaries*, 185, 189; Breines, *The Great Refusal*, 6.

63. Hamer in Howell Raines, *My Soul Is Rested* (New York: Bantam, 1978), 302.

64. Forman, *The Making of Black Revolutionaries*, 106.

65. Sellers, *The River of No Return*, 137.

66. Lewis in Beardslee, *The Way Out* . . . , 24–25.

67. Donaldson in Raines, *My Soul Is Rested*, 285; Curry, *ibid.*, 113; Forman, *The Making of Black Revolutionaries*, 291; Bond, CRDP (1968), p. 40; Cobb in Raines, 268.

68. Cobb in Raines, 270; Dave Dennis, *ibid.*, 305; Curry, *ibid.*, 112.

69. Sellers, *The River of No Return*, 180; Lewis in Beardslee, *The Way Out*, 30.

70. Edward Brown, CRDP (1967), p. 46; Pat Watters and Reece Cleghorn, *Climbing Jacob's Ladder* (New York: Harcourt, Brace and World, 1967), 294; Watters, *Down to Now*, 301, 131.

71. Watters, *Down to Now*, 404, makes this last point clearly.

72. Forman, *The Making of Black Revolutionaries*, 238.

Chapter 7: Violence and Self-respect:
Fanon and Black Radicalism

1. David Garrow, *Bearing the Cross* (New York: Morrow, 1986), 63. See also Peter J. Albert and Ronald Hoffman (eds.), *We Shall Overcome: Martin Luther King, Jr., and the Black Freedom Struggle* (New York: Pantheon, 1990) for several articles on King's influence on African liberation movements and ideas.

2. Staughton Lynd (ed.), *Nonviolence in America: A Documentary History* (Indianapolis: Bobbs-Merrill, 1966), 398–99.

3. Robert Moses in Robert Penn Warren, *Who Speaks for the Negro?* (New York: Random House, 1965), 91.

4/ Moses, *ibid.*, 95; Camus, "Neither Victims nor Executioners" (1946), in *Seeds of Liberation*, ed. Paul Goodman (New York: Braziller, 1964), 28.

5. James Forman, *The Making of Black Revolutionaries* (New York: Macmillan, 1972), 106; Stokely Carmichael in Warren, *Who Speaks for the Negro?*, 398.

6. Max Weber, "Politics as a Vocation," *From Max Weber*, ed. H. H. Gerth and C. Wright Mills (New York: Oxford Univ. Press, 1946), 122; see also Clayborne Carson, *In Struggle: SNCC and the Black Awakening of the 1960s* (Cambridge: Harvard Univ. Press, 1981), chap. 13.

7. For intellectual biographies or full-length studies, see David Caute, *Frantz Fanon* (New York: Viking Press, 1970); Peter Geismar, *Fanon: The Revolutionary as Prophet* (New York: Grove Press, 1971); Irene Gendzier, *Frantz Fanon* (New York: Vintage, 1974); Chester J. Fontenot, *Frantz Fanon: Language as the God Gone Astray*, University of Nebraska Studies: New Series no. 60 (Lincoln: Univ. of Nebraska Press, 1979); and B. Marie Perinbam, *Holy Violence: The Revolutionary Thought of Frantz Fanon* (Washington, D.C.: Three Continents Press, 1982).

Samuel Farber, "Violence and Material Class Interests: Fanon and Gandhi," *Journal of Asian and African Studies* XVI, #3–4 (1981): 196–211, is a Marxist treatment which highlights both men's "moralism" and their lack of attention to questions of material interests; while Paul Nursey-Bray, "Marxism and Existentialism in the Thought of Frantz Fanon," *Political Studies* 2, #2:152–68, not surprisingly finds that the two traditions fail to mesh. But Lewis Coser, "Fanon and Debray: Theorists of the Third World," in *Beyond the New Left*, ed. I. Howe (New York: McCall, 1970):120–34, is too concerned to discredit Fanon to be of much use. Three more recent treatments of Fanon—Homi Bhabha, "'What Does the Black Man Want?'"; Stephen Feuchtwang, "Fanonian Spaces," and Barbara Harlow, "Narratives of Resistance," can be found in *New Formations* 1 (Spring 1987):118–35. See also Elizabeth Fox-Genovese and Eugene D. Genovese, "Illusions of Liberation: The Psychology of Colonialism and Revolt in the Work of Octave Mannoni and Frantz Fanon," in *Rethinking Marxism*, ed. Stephen Resnick and Richard Wolff (Autonomedia), 127–50.

8. Alexandre Kojeve, *Introduction to the Reading of Hegel*, ed. Allan Bloom (New York: Basic Books, 1969); also Kojeve, "Hegel, Marx and Christianity," *Interpretation*, 21–42. For background on Kojeve's influence of postwar French thought, see Patrick Riley, "Introduction to the Reading of Alexandre Kojeve," *Political Theory* 9, #1 (February 1981): 5–47; Michael Roth, "A Problem of Recognition: Alexandre Kojeve and the End of History," *History and Theory* XXIV, #3 (1985): 293–306; and Mark Poster, *Existential Marxism: From Sartre to Althusser* (Princeton: Princeton Univ. Press, 1975). I stress Kojeve rather than Sartre because the position of the former pinpoints salient aspects of and problems in Fanon's thought more clearly than Sartre does. None of the literature on Fanon even mentions Kojeve, much less acknowledges his importance for or influence on Sartre.

9. Riley, "Introduction to the Reading of Kojeve," 8; Kojeve, "Hegel, Marx and Christianity," 32.

10. Hannah Arendt, *On Violence* (New York: Harcourt, Brace and World, 1970), 12–13, makes this point about "leftist humanism" derived from Hegel and Marx. In "A Problem of Recognition" Roth suggests that Arendt, having fled the Nazis in the early 1930s and come to Paris, also attended the Kojeve lectures in Paris (p. 294). See as well Riley, "Introduction to the Reading of Kojeve," 15.

11. Despite his use of Freud, Gendzier reports that Fanon felt "disdain for psychoanalysis, and for being psychoanalyzed" (*Frantz Fanon*, 18).

12. Fanon cites Lacan several times in *Black Skin, White Masks* (New York: Grove Press, 1967) and discusses the "mirror period" on pp. 161–63. His discussion of Hegel and Adler comes in chapter 7. For Kojeve's influence on Lacan, see Anthony Wilden, *The Language of the Self: The Function of Language in Psychoanalysis by Jacques Lacan* (Baltimore: Johns Hopkins Univ. Press, 1968). By distinguishing need and desire, the latter of which is always mediated by and through self and other, Lacan (and Lacanians) would presumably contend that the distinction between pleasure (the Freudian core of desire) and recognition (the Hegelian/Adlerian core of desire) is moot and thus meaningless. Still, there is a tendency of the French Freudians to lose the "body" and "pleasure" in exchange for the all-purpose term "desire."

13. Fanon, *Black Skin*, 219.

14. *Ibid.*, 100.

15. *Ibid.*, 222.

16. Bhabha, "'What Does the Black Man Want?'" 122.

17. Fanon, *The Wretched of the Earth* (New York: Grove Press, 1966), 88, and, generally, the chapter entitled "Spontaneity" (pp. 85–119). The central figure in Pontecorvo's *Battle of Algiers* is such a deracinated urban "guer-

rilla." In "Violence and Material Class Interests: Fanon and Gandhi," Samuel Farber draws the parallels between Fanon and Bakunin and further reading confirms some important similarities, though not, as far as I can tell, direct influence.

18. Patrick Taylor, *The Narrative of Liberation: Perspectives on Afro-Caribbean Literature, Popular Culture and Politics* (Ithaca: Cornell Univ. Press, 1989), 261.

19. Fanon, *Toward the African Revolution* (New York: Grove Press, 1967), 34; Gendzier, *Frantz Fanon*, 180; Fontenot, *Frantz Fanon*, 35.

20. Fanon, *Wretched*, 179, 188.

21. *Ibid.*, 161–63.

22. *Ibid.*, 30, 33, 29, 32, 52.

23. *Ibid.*, 63, 65.

24. *Ibid.*, 67.

25. *Ibid.*, 73.

26. Carson, *In Struggle*, 192, 198; Forman, *The Making of Black Revolutionaries*, 106; Huey P. Newton, *Revolutionary Suicide*, with the assistance of Herman Blake (New York: Harcourt Brace Jovanovich, 1973), 110; Eldridge Cleaver, *Post-Prison Writings and Speeches* (New York: Vintage, 1968), 17–18; Don Watts quoted in Aristide and Vera Zolberg, "The Americanization of Frantz Fanon," *The Public Interest* 9 (Fall 1967): 50.

27. Fanon, *Black Skin*, 173–76, 221; *Wretched*, 174.

28. Carson, *In Struggle*, chap. 17; Forman, "A Year of Resistance," in *Towards Revolution*, vol. II, ed. John Gerassi (London: Weidenfeld and Nicolson, 1971), 689.

29. Stokely Carmichael, "Black Power and the Third World" (1967) in Gerassi, *Towards Revolution*, 704–6; Cleaver, *Post-Prison Writings*, 157.

30. Fanon, *Wretched*, 172–73.

31. Elaine Scarry, *The Body in Pain: The Making and Unmaking of the World* (New York: Oxford Univ. Press, 1985), 47.

32. Quoted in Ronald Takaki (ed.), *Violence in the Black Imagination* (New York: Putnam's, 1972), 80. See also Lawrence J. Friedman, *The Gregarious Saints* (New York: Cambridge Univ. Press, 1982).

33. William Grier and Price Cobbs, *Black Rage* (New York: Bantam Books, 1969).

34. Marie Perinbam claims that Fanon's theory of "holy violence" is not novel, but stands in a long tradition of pre-modern religious and modern political violence (*Holy Violence*, 107). Though uneven in quality, Perinbam's book is important for the way it calls attention to the proto-religious dimension of Fanon's thought. See also Ferenc Feher, "Redemptive and Democratic Paradigms in Radical Politics" *Eastern Left, Western Left* (Atlantic Highlands, N.J.: Humanities Press, 1986), 61–76.

35. Barrington Moore, Jr., *Social Origins of Dictatorship and Democracy*

(Boston: Beacon Press, 1967), 505; Scarry, *The Body in Pain*, 140–42; Arendt makes the point about the need for commensurability between violence and the ends in question in *On Violence*, 55–56.

More generally, see William James, "The Moral Equivalent of War" (1910); Randolph Bourne, *War and the Intellectuals* (New York: Harper Torchbooks, 1964); as well as J. Glenn Gray, *The Warriors* (New York: Harper Torchbooks, 1970) and *On Understanding Violence Philosophically and Other Essays* (New York: Harper Torchbooks, 1970). As Jean Bethke Elshtain has observed, "Peace discourse that denies the violent undercurrents . . . is but the opposite side of the hard-line realist case," *Meditations on Modern Political Thought: Masculine/Feminine Themes from Luther to Arendt* (New York: Praeger, 1986), 108.

36. Arendt, *ibid.*; Gray, *On Understanding Violence*, 4.

37. Gray, *The Warriors*, 27–29, 45–47.

38. Eugene D. Genovese, "The Legacy of Slavery and the Roots of Black Nationalism" (1966), in *For a New America*, ed. James Weinstein and David Eakins (New York: Vintage, 1970), 415; Perinbam, *Holy Violence*, 8, 77–78.

39. Jean-Paul Sartre, "Preface," *The Wretched of the Earth*, 18–19.

40. Fanon, *A Dying Colonialism* (New York: Grove Press, 1967), 55.

41. Edward Peters, *Torture* (Oxford, U.K.: Basil Blackwell, 1985) makes the general point about the resurgence of physical torture which contradicts Michel Foucault's contention that physical has given way to psychological and moral intimidation in incarceration and punishment.

42. Scarry emphasizes the loss of voice, self, and world and the overwhelming presence of the body-in-pain under torture. It seems to me, however, that the (Hegelian) emphasis upon the struggle between self-conscious beings for recognition needs more emphasis by Scarry. One of the controversial claims of Scarry's work is that torture's point is generally not a utilitarian one, such as the extraction of information, but causing pain and ultimately destroying the world of the person being tortured. Peters widens such a narrow focus but he certainly includes intimidation among the purposes of torture; and it may be that such deconstruction of the world of the tortured may be the particularly modern or contemporary purpose of torture.

43. Eldridge Cleaver, *Soul on Ice* (New York: Delta Books, 1968), 12–15. Cleaver mentions his reading of or about Machiavelli, Bakunin, and Nechayev as crucial in his formulation of the idea of rape as an insurrectionary act.

44. Albert Memmi, *Dominated Man* (Boston: Beacon Press, 1968), 88. See Caute, *Frantz Fanon*, 10, for the point about the essentialist cast of Fanon's thought.

45. Kojeve quoted in Riley, "Introduction to the Reading of Alexandre Kojeve," 9; Kojeve, "Hegel, Marx and Christianity," 32.

46. Taylor, *The Narrative of Liberation*, 74, 80.

47. Perinbam, *Holy Violence*, 87.

48. Fox-Genovese and Genovese, "Illusions of Liberation," 148. Besides Feher, see Peter Clecak, *Radical Paradoxes: Dilemmas of the American Left* (New York: Harper Torchbook, 1975), chap. 7, for another critique of the idea of liberation from a left-wing point of view; and Philip Rieff, *The Triumph of the Therapeutic* (New York: Harper Torchbook, 1968) and *Fellow Teachers* (New York: Harper and Row, 1973) for a conservative critique of the ideologies of the "new" culture and the therapeutics of violence.

49. Cleaver, *Soul*, 205–10. See Carole Pateman, *The Disorder of Women* (Cambridge, U.K.: Polity Press, 1989) for the idea of the "fraternal" contract.

50. Rieff, *Fellow Teachers*, 43, 91–94; see also V. S. Naipaul, "Michael X and the Black Power Killings in Trinidad," in *The Return of Eva Peron* (New York: Vintage, 1981), 1–97.

51. See A. James Gregor, *The Fascist Persuasion in Radical Politics* (Princeton: Princeton Univ. Press, 1974), particularly chap. 8, for an attempt to draw the similarities between some forms of radicalism in the 1960s and fascism. Generally what Gregor identifies is the cluster of political values, institutions, and practices that have arisen in "underdeveloped" societies in this century. Fascism is the name of the European version of such developmental politics. Had it not been Hitler's association with fascism via the alliance with Mussolini, fascism might have become a relatively neutral category for the classification of political regimes. Missing from Fanon's thought and from most Third World ideologies is an emphasis upon racial superiority or upon political expansion and aggressiveness.

52. Ralph Ellison, *Shadow and Act* (New York: Signet Books, 1966), 360.

53. Jean-Paul Sartre, *Anti-Semite and Jew* (New York: Schocken Books, 1965), 69. Sartre assumes that Judaism does not refer to a religion, race, or ethnic group alone and that Jews lack a common and continuous secular history. Underlying Sartre's position is the further assumption that Jews would have willingly assimilated into Gentile society over the years had they been allowed. Thus to be Jewish is to be an exception by necessity. All this, to put it charitably, is highly questionable; uncharitably, it is nonsense.

54. Where post-structuralist readings of Fanon have a point is not so much in their claim that Fanon was a post-structuralist before the fact, but that his ideal of a "new man" of unified revolutionary consciousness mirrored the counter-ideal of the unified dominated consciousness prior to liberation. Homi Bhabha's reading of Fanon as concerned with, or at least pointing us mainly toward, the problems of the differences between "imaginary" identities works much better for *Black Skin* than it does *Wretched*. Though for Fanon a new identity is created through revolutionary struggle, that identity does not remain "up for grabs" but is intended to be relatively stable and/or encompass certain fixed characteristics and values. Fanon's theory of colonial domination falls into the category of theories which make it hard, if not

impossible, to see how liberation is subjectively possible and necessitates, as Maria Lugones has suggested, giving up the notion of a "unified" subject. See her "Structure/Antistructure and Agency under Oppression," *Journal of Philosophy* LXXXVII, #10 (Oct. 1990): 500–507.

55. Stanley Elkins, *Slavery* (Chicago: Univ. of Chicago Press, 1959). See also the Genoveses' "Illusions of Liberation," 144, for a similar position regarding Fanon and Elkins; and Orlando Patterson, *Slavery and Social Death* (Cambridge: Harvard Univ. Press, 1983), 97.

56. Gray, *On Understanding Violence*, 10.

57. See Feher, "The Pariah and the Citizen: On Arendt's Political Theory," in *Hannah Arendt: Thinking, Judging, Freedom*, ed. Gisela Kaplan and Clive S. Kessler (Sydney, Aus.: Allan and Unwin, 1989), 20.

58. Martin Jay, "The Political Existentialism of Hannah Arendt," in *Permanent Exiles* (New York: Columbia Univ. Press, 1985), 247–49, criticizes Arendt for the failure to integrate her ideas on violence with her idea of politics.

59. Arendt, *On Violence*, 67.

60. *The Battle of Algiers* suggests the incompatibility of underground military organizations and politics. In the former, each member of the resistance knew only three other members. In such a branching organization, commands were given and carried out, information conveyed, but rarely were opinions solicited or openly discussed.

61. Arendt, *On Violence*, 67–72. See also George Kateb, "Death and Politics: Hannah Arendt's Reflections on the American Constitution," *Social Research* 54, #3 (Autumn 1987): 605–16. Kateb claims that to Arendt "whenever the threat of death is missing, political action is not truly present" (p. 612). I would suggest that Arendt's earlier point is that one motive for political action is to defy time by carrying out memorable deeds which will last in the memories of others. In that sense politics does need to be shadowed by a sense of transience. But what she objected to in *On Violence* can best be understood as an obsession with death and violence itself, what might be called a necropolitical impulse.

62. James Forman, *The Death of Sammy Younge, Jr.* (New York: Grove Press, 1968), 24; *The Making of Black Revolutionaries*, 196. See also Arendt, *On Violence*, 72.

Conclusion

1. In his comments on political and social thought, Richard Rorty has contrasted the goals of transforming society versus reforming society, urging generally that liberals aim only for the latter. My point regarding the civil rights movement is that it doesn't fall comfortably within either position.

2. Albert O. Hirschman, *Exit, Voice, and Loyalty: Responses to Decline*

in Firms, Organizations, and States (Cambridge: Harvard Univ. Press, 1970).

3. It is of course more complicated than this. In *One-Dimensional Man* (Boston: Beacon, 1964), xv, Marcuse confessed that he was torn between the total domination thesis and the sense that resistance was possible; Foucault's notion of power is so protean and all-encompassing that repressive power can be checked by shaping and enabling forms of power; and Gramscians talk of "counterhegemony." Still, the impression one takes away from a reading of such thinkers is either the impossibility of mounting any significant opposition to the given order or that oppositional movements are only engaged in self-deception, since the dominant system uses them to cleverly reenforce its ultimate control.

4. Garry Wills, *Confessions of a Conservative* (New York: Penguin Books, 1980), 167.

5. Laurence Thomas, "Self-Respect: Theory and Practice," in *Philosophy Born of Struggle*, ed. Leonard Harris (Dubuque: Kendell/Hunt, 1983), 176.

6. Garry Wills, *Nixon Agonistes: The Crisis of the Self-Made Man* (Boston: Houghton Mifflin, 1969), 517.

7. Alasdair MacIntyre, *After Virtue* (Notre Dame: Univ. of Notre Dame Press, 1981), 175–89. As MacIntyre points out, a utilitarian view of ethics or politics cannot in principle accept that a practice such as politics might carry internal goods rather than be a matter of external pay-offs.

8. On this issue, see Ronald Dworkin's review of Michael Walzer's *Spheres of Justice* in the *New York Review of Books* (April 14, 1983), 4, 6; Walzer's reply in *NYR* (July 21, 1983), 43–44; and Dworkin's rejoinder (pp. 44–46). In another context, Seyla Benhabib has named these two positions "Neo-Aristotelian" and "Neo-Kantian." Walzer's neo-Aristotelian principles of justice are contextual and differ across practices and spheres, while neo-Kantian Dworkin wants to defend an idea of rights applicable across various practices and providing an independent standard of judgment. ("Judgment and the Moral Foundations of Politics in Arendt's Thought," *Political Theory* 16, #1 (Feb. 1988): 29–51.)

9. Hannah Arendt, *The Origins of Totalitarianism*, 2nd ed. (Cleveland: Meridian Books, 1958), 301. Though Arendt quite perceptively identifies this problem, her political thought places little emphasis upon rights as protections, i.e., negative freedoms.

10. William Beardslee (ed.), *The Way Out Must Lead In*, 2nd ed. (Westport: Lawrence Hill, 1983), 163.

11. Walter Benjamin, "The Work of Art in the Age of Mechanical Reproduction," in *Illuminations* (New York: Schocken Books, 1968). Harry Ashmore, at "Covering the South": A National Symposium on the Media and the Civil Rights Movement, April 3–5, 1987, panel 1 ("Early Days").

12. John Lewis, *ibid.*, Panel 2 ("The Mass Movement, 1960–64").

13. See David Garrow, *Protest at Selma* (New Haven: Yale Univ. Press, 1978) for a thorough discussion of the role of the media in creating pressure on Congress and the Johnson administration to do something in reaction to the events at Selma in early 1965.

14. See Ashmore, Eugene Roberts, and Rex Thomas for these comments in Panel 2 of "Covering the South."

15. Todd Gitlin, *The Whole World Is Watching* (Berkeley: Univ. of California Press, 1980), 28, 156.

16. *Ibid.*, 162, 166, 203.

17. Besides Gitlin, see Wini Breines, *The Great Refusal: Community and Organization in the New Left: 1962–1968* (New York: Praeger, 1982), 146, for the point about the preference for mass action over community organizing.

18. See particularly Fredric Jameson, "Postmodernism, or the Cultural Logic of Late Capitalism," *New Left Review* 146 (July–Aug. 1984): 53–92.

Index

Abolitionists, 29, 34, 75, 139, 185
action, political (*see also* non-violent direct action), 9, 10, 11, 27, 38, 105, 124, 150, 165, 203; and "goods," 11; and freedom, 25–26; in existentialism, 35; and Afro-American tradition, 37; and Afro-American music, 41–42; and self-transformation, 51, 100–101, 173, 179, 196; other-regarding, 66; and self-respect, 72–74; and violence, 81, 197–99; power to illuminate, 89, 106; personality and family, 123–24; and speech, 130, 197–98; collective forms of, 188; images of, 211
Adler, Alfred, 134–35; and Fanon, 178
Adorno, Theodor, 203
Africa, 38, 154, 158, 160, 167, 172, 173; Fanon on, 180
Afro-Americans, 16, 100, 103, 153, 175; and commitment to freedom, 16, 28–33, 34; political culture of, 28–34, 203; religion of, 28–29, 37–38, 41–42, 46; and autonomy, 30–31; as aliens, 33; music, 37, 41–42, 83; and name changes, 55; and self-formation, 74; writing, 83; self-consciousness and pride, 84–85, 91; cultural consciousness, 84–85; identity as racial, 84–85; divisions among, 90; as chosen, 99; and collective liberation, 117–18, 201–2; as civil disobedients, 126; and violence, 133–36; and colonial analogy, 140, 154–55, 183–84; as a community, 152, 164–65; as ethnic group, 154–55; distinctiveness, 155; and recognition, 160–61; as pariah people, 164; ideologists of, 164; unity of, 169;

Fanon on, 183; social and cultural life, 193–95
Afro-Caribbeans, 179
agape, 101, 134, 135, 136; King on, 98–99, 160; and political virtue, 118
Albany (Ga.), 3, 14, 41, 45, 57, 71, 132
Algeria, 173, 176, 180, 183, 190, 192, 194
Ali, Muhammed, 210
American Hunger (Wright), 76
Antigone, 138
Anti-Semite and Jew (Sartre), 194
apartheid, 162
Appeal, The (Walker), 31–32
Arendt, Hannah, viii, ix, 92, 107, 161, 204, 211; and public happiness, 9, 59; on freedom, 24–26, 198; on civil disobedience, 105–6, 128, 197; on political action, 105; on *The Declaration*, 109; on banality of evil, 123; on forgiving and forgetting, 136; on power and violence, 157; on the social question, 158; on pariah peoples, 164; on friendship, 165; and Fanon, 197–99; action and violence, 197–98; on speech and action, 197–98; death and politics, 199; exclusivity and the polis, 206
Arnett, Bishop, 32
Ashmore, Harry, 208; on television and the movement, 208–9
Asia, 38, 154, 158, 172, 173
Auden, W. H., 188
Auld, Mr. And Mrs. (*Narrative*), 77
"Aunt Thomasinas," 153
Autobiography of Miss Jane Pittman, The (Gaines), 51